The Passenger Cases and the Commerce Clause

LANDMARK LAW CASES

&

AMERICAN SOCIETY

Peter Charles Hoffer
N. E. H. Hull
Series Editors

RECENT TITLES IN THE SERIES:

Prigg v. Pennsylvania, H. Robert Baker
The Detroit School Busing Case, Joyce A. Baugh
The Japanese American Cases, Roger Daniels
The Battle over School Prayer, Bruce J. Dierenfield
Judging the Boy Scouts of America, Richard J. Ellis
Fighting Foreclosure, John A. Fliter and Derek S. Hoff
Little Rock on Trial, Tony A. Freyer
One Man Out: Curt Flood versus Baseball, Robert M. Goldman
The Free Press Crisis of 1800, Peter Charles Hoffer
The Treason Trials of Aaron Burr, Peter Charles Hoffer
The Woman Who Dared to Vote: The Trial of Susan B. Anthony, N. E. H. Hull
Roe v. Wade: *The Abortion Rights Controversy in American History*, 2nd ed., revised and expanded, N. E. H. Hull and Peter Charles Hoffer
Plessy v. Ferguson: *Race and Inequality in Jim Crow America*, Williamjames Hull Hoffer
Gibbons v. Ogden: *John Marshall, Steamboats, and the Commerce Clause*, Herbert A. Johnson
The Tokyo Rose Case, Yasuhide Kawashima
Gitlow v. New York, Marc Lendler
Fugitive Slave on Trial: The Anthony Burns Case and Abolitionist Outrage, Earl M. Maltz
The Snail Darter Case, Kenneth M. Murchison
Capital Punishment on Trial, David M. Oshinsky
The Michigan Affirmative Action Cases, Barbara A. Perry
The Supreme Court and Tribal Gaming, Ralph A. Rossum
Obscenity Rules: Roth v. United States *and the Long Struggle over Sexual Expression*, Whitney Strub
Mendez v. Westminster, Philippa Strum
The Sleepy Lagoon Murder Case, Mark A. Weitz
The Miracle *Case*, Laura Wittern-Keller and Raymond J. Haberski, Jr.
Bush v. Gore: *Exposing the Hidden Crisis in American Democracy*, abridged and updated, Charles L. Zelden

For a complete list of titles in the series go to www.kansaspress.ku.edu.

TONY ALLAN FREYER

The Passenger Cases and the Commerce Clause

Immigrants, Blacks, and States' Rights in Antebellum America

UNIVERSITY PRESS OF KANSAS

Published by the University Press of Kansas (Lawrence, Kansas 66045), which was organized by the Kansas Board of Regents and is operated and funded by Emporia State University, Fort Hays State University, Kansas State University, Pittsburg State University, the University of Kansas, and Wichita State University

Library of Congress Cataloging-in-Publication Data

Freyer, Tony Allan, author.
The Passenger Cases and the commerce clause : immigrants, blacks, and states' rights in antebellum America / Tony Allan Freyer.
pages cm
Includes index.
ISBN 978-0-7006-2008-1 (hardback)
ISBN 978-0-7006-2009-8 (paper)

1. United States. Supreme Court – History – 19th century. 2. Interstate commerce – United States – Cases. 3. Emigration and immigration law – United States – Cases. 4. United States – Commercial policy. 5. States rights (American politics) 6. Slavery – Law and legislation – United States – History I. Title.
KF8742.F74 2014
342.7308'2 – dc23
2014021373

British Library Cataloguing-in-Publication Data is available.

EU Authorised Representative Details: Easy Access System Europe
Mustamäe tee 50, 10621 Tallinn, Estonia | gpsr.requests@easproject.com

To Lyndsay Campbell, Morton J. Horwitz, and Forrest and Ellen McDonald

Let us waive that agitated national topic, as to whether such multitudes of foreign poor should be landed on our American shores; let us waive it, with the one only thought, that if they can get here, they have God's right to come; though they bring all Ireland and her miseries with them. For the whole world is the patrimony of the whole world; there is no telling who does not own a stone in the Great Wall of China. But we waive all this; and will only consider, how best the emigrants can come hither, since come they do, and come they must and will.

—Herman Melville, *Reburn* (1849)

CONTENTS

EDITORS' PREFACE

Distinguished legal historian Tony Freyer is both an antebellum legal historian and a historian of modern American race relations. In this long-awaited and first of its kind study of the Passenger Cases, Freyer brings these two fields together. The cases themselves are complex, involving Massachusetts and New York port restrictions on newcomers, but here they are unraveled with precision and insight. Entailing questions of states' rights and federalism, in Freyer's hands the opinions of the justices seem as fresh and relevant today as when they were promulgated in 1849.

Freyer's approach is both innovative and appropriate, for the nineteenth-century context of those opinions bears striking similarities to issues roiling modern jurisprudence and politics. The 1840s was the era of the great migrations from Ireland and Germany to American shores, and fears of disease, competition for jobs, and radical politics raced through New York and Massachusetts politics. It was the same fear that would make the two states home to the American Party (aka the "Know-Nothings") in the coming years—and the same fear that motivates anti-immigration forces today.

Although the opinions did not focus on slavery per se, everyone involved, from the legislators who framed the acts to the lawyers, litigants, and judges who adjudicated the suits, knew that slavery lurked in the shadows of the cases. If a state legislature could impose a tax on incoming passengers at its ports, could it also regulate slavery out of existence? Were slaves persons or objects in the stream of commerce? Framing the justices debate over the question were *Jones v. Van Zandt* (1849) and *Strader v. Graham* (1851), suits challenging state and federal laws on slavery. The Dred Scott case was moving through the Missouri courts heading for its own day of infamy. Slavery is no longer legal in the United States, but the penumbras of the "peculiar institution" continue to reach into political discourse at the highest levels.

In the Passenger Cases, a bare majority of the Supreme Court held that the states could not so legislate without violating the Commerce Clause of the federal Constitution. But the justices' eight opinions varied on everything from the meaning of commerce to the exclusivity of the power vested in the federal government. Similar questions of federalism vex jurists today, as states pass their own immigration laws as though regulation of immigration were not, like interstate commerce, vested in the federal government.

Freyer's work has achieved the ideal of every teacher of history—bringing the past into the present. Long overlooked, the Passenger Cases will once more be essential reading.

ACKNOWLEDGMENTS

I am happy to thank those individuals who have aided me in writing this book. Peter Hoffer suggested the idea that the Passenger Cases (1849) would be a suitable contribution to the Landmark Law Cases & American Society series, as long as the primary state regulation of immigrants before the Civil War was clear. Readers commenting on a project proposal emphasized the importance of delineating the antebellum commerce power theories in relation to slavery. Commentators at professional meetings urged the need to suggest the implications the history has for contemporary debates involving federal preemption in immigration regulations and state laws challenging it. My book attempts to balance these goals, though the origins, period prominence, and precedential obscurity of the Passenger Cases are the principal focus.

Lyndsay Campbell suggested that clarification of the Passenger Cases would be useful; long ago Morton J. Horwitz inspired me that I could satisfactorily address the subject, while Forrest and Ellen McDonald provided patient encouragement. I am grateful to each one of you. I thank also my colleagues at the University of Alabama School of Law who attended a presentation of an early draft of the project at a faculty colloquium in 2010; the commentator on another version of the project as part of a panel at the 2011 annual meeting of the Law & Society Association in San Francisco; and Jim Phillips and his colleagues for including a presentation of a portion of the project at the legal history seminar in the University of Toronto School of Law, October 2012. Several Earhart Foundation Research Fellowships enabled me to buyout teaching in order to write the book during early 2012; I am indebted to Dean Robert Olin and Associate Dean Carmen Burkhalter of the School of Arts & Sciences and History Chair Kari Frederickson for approving these assignments. University of Alabama School of Law Dean Kenneth C. Randall, the Edward Brett Randolph Fund, and the Alabama Law School Foundation, as well as the Office of Academic Affairs, which endowed the university research professorship I held, provided essential financial support over several years of researching the subject.

I am fortunate indeed that colleagues in the University of Alabama

Law Library have always answered my calls for help: Paul M. Pruitt, Robert Marshall, and Penny Gibson. Elizabeth Campbell, L3, UALS, provided research assistance; my office assistant, Donna Tucker, prepared the manuscript for publication. I am also indebted to Michael Briggs, and his successor as editor in chief of the series, Charles T. Myers, and their expert staff, at the University Press of Kansas. For answering particular research questions I thank too Daniel Hammer, Historic New Orleans Collection, the Special Collections librarian at the Tulane University, Scott A. Gray, Walter Nugent, Lois Ray Carlson, Mark Brilliant, and Allison Tierres. I am particularly grateful to Hebert Johnson for advice on revisions.

For continuing care and love I thank my wife, Zu, our son Allan and daughter-in-law Rachel in Durham, North Carolina, and my sister Joan and brother Jon in San Diego, California. Thanks also to my mother-in-law, Mrs. Elaine Faller. Finally reaching the end of this project, I am more conscious than ever before of the usual caution that others have contributed whatever good the book has, while I alone am responsible for any errors.

Introduction

Before the Civil War the U.S. Supreme Court established its umpire role prescribing powers of states and the federal government. Chief Justice John Marshall led the Court in establishing the independent judiciary as the arbiter of state-federal relations, but he avoided deciding the legal status of immigrants and free blacks under the federal commerce power. After Roger B. Taney became chief justice in 1836 the Court addressed the legal status of both groups in relation to state police powers and the commerce power. In the Passenger Cases (1849) the Court's 5–4 decision and eight opinions construing these state-federal powers influenced political responses to transatlantic famine migration, as well as fugitive slaves and western expansion of slavery at issue in the 1850 Compromise. Since the Civil War and Reconstruction growing federal regulation of immigration has supplanted state police powers. Even so, in *Arizona v. U.S.* (2012) Justice Antonin Scalia's dissent recalled the past: "Notwithstanding '[t]he myth of an era of unrestricted immigration' in the first 100 years of the Republic, the States enacted numerous [police power] laws restricting the immigration of certain classes of aliens, including convicted criminals, indigents, persons with contagious diseases, and (in southern States) freed blacks." In the Passenger Cases, however, the Supreme Court affirmed a commerce power that enabled Northern states to admit and confer limited citizenship upon immigrants and free blacks.

The following chapters focus on the origins, state court decisions, federal precedents, appellate arguments, and opinion making that culminated in the Court's split decision of the Passenger Cases, which in turn influenced the 1850 Compromise and the coming of the Civil War. The Court's majority and dissenting opinions, like the lawyers' arguments for each side, expressed divergent interpretations of law disputing the legal status of white immigrants and blacks under state police powers and federal commerce power precedents. The Court opinions and the legal arguments contested where state police powers ended and the federal commerce power began. The Court's divided decision provided political legitimacy for the 1850 Compromise: enactment of a stronger fugitive slave law, admission of slavery in Western territories based on popular vote of residents (popular sovereignty), and the abolition of the slave trade in Washington, D.C. The divided opinions in the Passenger Cases also influenced the immigrant and slavery crises that disrupted the balance between free and slave-labor states, culminating in the Civil War. The states did indeed enact laws enabling exclusion of undesirable white immigrants and free blacks. The prevailing state and federal court precedents, however, generally granted admission to both groups in Northern and Western free-labor states. John C. Calhoun, the great defender of Southern rights and slavery, predicted in 1849 that such free admissions encouraged sectional contestation of abolition, secession, and racial reconstruction.

The divided opinions of the Passenger Cases suggested an enduring institutional independence that future individual Supreme Court members shared. In his memoir, *The Court Years 1939–1975*, Justice William O. Douglas recalled learning the scope of this independence from Chief Justice Charles Evans Hughes, who told him that "you must remember one thing. At the constitutional level where we work, ninety percent of any decision is emotional. The rational part of us supplies the reasons for supporting our predilections." Legal historian Morton J. Horwitz sharpened Hughes's insight, arguing that, especially during transformative historical periods such as America's immigrant and slavery crises, judges' opinions formulated and channeled diverse, often conflicting class, ideological, political, cultural, and institutional motivations into instrumental results. Supreme Court opinions reflected the justices' attitudes about the commerce power and state police powers, which other courts and lawyers applied as precedents of law. Politicians, however, looked upon the Court's opinions more simply in terms of politics. Examination of the Supreme Court commerce power opinions within state and national immigrant and racial politics revealed multiple motivations shaping judicial doctrines and precedents that culminated in the decision of the Passenger Cases.

Most of the book concerns the antebellum Supreme Court's role prescribing state-federal regulation of immigrants in relation to free blacks that gave rise to the Passenger Cases and the decision's impact on the immigrant and slavery crises, the 1850 Compromise, and Southern secession. The precedential decline of the Passenger Cases signaled the Supreme Court's growing deference to federal regulation of immigrants, beginning with Justice Samuel F. Miller's opinions, especially *New York v. Henderson* (1875). The limited influence of Passenger Cases during the twentieth century suggested persistent institutional imperatives that helped to explain the Court's affirmation of congressional supremacy enforcing preferential racial quotas during the 1920s. Federal supremacy also instituted less-restrictive immigration regulations that limited the quota system between the 1940s and the 1960s. From World War II on the Court's recognition of federal supremacy in immigration regulation further sanctioned many rights aliens shared with U.S. citizens, including the right of travel traceable to the Passenger Cases. Since the millennium the Supreme Court has upheld federal regulatory supremacy in conjunction with a modicum of aliens' rights such as freedom of movement that undercut restrictionist demands and state laws attacking "illegal" immigrants. In the Passenger Cases, the Court had affirmed a limited commerce power and Northern states' police powers to achieve much the same result.

The first chapter examines the origins of the cases in the financial and social welfare stake Massachusetts and New York had in maintaining open immigration under a system of bonds and commutation fees—distinct from alien taxes—that shippers endorsed. By contrast, based on the Constitution's power over commerce and treaty making, Congress passed its first major Passenger Act in 1819, which attempted to regulate the conditions of immigrants aboard vessels traveling between U.S. and foreign ports. In addition, like the Constitution's framers before them, state leaders engaged in compromise politics sanctioning state police power regulation of immigrants and free blacks. The Marshall Court avoided addressing the legal status of immigrants and free blacks as "persons" in its first commerce power decision, *Gibbons v. Ogden* (1824). The Court did not consider the question where state police power regulations over such "persons" ended and the federal power began until the 1830s. State police powers also controlled Southern slavery. The Supreme Court engaged neither the interstate slave trade nor imprisonment of free British sailors in Southern ports under Negro Seamen Acts until abolitionists began arguing that the federal commerce power enabled Congress to end both practices.

Chapter 2 considers the state courts' decisions upholding the Massachusetts and New York alien tax, as an extension of police powers underpinning the bond-commutation system that already regulated the admission of immigrants into both states. Each state court construed the *Gibbons* precedent in light of the U.S. Supreme Court's police-power ruling established in *City of New York v. Miln* (1837), which recognized a "commerce-person" distinction. The opinion for the Supreme Court in *Miln* distinguished between "persons," such as immigrants, free blacks, and slaves subject to state police powers, and "commerce," which was regulated by the federal commerce power. While privately a Supreme Court majority did not support the "commerce-person" distinction, the implications of the *Miln* ruling prompted multiple opinions addressing Mississippi's abolition of the slave trade within its borders in *Groves v. Slaughter* (1841). By the mid-1840s the North-South sectional struggle over Texas annexation and the status of slavery in the Western territories acquired in the war with Mexico politicized the Supreme Court, blocking appointments as never before. The Court's divided opinions implicating the "commerce-person" distinction further exacerbated the abolitionists' claim that Congress could abolish the interstate slave trade and weaken Southern states' control of free blacks identified with the Negro Seamen Act.

Chapter 3 discusses the lawyers' appellate arguments in the Passenger Cases for and against the alien tax, including the great constitutional advocate Daniel Webster representing the shippers and New York attorney general John Van Buren defending the states. The discussion explores legal and political connections linking the lawyers' appellate arguments to state immigrant regulations and new U.S. passenger legislation amid the momentous famine migration and slavery struggles during the late 1840s. The chapter also addresses the License Cases (1847), which reinforced the 4–4 impasse in deciding the Passenger Cases. Chapter 4 draws these materials together in order to explain the 5–4 vote and eight opinions in the Court's decision-making process of the Passenger Cases, including the arrival of a fifth justice who broke the 4–4 deadlock. The announcement of eight opinions in February 1849 exposed the bitter dispute between Chief Justice Taney and Justice James M. Wayne, revealing that a majority of the Court had never supported the "commerce-person" distinction. The Court's majority and dissenting opinions in the Passenger Cases enunciated divisions over the federal commerce power and state police powers that nonetheless provided constitutional legitimacy that ameliorated divisive sectional politics, facilitating the 1850 Compromise.

Chapter 5 examines the shifting significance of the Passenger Cases from 1849 to 1870. Against the anti-immigrant nativists identified with the Know-Nothings, pro-Southern Democrats joined Northern Whigs and Republicans in paradoxical support of stronger federal passenger laws based on the federal commerce power and treaties. Some Northern Democrats also joined Whigs and Republicans in compromise local politics, enacting state personal liberty laws that extended limited legal equality and state citizenship to immigrants and free blacks. Compromise politics also defused the Know-Nothings' most extreme exclusion policies. Southerners' adamant opposition to personal liberty laws and Northern states' conferral of citizenship on blacks, however, were primary justifications for the South's secession. The Passenger Cases remained important during the Civil War and Reconstruction, especially in the California Supreme Court's reliance on the commerce power and treaties to overturn state discrimination against Chinese aliens. The Passenger Cases also sanctioned New York's immigration regulations prior to 1870, which preserved the states' bond-commutation system based on police powers.

Chapter 6 traces the more limited precedential influence of the Passenger Cases, beginning with Justice Miller's commerce power opinions striking down California, Louisiana, and New York laws in the *Henderson* decision of 1875, which overturned the states' bond-commutation system. As a result, Congress enacted and the Court affirmed federal bureaucratic supremacy that displaced the commerce power as the basis for federal taxation and regulation of immigrants. By the 1920s federal preferential-racial quotas triumphed. In *Edwards v. California* (1941), however, the Court upheld American migrants' right of travel—which also embraced aliens—under a dormant commerce power consistent with the Passenger Cases. From World War II through the Cold War and the civil rights movement, greater alien admissions displaced the preferential-quota system, culminating in the historic Immigration Act of 1965. Amid the cycle of recession and boom from the 1970s though the millennium and War on Terror, illegal immigrants prompted restrictionists' demands for stronger state regulation. But the Supreme Court affirmed federal supremacy and state-federal cooperation in *Graham v. Richardson* (1971) and the *De Canas Case* (1975), both of which cited the Passenger Cases. In *Arizona I* (2011) and *II* (2012), federal supremacy and state-federal cooperation triumphed. Justice Scalia's dissent in *Arizona II* appealed to the earlier history of states' employing police powers in order to exclude undesirable immigrants and blacks. The Passenger Cases provided a counter-history in which admission of these groups prevailed.

A reconstruction of the obscure pre–Civil War commerce power applied to states and immigrants in the Passenger Cases concerned certain broad themes. Most of the book examines the judicial interpretation of the Commerce Clause (1824–1870) that supported immigrant admissions over exclusions, though episodically, of course, the latter also were significant. In 1875 the Court initiated a new era of immigration regulation dominated by the federal government and federal supremacy rather than the commerce power analysis that prioritized balancing state-federal power. Concurrently, the post-Reconstruction Supreme Court until recently has sanctioned a pervasive federal hegemony over the regulation of virtually all commercial activity through an expanded view of the commerce power. And more recently, drawing upon the post–Civil War constitutional amendments and the Supremacy Clause, the Court enhanced the ability of immigrants to constitutionally challenge the federal government's administration of antiquated immigration laws. This volume thus has a special importance as the current conservative Supreme Court continues to struggle with defining state police powers in regard to newly arrived and illegal immigrants, including Justice Scalia's dissenting view that the antebellum commerce power generally did not limit states' exclusionary polices.

Focusing on the origins, precedents, lawyer arguments, decision making, and outcomes of the Passenger Cases highlights less conspicuous influences on immigration and antislavery crises and the

South's secession. This process demonstrates the functions and malfunctions of the pre–Civil War federal Constitution, along with the Supreme Court's function as its principal interpreter. The 5–4 division of the Court anticipated the better-known, but even more divisive, views of the justices in the *Dred Scott* case (1857). And in consideration of the post-Reconstruction evolution of a new standard by which to judge immigration issues, the Passenger Cases revealed the continuing impact of constitutionalism that strengthened more humane concerns for alien groups. The book thus leaves no doubt as to the hardships and suffering of immigrants both before and after the Civil War. These issues continue to complicate immigration law as much today as they did more than a century and a half ago. The persistence of these problems suggests that a "decent respect to the opinions of mankind" continues to demand a coherent, humane, and more consistent immigration policy.

The antebellum Constitution's view of immigration matters provides today's Court with much valuable information concerning the interplay of federal and state functions in dealing with immigration issues. As discussed in the Alien Tax Cases, the individual states bore the major responsibility of caring for the welfare of newly arrived residents; that required additional revenues, or alternative financial bonding arrangements to ensure adequate controls and the availability of public health protection. Amid the limited expansion of federal authority in the era, the impact of immigration—including the complex connections to the legal status of free blacks and slavery—remained a controversial issue at both the state and national levels. Thus the Passenger Cases provided a perceptive, albeit backward, look at the complexities of governmental control and involvement in this critical area of our national life that has remained important in present times, including the so-called revolution launched by the Fourteenth Amendment's revisions of citizenship that aliens could share with U.S. citizens. Finally, readers have indicated that the retrieval of the unfamiliar commerce power issues in this history suggests that more rather than less excavation of legal, social, and economic "details" and their analysis through repetition may be appropriate. I have done my best to strike a balance.

CHAPTER 1

Origins and Precedents in Law and Politics, 1819–1837

Between the 1819 U.S. Passenger Act and the 1837 Panic the states developed primary control over admitting or excluding foreign immigrants. From victory in the American Revolution to the Napoleonic Wars, shippers and agents financed relatively modest numbers of immigrants making the transatlantic passage by requiring labor contracts traded like property in Southern slaves. During the 1819 Panic Congress passed the U.S. Passenger Act, which attempted to regulate spatial conditions immigrants encountered aboard vessels. Although poorly enforced, the federal law instituted regulations governing immigrant ships that included data collection showing steady increases in the immigrants arriving annually into U.S. ports. In New York City, the nation's leading port, the number of foreign immigrants grew from 13,000 in 1830 to 58,000 in 1836. Since federal regulation ended with immigrants' disembarkation from aboard ship, state and local governments evolved complex police powers that facilitated admission of immigrants. These police-power regulations drew immigrants into local, state, and national party politics embracing free blacks and Southern slavery. Gradually, the state and federal judicial process led by the Supreme Court reshaped political struggles into legal and constitutional issues contesting the point where federal commerce power regulation over foreign immigrants ended and state police power regulations began.

The following narrative recognizes that state police powers in principle certainly permitted exclusion of undesirable immigrants. The evidence nonetheless supports the thesis that from 1819 to 1837 factors driving immigration from Britain and Europe to the U.S., combined with the data collected under the U.S. and New York Passenger Acts, enmeshed the immigrant trade in local and state politics. The state and federal judicial process reconstituted political struggles into legal issues that reached the Supreme Court, ultimately contesting the status of immigrants and free blacks as legal "persons," the resolution of which facilitated the immigrants' admission more than exclusion. The first section presents the law and politics constituting the shift in the immigrant trade from labor contracts to free-trade competition that coincided with Marshall Court interpretations of the Constitution's commerce power in Article 1, Sections 8–10. The second section focuses on New York City's police powers and extralegal politics governing legal "persons" under the state's alien tax and the 1824 Passenger Act; the third section presents the same political and legal context for the 1837 alien tax within the Massachusetts poor law. The fourth section examines Chief Justice Marshall's success in deciding *Gibbons v. Ogden* and two other commerce power precedents by avoiding the legal status of "persons," until his delayed decision of *New York City v. Miln* left the outcome to a reconstituted Supreme Court led by Chief Justice Taney.

The U.S. Passenger Act and the Law and Politics of the Transatlantic Immigrant Trade, 1819–1837

Before the 1819 U.S. Passenger Act, emigration from Europe to America gradually increased and payment for passage relied primarily on labor contracts. In 1818 Pennsylvania congressman Adam Seybert published statistics indicating that the annual number of foreign immigrants arriving in the United States averaged about 4,000 from 1784 to 1794; in 1810 the estimated annual average had risen to 6,000. As a result of agricultural blights in Europe and Britain the number of immigrants arriving in the United States reached an estimated 10,000 in 1817. New York immigrant commissioner Friedrich Kapp later described labor contracts used to pay for the transatlantic passage by 1818. The "great majority of immigrants" were "so poor that they could not pay their passage, and in order to meet the obligations incurred . . . for passage-money and other advances, they were sold, after their arrival, into temporary servitude." Thus, "prepayment of the passage was the exception," and the "subsequent discharge by compulsory labor the rule. The ship owners and ship merchants derived enormous profits from the sale of the bodies of emigrants, as they charged very high rates for the passage, to which they added a heavy percentage—often more than a hundred per cent—for their risks. But the emigrants suffered bitterly from this traffic in human flesh." The U.S. Passenger Act reflected national and local politics, including the Supreme Court that encouraged states to admit rather than exclude growing numbers of immigrants by the 1837 Panic.

Kapp ascribed passage of the 1819 U.S. Passenger Act to Southerners who resisted the sale of white immigrants' labor contracts. A Delaware congressman condemned a broker who sold Germans' labor contracts in the slave state in 1817. Delaware and Virginia slaveholder congressmen then introduced into the U.S. House legislation that regulated the space allocated poorer steerage-class passengers aboard vessels plying the transatlantic immigrant trade. In 1819 an immigrant labor broker unsuccessfully petitioned the U.S. Senate for assistance in recovering Germans who absconded from labor contracts resold in Tennessee and Alabama after Ohio courts had refused to enforce the exploitation of white workers. In the four Southern states slaveholders condemned the sale of white labor contracts as approximating too closely the interstate slave trade that troubled Congress as it struggled to separate Western slave and free-labor territories during the years preceding the 1820 Missouri Compromise. Also prior to the Missouri Compromise, Virginia congressional representatives briefly supported transporting free blacks to Liberia at public expense. Free blacks, however, would not subject themselves voluntarily to the deplorable conditions aboard vessels offered steerage-class whites. Accordingly, once a Virginia representative called for a final House vote, the Passenger Act passed both houses of Congress and received President James Monroe's signature in 1819.

The 1819 Passenger Act proved difficult to enforce. Congress, said Kapp, "fixed the space allotted to the emigrants to five tons, Custom House measurement, for every two passengers, and in case of contravention punished the captain with a fine of $150 for each passenger." The law also "declared the ship to be forfeited to the United States, if the number of passengers carried exceeded the said portion of two to every five tons. It further specified the amount of water and provisions to be taken aboard by emigrant vessels, and exacted a fine of three dollars for every day that any passenger was put on short allowance." The tonnage and "customs measurement" nonetheless applied standards borrowed from the transport of material goods to people designated as "legal persons" requiring reasonable living conditions. The shippers manipulated the spatial criteria for immigrants by averaging together cabin and steerage specifications, even though disproportionate numbers—including families—occupied the steerage class. In addition, the food "provision" ignored the grim reality that very few vessels had cooking facilities sufficient for the large numbers of steerage-class immigrants. Moreover, the tonnage and customs measurements did not recognize that steerage-class passengers could afford limited food "provisions," which often were inadequate over the weeks and months sailing vessels required to make the transatlantic crossing.

Although Kapp reported that the sale of white immigrant contract labor ended in the United States by 1819, shippers and agents crowded immigrants aboard vessels despite the U.S. Passenger Act. Like other critics in the United States and Britain, Kapp condemned the ship owners who "chartered the lower decks of their vessels to agents, for the payment of a certain sum for each ton of the whole space disposed of. The agents made the needful temporary arrangements for the accommodation of the passengers, and underlet the steerage, either to associations of emigrants, or parcelled [*sic*] it out to sub-agents or to single passengers." Aside from "assigning a space, however small, to the emigrants," agents "had no responsibility, and ran no risk whatever." Aboard vessels, individual and family steerage passengers "had no other right than to occupy the ten or twelve square feet which were allotted to them." These crowded conditions in conjunction with the limited provision for water, food, and the means for their preparation bred disease. Yet the "agents, in order to make the business lucrative, sent on board as many passengers as they could get hold of, without the smallest reference [to] the convenience of the steerage, the number of the births, the separation of the sexes, or anything except their own immediate profit."

The 1819 federal Passenger Act included one regulation, however, that was enforced. The law required federal customs collectors in all U.S. ports to make quarterly reports to the secretary of state giving the "number of passengers arriving in their collection districts, by sea, from foreign countries; also the sex, age, and occupation of such passengers, and the country in which they were born." This statistical data thus established the numbers and national origins of the immigrants arriving in U.S. ports. From 1826 to 1830, for example, the annual totals of those entering the United States were 10,837; 18,875; 27,283; 22,530; and 23,322. Over these same years shifting proportions of immigrants came from the British Isles, including England, Scotland, Wales, and Ireland, with 7,709 in 1826; 11,952 in 1827; 17,840 in 1828; 10,594 in 1829; and 3,874 in 1830. Kapp, suggesting similar humanitarian evidence reported in *Parliamentary Papers*, explained that the "fluctuations were due to the great commercial panic of 1826, and the distress in the manufacturing districts of England, as well as" another "famine in Ireland, which drove thousands from their homes, who, under ordinary circumstances, would never have thought of emigration." Political struggles, by contrast, brought numbers of German immigrants that periodically exceeded that of British immigration with annual totals from 1834 to 1837 of 17,654; 8,245; 20,139; and 23,036.

Limited regulation favoring agents' and shippers' profits, combined with increasing numbers of immigrants, encouraged ineffective policing of the immigrant trade in ports. Agents and shippers rebuffed criticisms of harmful conditions on vessels, declaring that immigrants often came aboard already in poor health as a result of sharp practices perpetrated in Liverpool and other British ports. Even so, from the 1820s on reformers and philanthropists repeatedly petitioned Parliament, urging increased policing and regulation targeting notorious operations of private "hotels," "hospitals," and "runners." These enterprises took advantage of an immigrant's weakened physical condition caused by famine as she or he waited for days or weeks to board ship. Parliament's gradual funding of more policing and official oversight did not match the scale of harmful conduct. Reliance upon episodic litigation for enforcement had little deterrent effect. Moreover, the British consul in New York witnessed the deplorable condition of immigrants arriving from Liverpool in vessels that had not complied with the 1819 U.S. Passenger Act. He recommended that Parliament adopt standards that more nearly approximated those in the U.S. law. Parliament's 1835 act, however, simply compromised low standards the London Ship Owners Society proposed with those from the U.S. Passenger Act, which made for ineffective legislation.

Disease resulting from crowded conditions aboard vessels directly affected American states' police powers. The most common shipboard diseases resulting from noncompliance with spatial regulations were cholera, or "ship fever," followed by typhus and smallpox. Kapp reported medical "facts" demonstrating "that the ships on board of which cholera broke out were those which were most crowded with passengers, and the vessels on board of which deaths from other diseases occurred were next most crowded, whilst the remainder, which were healthy, had the lowest average of passengers." Throughout history, governments empowered port officials to protect local people from possible diseases carried by those arriving on vessels from foreign ports. In Europe and Great Britain central governments delegated this police power to port officials, who administered quarantines and exercised authority to deport aliens deemed a threat to the general welfare. The U.S. Constitution established a federal-state system, however, in which the separate states rather than the federal government administered police powers governing the health, safety, and welfare of citizens and immigrant aliens alike. As the transatlantic immigrant trade gradually grew from the 1820s to the Panic of 1837, the U.S. and British passenger laws' weak enforcement thus had profound social welfare consequences for the costs and administration of the states' police powers.

While federal and British passenger acts encouraged the transport of both healthy and infirm immigrants to U.S. ports, state police powers separated individuals admitted from those excluded. As long as the annual volume of immigrants to *all* U.S. ports remained low at around 4,000, state port authorities could readily identify and decide whether to deport the small proportion of undesirables. The statistics collected under the federal Passenger Act indicated not only the increasing immigrant totals but also that New York City was by far the leading destination of all national groups, especially the Irish and Germans. Indeed, by the Panic of 1837 about two-thirds of all foreign immigrants disembarked in New York. The factual evidence also showed that German ports enforced spatial standards that reduced shipboard crowding better than did the British ports, creating divergent welfare conditions between German and Irish immigrants. New York officials initiated a police power system that accommodated the uneven health and welfare of immigrants seeking admission to the state. Shippers signed bond agreements guaranteeing that disembarking passengers were not diseased, destitute, criminal, or dangerous radicals who within as long as a decade might jeopardize the state's welfare.

The bond agreements were the first step in states' regulation of immigrants that encouraged admission rather than exclusion. The bonds required two sureties using negotiable notes, which in turn provided long-term credit designated for the support of almshouses. In addition, New York City officials granted shippers the option to "commute" the bonds by paying a fee for each immigrant carried aboard ship. Shippers could include the cost of the commutation fee in the ticket price. As the volume of the transatlantic immigrant trade increased during the 1830s, ticket prices reflected greater than ever competition, which led shippers often to pay the total commutation fees using negotiable bills and notes. Like the bond-sureties, the commutation fees provided New York City officials another source of credit, which defrayed social costs of administering the almshouses and other immigrant welfare services. The state also authorized city officials to support the immigrant regulation system with a portion of the auction duties collected from the sale of all imported goods entering the port. The state also enabled local officials to levy an "alien tax" on each and every foreign immigrant without regard to health, which funded the administration and services the city provided at the Maritime Hospital adjacent to quarantine on Staten Island. The system of bonds, sureties, commutation fees, auction duties, and the alien tax gave New York City officials a stake in admitting rather than excluding foreign immigrants.

The admission of foreign immigrants to U.S. ports also influenced citizenship. The Constitution granted the federal government the power to naturalize foreign immigrants residing within states and federal territories. Immigrants residing in federal territories acquired by treaty from foreign nations, in the Northwest Territory, which the states ceded to the federal government in 1787, or in the territories separating slavery and free labor in the 1820 Missouri Compromise acquired federal citizenship. The states Congress established from federal territories conferred state citizenship. For foreign immigrants who after admission continued to reside in New York, Massachusetts, or other states, this state and federal citizenship triggered complex issues of interstate privileges and immunities and qualification for federal court jurisdiction. Still, Justice Bushrod Washington noted in 1824, "every citizen of a state owes a double allegiance: he enjoys the protection and participates in the government of both the State and the United States." Robert Ernst, a historian of New York City immigrant life from 1825 to the Civil War, described the realities of acquiring what amounted to dual citizenship: "Immigrants were met at the boat; a 'naturalization bureau' was set up at the" city's Tammany Hall "Wigwam where aliens were advised and assisted in filling out naturalization papers; and it was common knowledge that many of these adopted citizens voted before they had fulfilled the Federal residence requirement of five years."

Chief Justice John Marshall's Supreme Court established constitutional precedents interpreting the federal commerce power and state police powers that facilitated state admission of immigrants. The Constitution's Article I, Section 8, enumerated the Commerce Clause enabling Congress "to regulate Commerce with foreign Nations, among the several states, and with the Indian Tribes." In *Gibbons v. Ogden* (1824) the Marshall Court held that Congress possessed an exclusive commerce power to license vessels plying interstate coastal waterways and to enact treaties and other international agreements such as the tonnage regulations imposed in the federal Passenger Act. This exclusive commerce power encouraged a steady flow of immigrants to U.S. ports and among the states and territories. Marshall's opinion in *Gibbons* also upheld *state regulation* affecting foreign trade, such as quarantine and use of local pilots, which the Court later upheld in the *Cooley* case (1852). Other commerce power provisions in Article I, Sections 8–10, included limited taxes, customs, and tonnage that authorized shared federal-state regulation, such as "essential inspections." During the early 1830s in *New York City v. Miln* Marshall delayed deciding whether state police regulations regulating admission or exclusion of immigrants designated as legal "persons" violated federal laws and an exclusive commerce power. By the 1837 Panic the *Miln* litigation embraced divisive immigrant, free black, and slavery politics in New York, Massachusetts, and the Supreme Court.

New York's 1824 Passenger Act and Alien Tax in Law and Politics, 1819–1837

New York's rise as the nation's leading port in the transatlantic immigration trade drew upon federal and state regulations that encouraged admission of immigrants. The statistics stipulated under the 1819 U.S. Passenger Act established that in 1821 New York had four times the number of immigrants arriving aboard vessels from foreign ports compared to each of its closest competitors: Boston, Philadelphia, New Orleans, or Baltimore. The comparatively larger number of immigrants entering New York City resulted in the state assembly passing the Passenger Act of 1824. The U.S. Passenger Act focused on the number, birthplace, gender, age, and occupation of immigrants. New York's 1824 Passenger Act, however, required shipmasters to provide written reports of each passenger's physical and mental condition. The reports were the basis for bond and surety agreements between shipmasters and the city; they also established a record enabling the mayor's office to discharge liability if the shipper instead paid the commutation fee. The reports also aided collection of the alien tax that supported the Maritime Hospital, though the tax was levied on passengers and crew alike without regard to health. Regulations instituted in U.S. and New York passenger laws enabled city officials and brokers to pursue corrupt practices through the bond, surety, and alien tax system, which in turn implicated state politics embracing immigrants, free blacks, and slavery in the 1836 presidential election.

The alien tax was integral to New York's system of immigration regulation. Though the alien tax had operated since the 1790s, the legislature altered it in 1829 in order to support the Maritime Hospital. The law required masters of vessels arriving in the city from a "foreign port" to pay a $1.50 tax levied on the captain, each crew member, and every steerage- or cabin-class passenger. Masters of coasting vessels running from New York City to ports in other states paid twenty-five cents "for each person on board," except that coasting vessels from "New-Jersey, Connecticut and Rhode-Island" paid the tax on only "one voyage in each month, computing from the first voyage in each year." Ship masters, in turn, were empowered to recover from the passengers and crew the amount of the tax. Shipmasters of vessels arriving from "foreign" ports paid the tax to the "health officer" representing the city's "commissioners of health." In order to collect the tax on board vessels, the "commissioners of health" also were required to "furnish a convenient boat with sufficient boatmen, for the use of the health officer." Masters of coasting vessels, by contrast, had no more than twenty-four hours after entering port to pay the tax at the health commissioner's New York City "office." The penalty for noncompliance was $100. If any shipmaster refused to pay the tax, the health commissioner sued for recovery in the city's name.

New York's alien tax extended the federal-state regulatory system linking police powers to federal commerce power regulations. The shippers' claim was not that the state tax on immigrants was an economic "burden," but instead that it conflicted with the federal passenger law, which regulated the same people aboard ship. The immigrant tax city "health commissioners" enforced funded the "Marine Hospital" built on state property occupying the "easterly shore of Staten-Island." The elaborate tax-collection process enabled maintaining and staffing the public hospital that ostensibly serviced immigrants in poor or diseased condition. Still, the alien tax was collected from shipmasters on vessels regulated under the U.S. Passenger Act, and from captains operating coastal vessels requiring a federal coasting license. Indeed, the ill-health of immigrants sent to the Maritime Hospital often arose directly from shipmasters' or shippers' failure to comply with the regulations stipulated in the U.S. Passenger Act. The health officer's alien-tax collection aboard vessels arriving from "foreign" ports also embraced the same state-federal regulatory system, including the U.S. Passenger Act, local pilots, the Staten Island quarantine, and health reports prescribed under New York's 1824 Passenger Act. Thus, city officials enforced the alien tax directly on shippers operating the transatlantic and coastal immigrant trade governed under the federal commerce power sustaining the U.S. Passenger Act within New York harbor, in order to maintain patients in the state Maritime Hospital on Staten Island.

In addition to the collection of the alien tax, the 1829 statute also stipulated Maritime Hospital governance targeting health-care accounting costs and enforcement. The "hospital monies" supported the institution's "physician," titled the "health officer," the "mates, nurses and attendants," and the "bedding, clothing, fuel, provisions, medicine, and such other articles." Although "[e]very sick person sent to the marine hospital, shall be there kept and attended to, with all necessary and proper care . . . no such person shall leave the hospital, until the health officer shall grant a discharge in writing." Moreover, the health officer could compel "in writing, any constable or other citizen to pursue and apprehend any person, not discharged who shall elope from the hospital," and to return "such person" to be "detained" at the hospital "until regularly discharged." Indicating further the potentially involuntary nature of hospital admittance, the statute also designated that "every person who shall so elope shall be considered guilty of a misdemeanor, punishable by fine or imprisonment." These penalties meant that the alien tax supplemented "those who [themselves] shall have paid hospital money, and such poor persons as the board of health shall exempt." In addition, others "sent to the hospital" able to "pay a reasonable sum for their board, medicine, and attendance" could be sued for the "recovery of such sum" in the "name of [the health commissioners'] office."

While the 1829 statute directly taxed shipmasters in order to fund the Maritime Hospital, its underlying police powers sustained systemic corruption. Like the bond-surety system, the statute imposed an enforcement process giving hospital and health officials a judicial cause of action in order to recover against shipmasters and shippers, as well as immigrants designated as "persons." In most cases, the 1829 alien-tax statute and the bond-security system also protected New York City officials from litigation except where culpable conduct could be expressly proven, such as in cases concerning the public accounting of moneys. Following the 1819 U.S. Passenger Act, the volume of the transatlantic immigrant trade steadily grew, replacing white contract labor with cabin- and steerage-class passengers paying more competitive ticket prices. As the city's income and credit grew from the increased immigrant trade, the state assembly granted New York City officials broader powers, including the 1824 Passenger Act and the alien tax. Commissioner Kapp later reported, however, that "old abuses were continued with the same impunity. In fact, the entire business became a private traffic between a set of low and subordinate city officials, on the one hand, and a band of greedy and unscrupulous brokers, on the other. It was . . . legalized robbery, the headquarters of which was at the City Hall."

New York City's corrupt practices and the volume of immigrant trade expanded together. Whereas the annual immigration to New York averaged about 4,000 between 1819 and 1824, by 1829 it had risen to about 14,000. The 1830 census registered "aliens, foreigners not naturalized" at about 8.77 percent of New York County's total population, compared to 2.74 percent for the rest of the state, and over twice that of Boston. In 1836 about 58,000 immigrants arrived in the city. Shipmasters and shipping firms accommodated the growing trade seasonally: part of the year they filled vessels with bulk cargos such as lumber or dry goods, but during a better-weather season they crammed the same vessels to full capacity with immigrants. Exposés of tragic conditions on board vessels transporting immigrants equated their plight with the Middle Passage in the international slave trade, which since 1808 Congress had formally outlawed. Such evils continued after the immigrants' disembarkation into New York City. Thus, Kapp reported, "as soon as emigration assumed greater proportions, [city] law [enforcement] became susceptible of the most flagrant abuses, which were actually practiced under it, and it did not afford the slightest indemnity for the maintenance of those who became chargeable to the city [under poor laws]." Indeed, "within a day or two after landing," many immigrants were "taken from wharves in large numbers, in a state of destitution, and sent to the Alms Houses."

The transatlantic immigrant trade and New York City's immigrant regulations also were entangled in party politics. Northern and Southern politicians knew that growing numbers of Irish immigrants entering New York City during the 1830s voted Democratic. These voters depended on Tammany Hall leaders turning the federal naturalization law to the purpose of recruiting immigrants who voted before completing the federal five-year residency requirement. Supported by Tammany Hall, the city's Democratic aldermen also administered the moneys and credit from the bond-surety system, the alien tax, and other sources in return for immigrant community votes. In addition, the 1830 census showed the breakdown between the city's free blacks and "alien foreigners" to be 13,959 and 17,773 respectively. New York enfranchised free black males, though because of a property-holding requirement the numbers were smaller than those in Massachusetts and other New England states. Nevertheless, by the mid-1830s the city's and the state's black voters supported temperance and education laws Whigs enacted, which Irish Catholic immigrants and the Democratic Party resisted. Thus, while New York City's white immigrant population gradually outstripped the numbers of free blacks, the latter's support for Whig's temperance and education measures ensured interracial conflict that both undercut social-class unity and strengthened political-party divisions.

The city's interracial party conflicts affected complex statewide politics encompassing the South. Although most Southerners had limited direct involvement in the immigrant trade, Southern leaders had supported the 1819 U.S. Passenger Act, following revelations that white immigrants were treated like black slaves. Southerners also supported the New York court ruling in 1834 that state law did not shield an escaped slave, Jack, from being returned to his master. North-South sectional politics also fostered Southerners' growing attention to Irish immigrants arriving in New York City. For decades New York usually allied itself with the Southern states in presidential elections. Victory for the intersectional alliance in the 1836 election, however, depended more than ever on city Democrats delivering the immigrant vote, as New Yorker Martin Van Buren campaigned against three different Whigs and South Carolina's anti-Jackson candidate. New York's internal sectional divisions nonetheless aligned western and upstate counties in which blacks joined Whigs voting against Democrats and their immigrant supporters. Although Van Buren won the election, the free black–white immigrant party conflicts that characterized New York City had become statewide. Accordingly, after 1836 Van Buren and other western or upstate Democrats gradually distanced themselves from proslavery Southern Democrats.

New York's 1824 Passenger Act and alien tax tested the separation between federal and state regulations admitting immigrants within city, state, and national politics. The New York law facilitated implementation of the bond-surety-commutation system and the alien tax, which encouraged the city's admission rather than exclusion of immigrants. Indeed, between 1830 and 1836 the number of immigrants entering New York port increased from 13,000 to 58,000, encouraging Tammany Hall's immigrant-voter recruitment, corruption in administration of immigration regulations, and party politics that divided free black and immigrant voters. Transatlantic shippers also benefited from the weak enforcement of the 1819 U.S. Passenger Act and Parliament's 1835 law. New York's Passenger Act and the 1829 alien tax nonetheless affected the same immigrants subject to regulation under the U.S. and British Passenger Acts and trade agreements. During the early 1830s a shipper challenged the state's Passenger Act in *New York City v. Miln* as a violation of the Marshall Court's commerce power precedents, U.S.-British laws, and trade agreements; the case also embraced issues concerning the Negro Seamen Act and interstate slave trade. As the *Miln* case wended its way to decision in the U.S. Supreme Court, the Massachusetts alien tax engendered a constitutional challenge to the same Marshall Court precedents, which had political ramifications for the state's immigrants and free blacks.

Law and Politics in Police Powers and the Massachusetts Alien Tax of 1837

The 1837 alien tax helped to finance the operation of the Massachusetts poor law. Since 1832 the number of immigrants entering Boston harbor had risen nearly threefold compared to the later 1820s. Roughly 60 percent of these immigrants were destitute Irish who, despite contract commitments to emigrate from Ireland to British North America, soon removed to Irish American communities such as Boston. Massachusetts courts also enforced the freedom of sojourner slaves Southern masters voluntarily brought into the state. These poorer immigrants and freed blacks encouraged levy of a $2.00 alien tax on ship captains for every foreign passenger entering the state's ports. The alien tax supported the Massachusetts poor law enabling most destitute persons to receive certain benefits, while those designated paupers, diseased, political radicals, or criminals could be deported. The tax extended to "alien passengers" a policy existing since colonial times "designed to guard this privilege of relief at the public expense, in cases of extreme indigence, from abuse, and to secure the State and its citizens from unreasonable burdens, whilst providing for exercise of a duty of humanity towards those, who in the ordinary course of life are placed within its borders." Like New York's immigrant regulations, the Massachusetts alien tax evoked immigrant and racial politics and constitutional challenges.

The state's empowering of port officials to collect the alien tax affected many of the same people regulated through federal laws and treaties. Boston port inspectors determined whether alien passengers arriving aboard vessels came within state police power rules that enabled excluding persons designated unfit for reasons of hygiene, immorality, criminality, or radicalism. The federal Passenger Act and U.S. treaties authorized state port officials to quarantine or deport immigrants in cases of known or suspected disease. The state inspection system also required shipmasters to post a $1,000 bond with sufficient security, affirming that the designated person or persons would not become public charges for ten years. Along with these police power regulations, the Massachusetts legislature in 1837 levied the $2.00 alien tax; Boston port officials authorized "boarding officers" to collect it from ship captains before the designated immigrants disembarked. State law and the Marshall Court commerce power precedents authorized the municipal operation of the bond-surety system, quarantines or deportation in cases of health hazards, and state regulation of pilots for vessels entering the state's harbors. The alien tax differed, however, in that it was essentially a revenue measure funding the state poor law levied through shipmasters on the same passengers subject to federal laws and treaties sustained by the commerce power. Such state-revenue measures could raise constitutional objections.

The Massachusetts alien tax passed in 1837 amid divisive politics embracing Irish immigrants. Federal customs officers routinely collected tariff duties until South Carolina "nullified" the federal tariff during the Nullification Crisis. Although Andrew Jackson's 1833 Force Act compelled South Carolina to capitulate, nullification set certain Massachusetts Democrats against Southern Democrats preceding the 1836 presidential election. Meanwhile, the growing numbers of Irish Catholic immigrants increasingly were segregated within certain communities near Boston, such as Worcester and Lowell. The federal five-year naturalization process nonetheless enabled Irish immigrants to readily acquire state citizenship. By the mid-1830s the

Boston *Courier* described recent Irish Catholic immigrants as belonging to the "Customs House party" of Democrats. The term suggested New York City "St. Tammanies'" political clout, which exploited Irish self-identification contained in the data customs officials collected under the U.S. Passenger Act. During the same period, poorer Irish constituted over 30 percent—a proportion greater than any other national group—of the residents in Boston's poor houses. The 1837 alien tax thus became law not long after sectional politics divided Massachusetts Democrats, while Irish voters exercised increasing influence among Boston Democrats and destitute Irish were primary beneficiaries of the state poor law that the tax supported.

Robert C. Manners, the British consul in Boston, urged shipmasters to legally protest paying the alien tax. The legal protests signaled not only Manners's support for the shippers' dislike of the levy, but also the lawful presumption that if courts declared it unconstitutional, captains and shippers could recover from the state the amount of paid taxes plus interest. Even so, the Boston boarding officer levied the alien tax while requiring from the shipmaster documentation stating the immigrant passengers' physical and mental condition. Municipal-port authorities also empowered boarding officials to deny disembarkation to immigrants from vessels whose master did not pay the alien tax. The method of protest thus reflected the reality that moneys paid the boarding officer might be recovered through litigation between the city official and the shipmaster or a ship owner. Such recovery was only possible, however, if a court declared the tax unconstitutional. In addition, unlike the bond-surety system, which was a contractual obligation generally based on negotiable commercial notes due at some later date, the tax required immediate payment. When Canadian officials imposed a similar tax, opponents' only recourse was to lobby provincial legislatures and Parliament, which did not succeed. Manners, however, raised constitutional claims that federal or state judges—and ultimately the Supreme Court—could use to overturn and ultimately force repayment of the alien tax.

The Constitution's federal power to naturalize aliens provided further national political context for the Massachusetts alien tax. The Federalists' controversial 1798 Naturalization Act had extended the alien residency period from five to fourteen years; the shorter period, however, was reinstituted in 1802. Another provision of the 1798 act that longer remained in effect stipulated that any white alien arriving in the United States should within forty-eight hours appear before a federal official authorized to grant a registration certificate. Aliens who previously were resident in the United States had six months to register. The 1802 act did away with the mandatory legal registration system at the time the alien entered the country, though a signed registration document could be used as evidence for the purpose of proving the five-year residency period. Conditional registration was repealed after Congressman James Buchanan's 1828 report informed the House of Representatives that the system was so widely ignored that it had little practical effect. Alarmed at how readily New York Tammany Democrats and other local political machines exploited the federal naturalization process in order to confer state citizenship upon immigrants, some nativist spokesmen lobbied Congress for a return to the fourteen-year period. These nativist initiatives achieved little success, however, during the 1830s.

The Massachusetts poor law supported in part by the alien tax provided assistance to all destitute groups irrespective of gender, race, or national origin. Since 1794 the state's poor law empowered each county to confer a "settlement" upon qualified male paupers—including the disproportionate numbers of Irish in the Boston poor house—wives and families, small property holders, transients (including seamen), free blacks, and a few slaves. The 1794 law also required the county to pay litigation costs in cases challenging the administration of the poor law. By 1837 dispossessed free blacks, white steerage-class immigrants, and even a former slave could qualify for the poor-law settlement, funded in part by the alien tax. The poor law covered litigation affecting settlement claims, which guaranteed equal judicial due process including blacks and white foreign immigrants alike. Notwithstanding this procedural equality, the state's personal liberty law permitted racial separation in public schools, as well as a school curriculum reflecting Protestant values, which discriminated against Catholics. Massachusetts courts' procedural equality nonetheless was sharply distinguishable from many other free states that practiced varying degrees of racial discrimination under black laws. The state's greater legal equality for blacks and white immigrants in the administration of justice and the poor law was still more pronounced in comparison with the strict white supremacy permeating Southern slavery.

The alien tax passed in 1837 amid fragmented party politics benefiting Democrat Marcus Morton. During the later 1830s Whig Party dominance of Massachusetts politics eroded in part because growing numbers of Irish immigrants in and around Boston provided pivotal support for Morton, who was antislavery, while some Massachusetts Democrats remained loyal to Southern Democrats' promotion of slavery. Within greater Boston, moreover, a faction of Scots-Irish Protestant workers within the Democratic Party resisted the growing numbers of recent Irish Catholic immigrants who worked for lower wages. In 1834 and 1837 the clash between the native workers of Scots-Irish Protestant descent and the recent Irish Catholic immigrants resulted in violence, including the burning of a "fashionable" school for young women run by the Ursuline Sisters in Charlestown. Nevertheless, the solid bloc of Irish Catholic voters, combined with the state's western farm workers identified with the "workingmen movement" and Anti-Masons, enabled Morton to receive a growing proportion of votes in gubernatorial elections. In the presidential election year of 1836 Morton's gubernatorial vote rose to 10,765, while his victorious Whig opponent, Edward Everett, gained just 4,605 votes. Three years later Morton finally was elected governor by a single vote.

The Whigs' eroded dominance of Massachusetts politics reflected a similar fluidity that aided passage of the 1837 alien tax. While Massachusetts Whigs were overwhelmingly Protestant, a persistent division involved support for a state temperance bill that empowered local officials to restrict consumer sale of alcohol beverages to the point of virtual prohibition. A faction of Whigs embraced prohibition, targeting Irish Catholics' alcohol consumption; the more restrictive legislation became law in 1838. In addition, Massachusetts was one of several New England states in which adult black males voted; because generally they were devout evangelical Protestants, these same blacks tended to support those Whigs demanding the restrictive temperance law. Some Whigs also joined black voters advocating political action to abolish slavery, contrary to William Lloyd Garrison's movement, which advocated abolition while eschewing politics. Also, Massachusetts Whigs generally opposed admitting proslavery Texas into the Union after it won independence in 1836. In the same year the Massachusetts Supreme Judicial Court decided *Commonwealth v. Aves*, which freed Med, a six-year-old slave girl, from a master who had voluntarily brought her to Boston. The court held that the state constitution and many court precedents since the 1772 *Somerset* case freed slaves in states that, like Massachusetts, had abolished the institution through positive and common law.

Despite Massachusetts' fragmented politics, the alien tax reflected bipartisan party support. The 1830 census suggested that blacks and recent immigrants occupied pivotal political constituencies: one person was designated a "slave," while 7,048 were "free colored persons," the number of "aliens (foreigners not naturalized)" was 8,787, and there were 603,359 "free white persons." The Panic of 1837 hurt individuals and families in all three groups; the alien tax contributed to the poor law, which offered a county "settlement" to members of each group on the basis of legal equality. This poor-law equal access passed amid Whigs' and free blacks' promotion of temperance laws targeting Catholics. Support for the alien tax and poor law also coincided with the antislavery stance of free blacks, many Massachusetts Whigs, and pro-Morton Democrats, including his Irish immigrant supporters. The shared antislavery stance of each state party's leaders also condemned the Southern Negro Seamen Act, which interfered with conservative Boston merchants' free trade employing free-black sailors. Still, the bipartisan antislavery politics consistent with the state's poor law was contrary to some Massachusetts Democrats' loyalty to Southern Democrats' defense of slavery. All groups' equal access to the poor-law "settlement" also passed in 1837 notwithstanding discrimination imposed in the Boston schools' "equal-but-separate" doctrine against free blacks and anti-Catholicism in the public school curriculum.

Amid contested immigrant and racial politics, Boston's British consul Robert Manners challenged Massachusetts' alien tax. During the 1837 Panic the tax raised costs on British and American shippers engaged in the immigrant trade; Manners represented these same commercial interests. The alien tax nonetheless helped to fund Massachusetts' poor law, encouraging port officials to admit rather than exclude immigrants. In addition, antislavery free blacks and many Whigs embraced the legal equality of poor-law access and judicial due process conferred upon freed slaves that the alien tax also aided. From the perspective of these and other Massachusetts authorities, the 1837 alien tax merely extended the state police powers sustaining the poor law. Manners undoubtedly perceived that the same police powers underpinned both Massachusetts' relative legal equality and the discrimination enforced by Southern Negro Seamen Acts, which the British government resisted. He also understood, however, that unlike the bond-surety or quarantine systems, the alien tax was essentially a revenue measure levied upon the same individuals regulated by the federal Passenger Act and U.S.-British treaties. Manners thus urged ship captains to pay the tax under protest, which laid the foundation for recovery if a court held that the alien tax was a revenue measure that clashed with Marshall Court precedents establishing an exclusive federal commerce power.

Law and Politics in the Marshall Court's Shifting Commerce Power from *Gibbons* to *Miln*

The Supreme Court did not construe the federal commerce power until *Gibbons v. Ogden* (1824). Prior to that decision Indian land claims, the international slave trade, and foreign consuls seeking federal court enforcement of admiralty jurisdiction over piracy and slave traders indirectly concerned commerce power issues. Meanwhile, Chief Justice Marshall, Justices Joseph Story and William Johnson, and others established the Supreme Court's independence despite political attacks. Indeed, *Gibbons* arose following Virginian John Taylor's criticism in 1823: the "consent of Congress [was] required to state laws in relation to duties . . . [b]ecause these were rights included in the principle of state sovereignty, subject to a limited federal control." Taylor's strict interpretation of commerce power provisions in Articles 8–10 also coincided with Charleston's defeat of Justice Johnson's attempted use of the exclusive federal commerce power to strike down South Carolina's Negro Seamen Act. Political contestation recurred during the Supreme Court's successive commerce power cases that avoided construing the status of free blacks or foreign immigrants as legal "persons." The tensions between politics and the Marshall Court's commerce power precedents delayed deciding in *New York City v. Miln* whether the state's 1824 Passenger Act clashed with the U.S. Passenger Act, treaties, and an exclusive commerce power.

The basic facts in *Gibbons* were that Thomas Gibbons, operating under a federal coastal license, ran steamboats between the New Jersey shore and Manhattan. Aaron Ogden held a license from the original monopoly the New York legislature conferred upon Robert Fulton's early steamboat. New York courts upheld the state monopoly against Gibbons on the ground that it was a legitimate exercise of police powers within the state that did not affect the interstate and international commerce power. Gibbons appealed the state police power and federal commerce power claims to the Supreme Court. In *Gibbons* Chief Justice Marshall's opinion for the Court began with vigorous language suggesting that Congress possessed an exclusive commerce power to regulate commerce defined beyond the mere trade in goods, embracing "intercourse" on an expansive scale. Marshall's actual holding, however, did not use the "exclusive" terminology; he overturned New York's steamboat monopoly on the narrow ground that it conflicted with the federal Coasting Act under which Gibbons held a license. Fundamentally, Marshall struck down the monopoly employing a limited interpretation of congressional power that supported the federal coasting statute as an exercise of federal supremacy. Marshall also affirmed state police power regulations requiring quarantine, the bond-surety system, or the employment of local pilots, enabling state collection of fees, limited by the expense to the state of the service provided.

Unlike Marshall's reliance upon the federal Coasting Act, Justice Johnson's concurring opinion in *Gibbons* targeted police power regulation of "persons." The South Carolina Association's vigilante action in Charleston obstructed Johnson's circuit case, *Elkison v. Deliesseline* (1823). Fear of the aborted 1822 Denmark Vesey slave conspiracy fired South Carolina's defense of the state's Negro Seamen Act that required free-black sailors to be imprisoned while their vessels remained in state ports. Penalties for noncompliance included enslavement of free-black seamen. Johnson's circuit decision held that the state law was contrary to an exclusive commerce power, though free-trade reciprocity with Britain was not stressed. Negotiations among British, U.S., and state officials won Elkison's release. The local defiance, however, spurred Johnson's sweeping concurrence in *Gibbons*, emphasizing an exclusive commerce power that denied state interference with "persons" moving in interstate commerce. Johnson did not mention free-black seamen. He rejected, however, that state sovereignty empowered police power regulations obstructing "the right of controlling personal ingress or migration, as implied" in the commerce power affirmed in the Constitution's Article I, Section 9, regulating the international slave trade. Johnson's opinion impliedly embraced not only "slaves," but also "persons of all descriptions," including black seamen.

Marshall's affirmation of the federal Coasting Act and an exclusive commerce power also addressed Justice Smith Thompson's silent opinion. Appointed to the Marshall Court in 1823 during the appeal of *Gibbons*, Thompson did not participate in the case because of family-health reasons. As a state judge, however, Thompson had served on the New York court that upheld the steamboat monopoly, suggesting a theory of concurrent-commerce power. New York's chief justice, James Kent, had conceded that "it may be difficult to draw an exact line between those regulations which relate to external and those which relate to internal commerce, for every regulation of one will, directly or indirectly, affect the other." Kent regarded a "safe rule of construction" to be that "if any given power was originally vested in this state, if it has not been exclusively ceded to congress, or if the exercise of it has not been prohibited to the states, we may then go on in the exercise of the power until it comes practically in collision with the actual exercise of some congressional power." Wherever such a "collision" occurred, the "state authority will so far be controlled, but it will still be good in all those respects in which it does not absolutely contravene the provisions of the paramount law." Avoiding a determination of where a "concurrent power" might begin or end, Marshall nonetheless applied Kent's reasoning, resting his *Gibbons* opinion squarely on the federal coasting law, sustained by an exclusive commerce power.

Marshall directly confronted Thompson's dissent in *Brown v. Maryland* (1827). The state imposed a license tax on Baltimore importers, testing congressional regulation of foreign commerce. A key issue was whether the license tax came within the proviso of Article I, Section 10, that "no state shall, without the consent of Congress, lay any imposts, or duties on imports or exports, except what may be absolutely necessary for executing its inspection laws." In the latter category, Congress had permitted state regulations such as quarantine and requirements for local pilots. Consistent with the precedent of *Gibbons*, Marshall curbed state police powers through a compromised exclusive commerce power. The state license tax was invalid as applied to imported goods contained in "original packages" arriving in Baltimore from abroad; it thus was not "absolutely necessary" for "inspections." The license tax was valid, however, imposed on goods removed from those packages for resale among local retailers. Justice Thompson's dissent termed the distinction artificial. Any tax on importers was passed on to consumers through retail prices levied according to the police power; since the latter was constitutional, so was the former. Still, just as he had avoided the slavery and free-black issues Johnson's concurring opinion had implied in *Gibbons*, Marshall's *Brown* opinion did not suggest police power regulation of "persons" such as immigrants, free blacks, or slaves moving in interstate or foreign commerce.

Marshall avoided the federal commerce power in *Willson v. Blackbird Creek Marsh Co.* (1829). Employing police powers, the Delaware legislature incorporated a construction company to drain a swamp by building a dam across a navigable stream. The sloop *Sally* "licensed" under U.S. "navigation laws," including the Coasting Act, collided with the dam. The Blackbird Creek Marsh Co. won $20,000 in damages from a jury, which the state's highest court affirmed. Under section 25 of the 1789 U.S. Judiciary Act, Captain Thompson Willson appealed to the Supreme Court claiming that the company's dam breached the federal commerce power embracing navigable waterways. Willson's argument suggested that since no claim based on a federal statute was argued, the dam violated a dormant commerce power. The vessel nonetheless operated under the federal coasting license like that Marshall had used to strike down the New York monopoly in *Gibbons*. Marshall, however, ignored both the federal coasting statute and the nascent dormant commerce power, upholding the state's police power. The Marshall Court's decision in *Willson* favored police powers supporting state development projects like New York's Erie Canal. Marshall's affirmation of state police powers also avoided the implication that white immigrants or free blacks designated as legal "persons" crossing state lines or arriving from abroad aboard ships might be regulated by an exclusive commerce power.

Political pressures suggested why Marshall's commerce power

precedents did not address the legal status of "persons" within the federal commerce power or police powers. Marshall maneuvered within state-sovereignty challenges from Virginia, Ohio, and Kentucky. In particular, Kentucky senator Richard M. Johnson repeatedly introduced legislation to eviscerate the Supreme Court's appellate jurisdiction. When the *Gibbons* litigation coincided with South Carolina's defiance of Johnson's *Elkison* decision, Marshall confided in Justice Story: "Thus, you see fuel is constantly added to the fire at which the exaltées are about to roast the judicial department," using laws "not very unlike in principles to that which our brother [Johnson] declared unconstitutional." Similarly, Marshall said, in Virginia "a case has been brought before me in which I might have considered its constitutionality had I chosen to do so; but it was not absolutely necessary, and as I am not fond of butting against a wall in sport, I escaped into the construction of the statute." Marshall's same strategic avoidance rested *Gibbons* narrowly on the federal coasting law rather than solely on an expansive exclusive commerce power. Similarly, in *Brown v. Maryland* Marshall rejected that a state's "essential inspections" embraced the "original package" doctrine that endorsed a compromised exclusive commerce power. The *Willson* decision dismissed both an exclusive and a dormant commerce power, upholding broad state police powers.

Although Marshall's three commerce power decisions ignored the status of free blacks or immigrants designated as legal "persons," the issue was unavoidable in *New York City v. Miln*. New York's 1824 Passenger Act enabled city officials to require from ship captains health reports for growing numbers of immigrants. City officials fined shipmasters who refused to file the reports. In 1829 these authorities sued on a debt action in state court to recover fines amounting to $15,000 from William Thompson, captain of the *Emily*, and his consignee George Miln. As a foreign national, Miln removed the case to the U.S. Circuit Court for the Southern District of New York. Both parties agreed that recovery of the fines raised the question whether New York's Passenger Act was a valid police power regulation, or did it violate an exclusive commerce power upon which rested federal treaties and the federal Passenger Act? Justice Smith Thompson and federal district judge Samuel Betts constituted the U.S. Circuit Court. In order to certify the appeal to the Supreme Court, Thompson and

Betts divided over the scope of the police power and the commerce power. The question in *Miln* directly addressed the legal status of white immigrants as "persons" under police powers for purposes of determining their admission to or exclusion from the state. Marshall delayed deciding *Miln* partially in order to gain support for overturning New York's Passenger Act as contrary to an exclusive commerce power.

Marshall died in 1835, leaving *Miln* undecided until Roger B. Taney was chief justice in 1837. Meanwhile, the federal judicial process channeled state and national politics embracing immigrants and free blacks as legal "persons" into the issues *Miln* presented: whether New York's Passenger Act and police powers clashed with the federal Passenger Act, treaties, and an exclusive commerce power. In 1837 Boston's British consul Manners also initiated the legal-protest strategy challenging the alien tax within the state's poor law, which brought into the state judicial process immigrant, free-black, and antislavery politics linked to the federal passenger law and exclusive commerce power. Massachusetts' alien tax raised basically the same constitutional questions as its New York counterpart. The Supreme Court's 1837 *Miln* decision thus would shape the law and politics of each state court's opinions admitting or excluding immigrants, free blacks, and slavery. But the *Miln* decision depended on attitudes Jackson's Court appointees John McLean, Henry Baldwin, and James M. Wayne held toward *Gibbons* and Marshall's other commerce power precedents. Only Justice Story supported an expansive exclusive commerce power. For Justice Thompson *Miln* presented the opportunity again to promote the concurrent-commerce power, while it offered Jackson's last Court appointees, Taney and Philip Barbour, the means to address Marshall's police power and commerce power precedents for the first time.

From the U.S. Passenger Act to the delayed decision of *Miln*, the law and politics of states' admitting or excluding immigrants concerned legal "persons." According to commissioner Kapp, up to 1819 shippers and agents controlled immigrant labor contracts that financed the transatlantic passage. Following the Napoleonic Wars, however, British and European agricultural and industrial dislocation brought steady increases in the number of immigrants transported to American ports, especially New York City. This trade shifted to ticket-price competition, with the U.S. Passenger Act and U.S.-British trade agreements prescribing weak shipboard spatial regulation of immigrants' welfare. State police powers, by contrast, governed bonds, sureties, commutation fees, alien taxes, and other regulations facilitating immigrants' admission to rather than exclusion from states. The financial and credit advantages states gained from these regulations rested on information shippers supplied port officials, which emphasized the immigrant's national origin and physical condition as "persons" rather than "commerce." Electoral politics and extralegal practices also promoted admitting immigrants as voters and cheap labor, despite resistance from white-native and free-black workers and citizens. By the 1837 Panic the state and federal judicial process reshaped the immigrant and racial politics into legal issues pitting state police powers against the federal commerce power in the *Miln* and the Alien Tax Cases.

CHAPTER 2

Federal and State Court Litigations, 1837–1843

During the depressed economy of 1837–1843, federal and state court litigation channeled political conflicts into state police powers and federal commerce power governing states' admission or exclusion of white foreign immigrants, free blacks, or slave traders. Despite economic distress, federal and state courts generally affirmed admission of foreign immigrants and free blacks in Northern states, while the Supreme Court proclaimed Southern state supremacy in the exclusion of free blacks and the regulation of slavery. The first section of this chapter locates the Taney Court's 1837 *Miln* decision—including the disputed "commerce-person" distinction—within New York's admission of white immigrants and the interracial politics driving Southern exclusion of free blacks. The second section considers *Norris v. City of Boston* (1839–1842) challenging the linkages between the 1837 alien tax and the Massachusetts poor law that instituted formal legal equality governing the state's admission of white immigrants, free blacks, and slaves as legal "persons." The third section considers *Smith v. Turner*, testing the state's alien tax within New York City's troubled immigrant affairs and racial politics, including the police power status of legal "persons" admitted to the Maritime Hospital and quarantine on Staten Island. The fourth section examines the Taney Court's divisions in *Groves v. Slaughter*, supporting Mississippi exclusion of slave traders and its implications for the appeals of the Massachusetts and New York Alien Tax Cases by 1843.

New York City v. Miln (1837) and the "Commerce-Person" Distinction

In 1837 the Supreme Court decided *Miln* amid an economic panic. Still, a record total number of 84,000 immigrants entered all U.S. ports. Justice Thompson and the U.S. Circuit Court had divided in order to bring the matter before the Supreme Court. The question was whether the immigrant reports required under New York's 1824 Passenger Act violated federal laws and the commerce power. When Chief Justice Marshall died in summer 1835 the question divided the Court, perhaps as closely as 3–3. In 1836 the Senate, which earlier had blocked President Jackson's choice of Roger B. Taney to be associate justice, confirmed him as chief justice. Virginian Philip Barbour was then confirmed as associate justice. Jackson's earlier appointees, Justices McLean, Baldwin, and Wayne, undoubtedly knew Marshall had delayed deciding *Miln*, partially at least because he had hoped to persuade some or all of them that the state-report proviso violated federal laws and the exclusive commerce power. By the January term a newly constituted Taney Court had heard *Miln* reargued to include briefs bearing on not only police powers and the commerce power regulating admission or exclusion of immigrants, but also the status of Southern laws barring free blacks. Justice Story dissented. Taney rejected Thompson's opinion upholding a concurrent-commerce power, while the Jackson appointees disputed among themselves whether "persons" were "commerce" subject to regulation by police powers or the commerce power.

The final arguments in *Miln* noted the basic facts and issues, as well as the need to overcome the Court's preexisting divisions. Upon arrival in New York from Liverpool, William Thompson, master of the *Emily*, did not file the reports for 100 passengers mandated under the state's 1824 Passenger Act. Consignee George Miln removed the case to the U.S. Circuit Court for the Southern District of New York. District judge Samuel R. Betts and Justice Thompson divided on the narrow question whether the reporting provision of the state's 1824 Passenger Act "assumes to regulate trade and commerce between the port of New York and foreign ports and is unconstitutional and void." The case was appealed to the U.S. Supreme Court, employing the procedural certificate of division. Lawyers and members of the Supreme Court agreed that this particular appellate procedure was significant because it shaped the ultimate decision around the narrow question rather than other possible issues, such as the constitutionality of New York's alien tax. Lawyers for either side argued to bring the state immigrant reports within the state's police powers or to show a conflict with a federal law such as the federal Passenger Act based on an exclusive commerce power, as Marshall had suggested in the *Gibbons*, *Brown*, and *Willson* precedents. Still, said one, the "very hesitation of a court constituted as this was, admonished him of the doubts and difficulties attending the solution of the question."

The central question was whether federal "power regulating commerce" was "so exclusive that all states' laws affecting or regulating commerce" were "necessarily void, even where no conflict exists." Chief Justice Marshall had overturned the state steamboat monopoly in *Gibbons* based expressly on the U.S. Coastal Licensing Act, rather than relying solely upon an expansive exclusive commerce power. All three Marshall Court commerce power precedents also affirmed state "harbour regulations," state "pilot" laws, "health" laws, and the "laws of police as to the conduct of crews of vessels while in port." In addition, legitimated police powers included "a class of laws peculiar to the southern states, prohibiting traffic with slaves, and prohibiting masters of vessels from bringing people of colour in their vessels." Moreover, "if the power to pass laws regulating the admission of passengers from Europe, fall under the power of regulating foreign commerce, that of regulating the arrival of passengers by land, falls under the power of regulating commerce between the states. If the one be exclusive, the other is exclusive; and all vagrant laws, all poor laws, and police regulations, become at once, solely of federal jurisdiction." Should the Court permit these wide-ranging results, "the laws of the southern states in relation to the intercourse and traffic with slaves, and to the introduction of coloured persons into those states, also become the subjects of federal jurisdiction, and the state laws are abrogated."

The lawyers' arguments in *Miln* reflected persistent contention over free blacks and slavery. Attorney General Roger Taney had said in 1831–1832 that the legal status of "persons," such as free blacks and foreign immigrants, was "subject always to the laws" of the United

States or foreign "countries" or was between Northern and Southern states. In America the "African race" was "a separate and degraded people to whom the sovereignty of each state might accord or withhold such privileges as they deemed proper." Suggesting without naming New York, Massachusetts, and other New England states that conferred adult manhood suffrage upon qualified free blacks, Taney said that "where they are nominally admitted by law to privileges of citizenship, they . . . [are] permitted to be citizens by the sufferance of the white population." The arguments in *Miln* also followed Britain's 1834 abolition of slavery in the West Indies. Since 1830, too, successive editions of David Walker's *Appeal to the Coloured Citizens of the World* spread openly from Boston through Northern free states and surreptitiously across the South, despite aggressive censorship. Walker advocated black-liberation consciousness and citizenship like the freemen rising from Britain's abolition movement. Nat Turner's Rebellion in Virginia, William Lloyd Garrison's uncompromising Protestant abolitionism, the murder-martyrdom of abolitionist Quaker Elijah Lovejoy in 1836, and resistance to Negro Seamen Acts also stoked proslavery anger.

The narrow procedural posture in *Miln* framed by the circuit court's certificate of division suggested the Taney Court might avoid racial contention as had Marshall's commerce power decisions. Since *Miln* came up from Thompson's circuit, Chief Justice Taney initially assigned writing the Supreme Court's opinion to the New Yorker. Thompson crafted an opinion that upheld the state's passenger-reporting provision under the concurrent-commerce power, as a legitimate exercise of police powers regulating admission or exclusion of immigrants. He reasoned that New York City officials administered the report requirement ashore after immigrants had disembarked from vessels. The reports did not violate the 1819 U.S. Passenger Act based on an exclusive commerce power regulating those same immigrants while being transported at sea or while still aboard ship in port. The distinction between "internal" and "external" commerce could locate the reports within the former, which Marshall held in *Gibbons* and the other two precedents to be clearly subject to police power regulations. Thompson emphasized that in "the leading cases upon this question, where the state law has been held to be unconstitutional, there was an actual conflict between the legislation of congress and that of the states, upon the right drawn in question." In "all such cases the law of congress is supreme; and the state law, though enacted in the exercise of [lawful police] powers . . . must yield to it."

Yet as Thompson pronounced the concurrent-commerce power, he also distinguished it from the "dormant power." Thompson thus stated the "very important principle" that the "states retain the exercise of powers; which, although they may in some measure partake of the character of commercial regulations, until congress asserts the exercise of the power under the grant of the power to regulate commerce." His focus upon the necessity for a state law in conflict with an express statute of Congress also explained why the state report proviso did not conflict with the "dormant" commerce power, which was enforceable without congressional action. Even so, Thompson pressed the point of regulating immigrants' admission or exclusion from the state: "Can anything fall more directly within the police power and internal regulation of the state, than that which concerns the care and management of paupers or convicts, or any other class or description of persons that may be drawn into the country, and likely to endanger its safety, or become chargeable for their maintenance?" He noted that Marshall's *Gibbons* and two other precedents left unsettled the point where the commerce power ended and the police power began. Thompson's concurrent-power rule, by contrast, "defined limits to the exercise of this power to regulate commerce; or what shall be considered commerce with foreign nations, and what regulations of domestic trade and police."

Taney, however, did not accept Thompson's concurrent-commerce power as the basis for the Court's majority opinion in *Miln*. Taney undoubtedly knew that sitting as a state judge, Thompson had applied the concurrent-commerce power to uphold New York's steamboat monopoly. Indeed, the need to deny that theory had partially motivated Marshall's reliance in *Gibbons* upon the federal Coasting Act as exemplifying an exclusive congressional power superseding state law. Yet in *Miln* the issue was not only whether the state report proviso conflicted with an express federal law and commerce power; it also concerned the legal status of citizens as free "persons," moving in interstate coastal waterways from other U.S. ports. Presented in this light, such "persons" could embrace American and British free-black sailors or free blacks emigrating from the West Indies after Britain's abolition of slavery in 1834. As attorney general, Taney had conceded that through the "sufferance of the white population" free Northern states held the sovereign right to confer citizenship upon free blacks. Shippers from New York and Massachusetts employed such free black citizens to transport white immigrants from Europe and blacks from the West Indies; the same vessels also navigated America's interstate coastal and inland waterways. From Taney's perspective, then, Thompson's concurrent-commerce power did not state firmly enough the extent to which states could exclude free blacks, especially if they were citizens.

Story's *Miln* dissent embracing "citizens" seeking admission to ports further aggravated Taney. Story urged that Marshall believed the New York immigrant reports to be in violation of the exclusive commerce power underpinning the 1819 federal Passenger Act and other laws. Thus, Story concluded, "whatever restrains or prevents the introduction or importation of passengers or goods into the country, authorized and allowed by Congress; whether in the shape of a tax or other charge, or whether before or after their arrival in port, interferes with the exclusive right of congress to regulate commerce." Story's reading of *Gibbons* and the two other earlier precedents in order to strike down New York's reporting provision represented the exclusive commerce power Marshall had preferred and Taney opposed. Story's reasoning in dissent about interstate travel of "persons" designated "citizens" also could have alarmed Taney. Story targeted the language in the New York law "that whenever any person brought in such ship, and *being a citizen of the United States* [emphasis in original], shall be by the mayor . . . deemed likely to be become chargeable to the city; the master or owner shall, upon order for this purpose, remove every such person without delay to the place of his last settlement." Story had hoped to overturn this language enabling state officials to deport naturalized citizens—including free blacks—whereas Taney believed that the very same state power was essential, especially in the South.

Taney reassigned the *Miln* opinion to Barbour. During the final argument counsel had noted new "Laws relating to Coloured Passengers and Seamen" that Georgia, Virginia, Louisiana, and South Carolina passed in 1834–1835 following British abolition of slavery in the West Indies. Thus, while Barbour formally grappled in *Miln* with white immigrants regulated under New York police powers authorizing admission to and exclusion from the state, he also faced possible implications of the decision for Southern states' laws excluding "foreign" free blacks. The latter suggested Barbour's language distinguishing *Brown* and the "original package" doctrine: "But how can this apply to *persons*? They are not the subject of commerce; and, not being *imported goods*, cannot fall within a train of reasoning founded upon the construction of a power given to congress to regulate commerce, and the prohibition from imposing a duty on imported goods" (emphasis in original). Like Marshall in *Gibbons*, no member of the Court in *Miln* mentioned free blacks. Barbour, however, was expansive concerning exclusion of "persons" from states. He implied that the primary "object of the legislature was, to prevent New York from being burdened by an influx of persons brought thither by ships, either from foreign countries; or from any other of the states . . . to prevent them from becoming chargeable as paupers." This reasoning reflected Taney's publically expressed views about the need for states to exclude undesirable "persons."

Shortly after Barbour's *Miln* decision upholding the New York law, Baldwin published *A General View of the Origin and Nature of the Constitution and Government of the United States* (1837). In his discussion of *Miln* Baldwin did "not inquire whether" the commerce power was "exclusive in congress, or may be, to a certain extent, concurrent in the states." Targeting instead the *Miln* holding on "persons," Baldwin limited the "inquiry" to the "framers'" provision that "[n]o state shall, without the consent of congress, lay any imposts or duties on imports or exports, except what may be absolutely necessary for executing its inspection laws." Distinguishing between the commerce power restricted by enumeration and state police powers underpinning "inspection and analogous laws," the states "may regulate the importation and exportation of the subjects of foreign commerce, so far as is necessary for the execution of such laws," following Marshall's "original package" doctrine. Since state police powers regulated admission or exclusion of indigents, Baldwin rejected Barbour's separation of "persons" from "commerce," declaring, "To my mind there can be no such cause for discriminating between an imported and domestic pauper; one is as much an article of commerce as another, and the same power which can force them into a state from a vessel, can do it from a wagon, and regulate their conveyance on the roads or canals of a state, as well as on its rivers, havens, or arms of the sea."

The reason for Baldwin's separately published *Miln* opinion was known only within the Taney Court. In a hurried private conference the Court's members claimed to have missed Barbour's introduction into the majority opinion the distinction that denied "persons" were "commerce." When Baldwin discovered and asked Taney to have Barbour remove it, Taney balked, insisting that Barbour had left town and the opinion would be published as written. Baldwin condemned Barbour's "commerce-person" distinction in principle as contrary to the limited exclusive commerce power Marshall had affirmed in *Brown v. Maryland*; he also rejected its gratuitous introduction into the *Miln* majority opinion, as well as Taney's cavalier handling of the incident. Justice Wayne firmly embraced Baldwin's criticism; for the rest of his years on the Court it influenced adherence to the limited exclusive commerce power Marshall had pronounced in *Gibbons*, *Brown*, and *Willson*. Amid ever-percolating ambition to become president, Justice McLean accepted Baldwin's and Wayne's criticism; it encouraged a willingness to pronounce commerce power opinions that resisted Taney's views. The three Jackson appointees had not participated in Marshall's commerce power decisions. But they served during the delayed *Miln* arguments, which enabled them to appreciate Marshall's strategic avoidance of issues involving free blacks and slavery, which Barbour's "commerce-person" distinction could inflame.

The four *Miln* opinions reflected contending commerce power theories. Only Story's dissent held that the state's reporting regulations violated an exclusive commerce power underpinning the 1819 U.S. law regulating passengers aboard ship. More troubling for Taney was the implication that Story's dissent accepted free-black citizenship. Thompson's concurrent-commerce power held that state and federal regulation of the same individuals was possible as long as the express federal or state purpose was distinguishable; his opinion also came closest to formulating a dormant-commerce power theory. Neither theory, however, received the Court's support. Taney endorsed Barbour's separation between "persons" and "commerce," enabling Northern states to exclude white indigent immigrants and Southern states to do the same with free blacks. Baldwin, Wayne, and McLean rejected the "person-commerce" distinction regarding the commerce power, but upheld that police powers enabled states to *admit* or *exclude* persons from foreign and interstate-operating vessels regulated under federal laws. Known only among the members of the Court, the disputed distinction between "commerce" and "persons" ultimately cast a shadow over the appeal of the New York and Massachusetts Alien Tax Cases, and the Taney Court's next commerce power decision, *Groves v. Slaughter*.

The Massachusetts Alien Tax Case: *Norris v. City of Boston* (1839–1842)

Although the *United States Reports* later stated that the *Norris* case arose in 1837, the Massachusetts reports gave the year as 1839, when a depression engulfed the nation. The state's esteemed chief justice, Lemuel Shaw, thus knew the impact the tax had on admitting immigrants receiving the poor-law settlement and its relation to state-police and commerce power precedents, especially *Miln*. Yet his opinion encouraged admission rather than exclusion. The facts were that captain James Norris, commanding the schooner *Union Jack* operating from the port of St. John, New Brunswick, a British colony, arrived in Boston during June 1839. On board the schooner were "nineteen persons" listed as passengers, "aliens to each and every of the States of the United States, but none of them were lunatics, idiots, maimed, aged or infirm." Before the immigrants departed the vessel, Boston agent Calvin Bailey demanded and received from Captain Norris $38.00, in payment of the $2.00 alien tax levied on each passenger. Consistent with British consul Robert C. Manners's strategy, Norris paid "under a protest" that the 1837 tax was "unconstitutional and in violation of the treaties between" the United States and Great Britain. The Court of Common Pleas upheld the alien tax; Norris made exceptions, which were appealed to the state's highest court. By the time of Shaw's decision in 1842, the number of immigrants arriving in Boston was more than double that in 1839, which influenced state and local politics.

The *Norris* appeal came before the Supreme Judicial Court of Massachusetts and Chief Justice Shaw. The prominent Rufus Choate represented Norris versus the state's attorney general and the city attorney of Boston. The constitutional "question" the appeal presented, Shaw said, far exceeded in significance the "small" tax levied under the law. Still, amid the depression the tax helped to fund the state's poor-law benefits each town or city guaranteed qualified persons; at the same time, it increased shippers' costs as numbers of immigrants declined compared to the early 1830s. Moreover, the tax was integral to the administration of the state's entire poor law, embracing indigent persons from within and arriving from outside the state, as well as other "persons" termed physically or mentally "infirm," who were not included in the litigation. Thus, Boston officials' agents such as Calvin Bailey collected the state tax levied for police power purposes on ship captains like James Norris for immigrant passengers as a *condition for disembarkation* from vessels, such as the *Union Jack*, operating in interstate and foreign trade. These passengers, crew, and vessels also were regulated by federal laws and the commerce power. The federal laws at issue were the 1799 baggage regulations and the 1819 Passenger Act based on the Constitution's Article I, Sections 8 and 10, in pursuance of certain commercial treaties between the United States and Great Britain.

Shaw's opinion considered the state police powers underpinning the alien tax and poor law versus the commerce power and federal regulations. Thus Shaw said that the 1837 law prescribing the tax, "having been passed under all the forms required by the [Massachusetts] constitution to give it force of law, must be regarded as valid, unless it can be clearly shown to be contrary to the constitution of the United States. Whether it is so, is therefore the only question in the case." The court's answer to "this question must depend mainly upon a comparison of the statute of the Commonwealth with the laws of the United States, to determine whether they are in conflict," including the "object and purpose for which" the state's poor law and tax "were established." Indeed, the 1837 law providing for the alien tax and its collection merely extended legislative poor-law policies reaching back to the colonial "period long anterior to the establishment of the constitution of the Commonwealth." The legislative and constitutional "object" of these policies was "to make provision for the relief of poor and destitute persons, being within the limits of the State . . .

whether such persons were citizens and subjects of the State or not." Moreover, local knowledge and administration of authorities in each town determined whether "such persons" were residents.

The poor law's presumption that determination of residency was left to local community control reinforced express policies governing admission or exclusion. Thus, the residency qualifications sought "to prevent the increase of this [poor law] burden upon the State" through two broad administrative policies: either "by prohibiting the introduction of paupers from other places, or to admit such introduction upon conditions intended to secure the State from this burden." Although local community officials took seriously the "prohibition" policy, Shaw indicated that exclusion was exceptional, embracing primarily known criminals or those infected with disease. Otherwise, even regarding people with severe mental and physical disabilities, local authorities applied reasonable discretion consistent with the "general provisions of the [Massachusetts] poor laws" that "make it the duty of the proper officers of cities and towns to furnish immediate relief to any poor person being within their limits, without regard to . . . whether such persons have a settlement in such town or any other town, of the State or not, or whether he [or she] be the citizen or subject of any other State or country." Accordingly, the 1837 alien tax law encouraged exclusion from the state in only exceptional circumstances; instead, the law's primary police power purpose was to ensure sufficient poor-law funds enabling local officials' increased regulation of passengers disembarking from foreign vessels.

Shaw's opinion recognized that city agents' administration of the alien tax imposed upon ship captains such as Norris a new regulatory requirement. Prior to 1837, "in cases where the alien passenger [was] not, at the time [of arrival in port], infirm, or otherwise disabled, so as to require immediate relief," the shipmaster could choose "to pay five dollars to cover the risk that such passenger will become a pauper and chargeable to the public—as a commutation for the duty of giving bond, with surety, conditioned to indemnify the public against the same peril." The commutation thus permitted the shipmaster a choice between a $5.00 payment or a long-term bond and surety that was enforceable in court after passengers disembarked. In *Norris*, however, the constitutional question was whether a tax that "unconditionally required" the shipmaster "to pay two dollars for each of such passengers, before he can be permitted to land them, conflicts" with federal regulations governing the same persons and vessel. In *Gibbons* and *Brown*, said Shaw, the Marshall Court acknowledged that states possessed police powers over shipping to carry out inspections and quarantines, the removal of gunpowder, and local regulation of pilots, which might affect interstate or foreign commerce without raising constitutional objections. Marshall's holding in *Willson v. Blackbird Marsh Co.* upheld such police power purposes despite possible conflicts with the federal coasting law or dormant-commerce power.

In *Norris*, Shaw held, the governing precedent was *Miln*. The Supreme Judicial Court did not need to depend on the other "obviously analogous cases," because in *Miln* the U.S. Supreme Court "expressly decided . . . that the States have the power to pass laws regulating the introduction of persons who may become paupers; that the power existed before the formation of the [1787] constitution . . . and was not taken away by it." Even Justice Story's dissent conceded, Shaw said, that state police powers enabled poor laws excluding paupers unless there was an express conflict with a federal "act regulating commerce." Shaw then reasoned that the 1837 tax came within the Supreme Court's *Miln* majority decision and not Story's dissent. The tax extended the state's poor law requiring both "relief of the indigent and the protection of the State. If the law operates upon passengers before they have actually landed, this is merely a matter of convenience, like the collection or security of the duties on goods." Accordingly, Shaw held, "the real and sole object of this [tax] law, on the part of the legislature, was in good faith to carry into effect that part of the poor laws of the State, which provides relief for every suffering member of the human family, who is, at the time, within its limits, including the foreigner, however, recently brought within its limits." Thus, within the "poor law system" the tax "operates upon such aliens, before they are landed" consistent with the "duty of simple humanity."

Shaw's reliance on *Miln* to support immigrants' admission into the state embraced the "commerce-person" distinction. He ignored Justice Barbour's contention in *Miln* that virtually the sole purpose of the New York law was to exclude undesirables. Rather, Shaw construed Barbour's opinion to mean that it "did not consider the term *imports* as applying to *persons.*" Accordingly, such "persons . . . not [being] the subject of commerce, and not being imported goods, cannot fall within a train of reasoning founded upon the construction of a power given to congress, to regulate commerce" or the "prohibition to the States, from imposing a duty on imported goods." Also, it was unnecessary to consider whether an "exclusive" federal commerce power possessed a silent or dormant force separate from a federal statute. Norris's lawyer, Rufus Choate, argued that the 1837 alien tax violated the 1799 federal regulations of baggage carried in foreign trade and the 1819 act regulating transatlantic transport of passengers, both of which had support in commercial treaties between Great Britain and the United States. Even so, the "commerce" versus "person" distinction placed the latter within the state's legitimate poor-law regulations, which coexisted but did not conflict with the federal regulations. Finally, because the amount Norris paid was "small," neither Shaw nor his colleagues accepted the "argument much pressed" that the tax was a revenue measure.

The *Norris* decision had implications for state interracial politics. Consistent with British consul Manners's strategy, Norris's protested payment of the alien tax in 1839 and the Shaw court's adverse decision in 1842 resulted in appeal to the Supreme Court. Choate's appellate argument suggested that Shaw's emphasis on immigrants' admission to rather than exclusion from the state could be useful in narrowing Barbour's "commerce-person" distinction in *Miln*. The constitutional contention concerning legal status of "persons" also reflected Massachusetts political tensions embracing recent immigrants and free blacks. The state's poor law, as noted above, established comparative legal equality for free blacks, as well as those immigrants satisfying the federal five-year naturalization requirement. Poor-law assistance and alien-tax contributions also aided wider free-black and white-immigrant communities of voters amid splintering party politics. By 1842 free blacks supported the new Liberty Party's demanding slavery abolition and the Whig Party's temperance stance. Democrats led by Marcus Morton could win local or state elections only with the support of disaffected Whigs and recent immigrants; they needed also to avoid the hard-line pro-Southern slavery position identified with Democratic supporters of John C. Calhoun. Shaw's *Norris* opinion favoring immigrants' admission to Massachusetts and Choate's appeal thus ensured that the case possessed continuing significance in state and national racial politics.

The New York Alien Tax Case: *Smith v. Turner* (1841–1843)

The facts in the New York case seemed straightforward. George Smith was captain of the British vessel *Henry Bliss*, engaged in the immigrant trade between Liverpool and New York. William Turner was the New York City health officer responsible for collecting the penalty of $1.00 per passenger in lieu of the $1.50 alien tax that supported the Maritime Hospital located on Staten Island. Under the New York statute described above, the Maritime Hospital, the tax supporting it, and the penalty for nonpayment established a regulatory system administered by private health officials subject to city regulations. Amid the generally increasing annual immigrant trade reaching New York port, the Maritime Hospital was integral to the quarantine facility abutting it on Staten Island. In June 1841 the *Henry Bliss* arrived in port with 295 steerage-class passengers on board; after the passengers disembarked, Smith did not pay the alien tax. Turner sued to recover the penalty totaling $295. Smith's lawyer filed a demurrer, claiming that the statute imposing the tax was unconstitutional and void because it violated federal laws and treaties. At trial and on appeal in state court the "single question" was "whether the statute of the legislature of New York upon which the act is founded is an unconstitutional and invalid law." The decision for Turner encouraged admission of immigrants to the Maritime Hospital and quarantine; it also coincided with corruption in local immigrant and racial politics.

The New York statute prescribing the alien tax and nonpayment penalty authorized Turner's suit for recovery from Smith. In the supreme court of the state, Turner sued on an action of debt claiming $295; Smith's defense did not question the fact that he refused to pay the debt. Rather, the purpose of Captain Smith's demurrer was to establish the constitutional basis for challenging the statute upon which rested both the alien tax and the nonpayment penalty. If after the lengthy appellate process Smith won, the practical result would be that nonpayment of the alien tax and penalty constituted a legal protest establishing the precondition in the future for a possible damage award. Nevertheless, from the perspective of Turner and the city,

Smith's winning was unlikely given that state police powers prescribing the alien tax and penalty directly funded the Maritime Hospital; the same police powers indirectly resulted in defraying the cost of maintaining the New York port quarantine, which seemed consistent with Marshall's holding in *Gibbons*. The two facilities were located in the same place on Staten Island. New York statutes also provided that the same health officer was "to reside at the quarantine ground, to board and examine any vessel arriving . . . and to have the charge of the hospital at the quarantine ground." At trial the facts that the New York law linked the hospital and quarantine within police powers enabled the court's decision for health officer Turner.

Following the lower court's adverse decision in September 1842, Captain Smith appealed to the Court for the Trial of Impeachments and the Correction of Errors in New York, the state's highest court. His argument was that although the quarantine relied on police powers that Marshall's *Gibbons* decision held coexisted with the federal commerce power, it was a health measure distinct and separate from the alien tax and the nonpayment penalty. State high courts, the U.S. Supreme Court, and foreign tribunals upheld quarantines as essential to protecting communities' health and welfare, especially regarding the possible transmission of dangerous diseases in ships. The lower court erred, however, in deciding that the tax was "a part of the quarantine system" operating in New York port. Whether the health officer received the tax on foreign passengers or sued for nonpayment, the funds procured did not "enable the authorities of New York to prevent the introduction of disease" since as in the present case the immigrants had left the vessel and entered the city. Indeed, contrary to the acknowledged preventive purpose of the quarantine system, the New York alien tax funded the "expenses attending the exercise of the power of the State to protect its citizens from the consequences of disease already in the city." Thus, "by appropriating" a state tax on foreign passengers "to objects totally unconnected with the system of quarantine" it clashed with the commerce power sustaining federal regulation of passengers arriving in vessels from abroad.

Turner rebutted the claims that the quarantine and tax exercised separate police powers and addressed the federal commerce power based on *Miln*. Legislation linking the quarantine and hospital dated from the 1790s, when Governor John Jay and state legislative committees including DeWitt Clinton and Aaron Burr had the quarantine moved from Governors Island to Staten Island. The distance between the city and quarantine increased, respectively, from three-quarters of a mile to nine miles. The same legislation "also required . . . a wall to be thrown around it [quarantine] as high and impassable as that of a state prison, [so] that no one might enter or escape without permission of the health officer. It also directed that a marine hospital should be built within the wall, and adequate accommodations prepared for all who should be sent to quarantine." Although the connection between quarantine and hospital did not itself justify the tax, the process by which the health officer enforced its collection was part of immigration regulations like the bond-surety system and pilots. Moreover, the health officer assessed the amount of the "alien" passenger tax aboard vessels arriving from foreign ports, based on the ship captain's reports administered under the New York law the U.S. Supreme Court upheld in *Miln*. The police powers affirmed in *Miln* were interdependent with those sustaining the alien tax, so that the constitutionality of the one followed from the constitutionality of the other.

Turner's main argument included further claims. Story's dissent in *Miln* suggested that New York's alien tax was unconstitutional because it was collected from the same foreign steerage-class passengers that the 1819 U.S. law regulated. Turner's answer was that the federal act "regulates the number of passengers who may be taken on board by the tonnage. It was made in the exercise of the undisputed . . . power of Congress over vessels on the ocean." Following the *Miln* precedent, the state alien tax and federal regulation embraced the same passengers who had departed vessels after arriving within New York harbor. These same "persons" were not "commerce," especially regarding their police power status as potential bearers of disease isolated in quarantine and possibly admitted to the Maritime Hospital. Turner's argument also addressed the contention that the "exclusive" federal commerce power need not impose "any conflict with any written law, any actual regulation, but with 'a non-regulation,'" dubbed a "dormant" power. Marshall had declined to follow such a dormant-commerce power in *Willson v. Black Bird Creek*. Similarly, Madison's recently published accounts of the 1787 Constitutional Convention had indicated that he believed "commerce" to be a "unit" embracing items both actually regulated by Congress and potentially regulated under a dormant commerce power.

In October 1843 the New York Court for the Trial of Impeachments and the Correction of Errors affirmed the lower court's decision in *Smith v. Turner*. The lower court's decision and appeal occurred during crisis years in New York City's administration of immigrant affairs, indirectly involving the alien tax. At the same time a turnover occurred in the state's court reporter that delayed publication of certain cases, including the alien tax decision. Not until after the appeal was underway did the new reporter publish New York's highest court decision for health officer Turner. The court applied Marshall's reasoning in *Gibbons* upholding quarantines as indisputably among those police powers left to the states, notwithstanding possible impact on federal regulations such as the federal Passenger Act. The state laws linking quarantine and the Maritime Hospital through the same health officer in the same locale on Staten Island supported a legislative policy refuting Smith's claim. Moreover, the alien tax relied on the immigrant-reporting system upheld as a legitimate exercise of New York police powers governing "persons" in *Miln*, consistent with the state immigrant regulations that embraced the bond-surety system and pilots. The New York high court relied on these precedents, rather than Story's dissent in *Miln* or a dormant-commerce power that even Marshall had expressly avoided.

The state high court's decision awarding Turner recovery of the alien tax–nonpayment penalty coincided during 1842 with revelations of malfeasance in New York City government. As the economic depression ebbed, Commissioner Friedrich Kapp later reported, "daily increasing immigration" arrived into New York port, reaching a new high of 74,000. The immigrant reports describing passengers' physical and moral condition upheld in *Miln* and the alien tax case exposed the eighteen-year void in accounting for moneys collected through the bond-surety system. A city alderman called for a "committee investigation" into and "report upon the subjects of reporting, bonding, and commuting of passengers, and the course pursued in relation to aliens and others who made application to" the almshouse commissioners "for relief." In 1843 the committee published an extensive factual record. It revealed that the "profits growing out of the bonding system to brokers became larger, and with keen attention to pecuniary gain, these unscrupulous men appropriated to themselves what, of right, belonged to the City," amounting annually to over $46,744. Under state law the moneys collected from the alien tax and nonpayment penalty concerning the Maritime Hospital were accounted for separately from the bond-surety system and so were not subject to the exposed corruption. Still, the exposé confirmed the growing admission of immigrants in *Smith v. Turner*, which was being appealed to the Supreme Court.

Shortly after the New York court upheld Turner in October 1843, U.S. Supreme Court Justice Thompson died. The Court's vacancy left appeal of the state's alien tax case dependent upon President John Tyler's nomination of a New Yorker. Embroiled in North-South confrontation over Texas annexation, the Senate rejected an unprecedented number of Supreme Court nominees; not until 1845 did New York judge Samuel Nelson finally replace Thompson. Meanwhile, New York's immigrant and racial politics fractured the Democrats and Whigs because the Liberty Party drew not only free blacks and abolitionists, but also disaffected white voters from the two dominant parties. The Hunker faction of the New York Democratic Party supported Southern Democrats' proslavery and Texas-annexation platform. The Barnburner faction of New York Democrats, including Martin Van Buren, opposed the Southern platform, in part to stem state Democrats going to the Liberty Party. Competition within and between Whig or Democratic state parties fostered shifting legislative majorities that enacted local education and judicial due process guarantees benefiting recent Irish immigrants and free blacks, although the two groups opposed each other. Within increasingly conflicted immigrant, free-black, and antislavery politics, the delayed appeal of the New York alien tax case after 1843 also followed the Supreme Court's commerce power decision involving slavery, *Groves v. Slaughter* (1841).

State Exclusion and the Interstate Slave Trade: *Groves v. Slaughter* (1841)

The announcement of *Groves* in 1841 publicized the Supreme Court's divisions over the commerce power, which concerned antislavery and immigrant politics. *Miln* and the alien tax decisions upheld immigrants' general admission to states. In *Groves*, however, the Taney Court splintered over state police powers and the commerce power after agreeing that Mississippi could exclude slave traders. In the three immigrant cases federal and state judges employed the "person-commerce" distinction of *Miln*, encouraging Northern states' admission of white foreigners, though under exceptional circumstances state police powers also enabled exclusion. The states' general admission of foreign immigrants coincided with free blacks' disfranchisement in Pennsylvania and the national fugitive-slave controversy from the late 1830s to *Prigg v. Pennsylvania* (1842). In that case Maryland, other slave states, and Northern sympathizers achieved Margaret Morgan's return to slavery despite her years of liberty in the free state of Pennsylvania. The Court's 1841 decision of *The Amistad*, however, freed and ultimately led to the return home of Africans entrapped by slave traders. The multiple opinions in *Groves* focused law and politics on Mississippi's constitutional slave-trade prohibition; the Court's divisions implicated admission or exclusion of slaves, free blacks, and immigrants as legal "persons" governed by police powers rather than "commerce" regulated under the commerce power.

Moses Groves and Robert Slaughter were parties to ordinary negotiable credit contracts on which the interstate slave trade depended. Groves, a resident of Louisiana, in 1836 endorsed a promissory note for $7,875 guaranteeing interstate slave trader Slaughter payment for slaves sold in Mississippi. Groves endorsed the note as an accommodation securing the long-term credit that Mississippi slaveholders required to facilitate cotton planting and final sales through middlemen. Preceding the Court's *Groves* decision, the number of slaves involved in such Mississippi commercial contacts had increased from approximately 65,000 in 1830 to 195,000 by 1840. The 1832 Mississippi constitution, however, proclaimed: "The introduction of slaves into the state, as merchandize, or for sale, shall be prohibited from and after the first day of May 1833: provided, that actual settler or settlers shall not be prohibited from purchasing slaves, in any state within this Union, and bringing them into this state for their own use, till the year 1845." The economic impact of the constitutional prohibition was not unlike a protective tariff that raised slave values *within* the protected Mississippi market, while the same state-resident masters purchased slaves at competitive prices in the interstate human-property market. Still, the narrow question in *Groves* was whether the constitutional prohibition was self-enforcing, or did it require legislation establishing the right to a formal legal action?

On the narrow question whether the Mississippi constitutional prohibition voided Groves's contractual obligation, a divided Supreme Court affirmed the lower federal court decision for Slaughter. Justice Thompson's majority opinion for the Supreme Court thus held that since the state's constitutional prohibition was not enforceable without enabling legislation, Groves's endorsement established the legal obligation to pay Slaughter. Although the legislature passed an enabling law in 1837, it applied only to future contracts, not retroactively; Groves had endorsed the promissory note instituting Slaughter's claim in 1836. Without written opinions, Justices Story and John McKinley dissented, stating only that the promissory notes "sued upon" were "void." In addition, Story, McKinley, Thompson, and James Wayne had the Court's reporter include in the published record of *Groves* the proviso that these four justices "concurred with the majority of the court in opinion, that the provision of the constitution of the United States, which gives the regulation of commerce to congress, did not interfere with the provision of the constitution of the state of Mississippi, which relates to the introduction of slaves, as merchandize, or for sale." Moreover, in response to Justice John McLean's surprise presentation of a concurring opinion, Chief Justice Taney and Justice Baldwin published refutations framed as concurring opinions.

Present in Court during the *Groves* decision, John Quincy Adams made a diary entry noting McLean's unexpected presentation of a concurring opinion and Taney's rebuff. The exchange exposed McLean's, Taney's, and Baldwin's disagreement regarding state-police and federal-commerce powers subsequently published in the *U.S. Reports*. Southern and Northern proslavery Democrats, as well as antislavery proponents like Adams, then understood how closely the commerce power divided the Court, especially given that Barbour had died and John Catron did not participate due to illness. The contestation in *Groves* coincided exactly with Adams's and abolitionist lawyers' defense of Africans from *The Amistad*. Adams and other antislavery proponents also were aware that the Mississippi prohibition of slave traders at issue in *Groves* was like Southern states' police powers deployed to exclude free blacks. The Southern states' exclusionary police powers clashed with abolitionists' assertion of an exclusive congressional commerce power enabling abolition of the interstate slave trade. Ironically, the Southern states' police powers used to *exclude* designated undesirables also were indistinguishable from the personal liberty laws free states such as McLean's Ohio, New York, and most New England states enacted in order to *protect* free blacks and slave-fugitives from slave catchers.

Following *Gibbons*, McLean affirmed that Congress possessed exclusive regulation over foreign and *interstate* "intercourse," including "passengers or articles of commerce," and legal "persons." In addition, although a "power may remain dormant" there was no Supreme Court precedent expressly resting on that holding. Comparing the state slave-trade prohibition at issue in *Groves*, McLean found that every relevant section of the U.S. Constitution, including the 1808 international slave trade provision, "treats slaves as persons." Moreover, the Mississippi constitutional prohibition specifically applied to "slaves as merchandize," which thus did not conflict with the U.S. Constitution's "controlling quality of persons" that "acts upon slaves as persons, and not as property." Moreover, McLean said that Ohio's constitution went farther than Mississippi's prohibition, in that it not only "prohibits the introduction of slaves into the state . . . as merchandize . . . but it declares that slavery shall not exist in the state." Thus, neither Ohio's abolition of slavery nor Mississippi's prohibition of the slave trade as "merchandise" conflicted with the "persons" terminology in the U.S. Constitution. Ultimately, every "state" had the "right to protect itself against the avarice and intrusion of the slave dealer," McLean concluded; it was a right derived from the "law of self preservation . . . vital to every community, and especially to a sovereign state."

Taney chided McLean for not accepting Thompson's narrow opinion in *Groves*. McLean's announcement that Ohio and Mississippi exercised police powers over slavery for opposite purposes aroused the abolitionists "in relation to the power of congress to regulate the traffic in slaves between the different states." McLean having raised the issue, Taney was "not willing, by remaining silent, to leave any doubt" that in "my judgment, the power over this subject is exclusively with the several states; and each of them has the right to decide for itself, whether it will, or will not, allow persons of this description to be brought within its limits, from another state, either for sale, or for any other purpose." The states thus "determine[d]" a black "person's" slave or free "condition and treatment within their respective territories; and the action of the several states upon this subject cannot be controlled by congress . . . by virtue of its power to regulate commerce." Given the "interest which a large portion of the Union naturally [felt] on this matter," Taney also addressed the related question: "would a regulation of commerce, by a state, be valid, until congress should otherwise direct?" Taney suggested that congressional silence concerning the interstate slave trade and the Negro Seamen Acts implicit in the "person-commerce" holding of *Miln* left "open" an "abstract question" the public would "frequently and earnestly discuss," but the Court would not do so unless and until it came "here for decision."

"I am not willing to remain silent," Baldwin said, "lest it may be inferred, that my opinion coincides with that" of Taney, McLean, or other justices. Following *Gibbons*, *Brown*, and his separately published *Miln* opinion, Baldwin accepted the Court's majority *Groves* decision favoring Slaughter regarding the state's prohibition of the interstate slave trade: it was "not" a "regulation of police" protecting the "health and morals of the people." Instead, it "aimed at the introduction of slaves, as merchandise from other states." Admittedly, Mississippi's prohibition implicitly raised the abolitionists' assertion that it violated congressional power to regulate interstate commerce in slaves, identified in the Constitution only as "persons." Baldwin acknowledged that "[o]ther judges consider the constitution as referring to slaves only as persons," and "not" to "be recognized as subjects of commerce." Even though "I may stand alone among the members of this court, [it] does not deter me from declaring that I . . . consider slaves as property, by the law of the states" and "from the first settlement of the colonies." The idea that slaves were "persons merely and not property" was ultimately "fatal to the whole system." Baldwin then embraced a due-process theory Slaughter's lawyer Daniel Webster presented: the Constitution's "fifth amendment" ensured slaveholders "just compensation" for property-takings should Congress interfere with the interstate sale or transport of slaves as "merchandise."

McLean's concurring opinion in *Groves* had a public reception somewhat like that of the abolitionist victory in *The Amistad*. In that decision a 6–1 majority held that the distinction between transportation of "persons" and carriage of goods clashed with constitutional and statutory definitions of "importation" in connection with the international slave trade; it also applied a natural-law presumption against the undocumented status of slavery. Baldwin dissented without opinion. The rest of the Court supported Story's opinion affirming the Africans' freedom and return home. The decision reinforced the Constitution's 1808 international slave-trade clause that smugglers increasingly violated and Southern as well as Northern federal courts ineffectually prosecuted. Similarly, McLean's concurring opinion in *Groves* received some Southern support because it preserved slave states' control over "persons" consistent with Georgia's, South Carolina's, and Louisiana's police powers excluding free blacks from admission to the states. Thus, the Mississippi *Columbus Democrat* lauded McLean's concurring opinion in *Groves* in May 1841, declaring, "All the abolitionists who respect the unanimous opinion [regarding the exclusive commerce power versus the interstate slave trade] will now abandon so much of their petitions as call on Congress to regulate or prohibit transportation of slaves. One point of the abolition controversy (and the most important) is now solemnly settled in favor of the South."

Although the Court was comparatively united in *The Amistad* opposing the international slave trade, the interstate slave trade and exclusion of free blacks exposed divisions in *Groves*. A majority of the Court held that the state legislature had not formally invalidated Groves's debt to Slaughter. From the majority, Thompson and Wayne agreed with dissenters Story and McKinley that the commerce power did not interfere with the Mississippi constitution's slave-trade prohibition. McLean's unexpected opinion, however, asserting state police power control of "persons" and limited exclusive commerce powers governing "passengers," was consistent with Henry Clay's argument for his client Slaughter. In the same period Clay and McLean were identified, respectively, as the leading and a minor Whig Party presidential candidate for 1844, amid John Tyler's weak presidency. Also, Grove's lawyer, Mississippi Democrat U.S. Senator Robert J. Walker, articulated the disunion sentiments certain Southern Democrats felt resulting from abolitionists' attacks on both the interstate slave trade and arbitrary exclusion of free blacks through the Negro Seamen Acts. Taney's pro-Union opinion, supported by his citation of the less controversial *Miln* decision, attempted to mollify these party divisions. Finally, Webster urged the innovative due-process theory protecting slave property in the interstate slave trade; but only Baldwin adopted it to buttress his rejection of the "person-commerce" distinction.

During the same period the Taney Court divided over exclusion of slave traders and free blacks in *Groves*, some Northern states strengthened personal liberty laws and admission of immigrants. The insistence in McLean's concurring opinion that his state's police powers abolished slavery coincided with Ohio, Pennsylvania, and some other border free states' extending increased legal equality to free blacks and alien immigrants as "persons." In Ohio, particularly, the improved equality in court paralleled the state appellate courts' construing constitutional-franchise provisions broadly, enabling some blacks to vote. Ohio Whigs and Democrats also expanded the legal status of "persons" to more readily confer citizenship upon recent immigrants. In Pennsylvania, though free blacks were disfranchised in 1838, Quakers and other Protestants incensed over the attack on the state's personal liberty law in *Prigg* worked with Whigs and some Democrats to extend legal equality for free blacks and fugitive slaves as a defense against slave catchers. At the same time, Pennsylvania's immigrant communities demanded and won limited conferral of state citizenship upon recent immigrants. As had occurred in Massachusetts and New York, the political trade-offs between Ohio and Pennsylvania Whigs and Democrats favored admission over exclusion of free blacks and recent immigrants as "persons," which conferred inconsistent yet noteworthy claims of citizenship.

The public divisiveness accompanying *Groves* left uncertain the "commerce-person" distinction in *Miln* as applied to the appeals of the Alien Tax Cases. The Massachusetts legislature's imposition of the 1837 alien tax was consistent with the expansive police powers affirmed in *Miln*, though Manners's protest strategy logically followed Story's dissent. Chief Justice Shaw's *Norris* decision sustaining the tax as a poor-law regulation of "persons" prompted Rufus Choate's appeal in 1842. The *Miln* holding on "persons" provided direct precedent for the New York alien-tax litigation from 1841 to 1843, including health officer Turner's success, amid publicized corruption of city officials, and Captain Smith's protest that suggested Manners' strategy. The delay in deciding *Miln* followed by Baldwin's, Wayne's, and McLean's confidential rejection of Barbour's separation between "commerce" and "persons" indicated that the Court's changing membership would shape the eventual outcome of the Alien Tax Cases. By 1843, not only had Southerners Catron, McKinley, and Peter V. Daniel joined the Court, but Thompson and Barbour had died and Baldwin's mental stability eroded, leaving Story, Wayne, McLean, and Taney active from the *Miln* decision. The Court's disputation in *Groves* regarding states' admission or exclusion of slaves and free blacks, which impinged upon white immigrants' legal status, became more aggravated during the appeals of the Alien Tax Cases after 1843.

CHAPTER 3

Alien Tax Cases Appealed in Crises, 1843–1848

An unsettled Supreme Court heard appeals of the Alien Tax Cases amid transatlantic immigrant and antislavery crises. Between 1843 and 1845 Smith Thompson, Henry Baldwin, and Joseph Story passed on; nevertheless, the Senate refused to confirm President Tyler's several Supreme Court nominees, except for New Yorker Samuel Nelson. By 1846, however, the Senate confirmed Democrat James Polk's appointments of Levi Woodbury, New Hampshire's pro-Southern Democratic senator, and Pennsylvania lawyer and Democrat Robert C. Grier. In 1845 Massachusetts and New York shippers hired Daniel Webster for the final appeals of the Alien Tax Cases. The transatlantic potato famine and North-South sectional agitation over the interstate slave trade, free blacks, and the war with Mexico engulfed the appellate process. Over successive terms from 1845 to 1848, Webster argued against the tax in *Norris v. City of Boston* and *Smith v. Turner.* New York attorney general John Van Buren, a Barnburner politician like his father, the former president, led the lawyers defending the states' alien tax. Following the uncertain precedent of the Licenses Cases (1847), the final appellate arguments of the alien tax litigation reshaped the famine-immigrant struggles and slavery–free black conflicts into contending theories of police powers and the commerce power. In addition, inflationary pressures upon the money used to cover the state fees and taxes accompanied improved economic conditions during the late 1840s.

The appellate arguments of the Alien Tax Cases were disrupted. While Webster argued the shippers' appeals over three Court terms, the *U.S. Reports* noted it was "certain that some . . . counsel never heard the arguments" in the "different terms at which the arguments were made." In 1845 the appeals focused on state-police versus federal-commerce power regulations of foreign immigrants after years of economic depression. By 1846, however, the potato blight plagued western Europe and Ireland, resulting in unprecedented numbers of destitute immigrants leaving for the United States and British North America. As the famine spread, Irish and Germans entered New York, Boston, and other ports, bringing disease that aggravated preexisting poverty. Local and state officials addressed the painful social welfare problems through police powers implemented in expanded poor-law regulations. The sheer numbers of impoverished persons arriving in all U.S. ports from 1846 to 1848 totaled about 626,000; in New York and Boston, respectively, the totals were 403,000 and 55,000. The new arrivals disrupted the state-federal regulatory system encompassing people and vessels, obscuring the constitutional separation between the federal commerce power sustaining the U.S. passenger laws and the state police powers underpinning the alien tax. Anti-immigrant and slavery politics and the rights of American and British free blacks further agitated the constitutional boundary.

The transatlantic famine migration reshaped the admission and exclusion issues inherent in the appeals of the Alien Tax Cases. In 1844 the number of new annual arrivals in New York alone had risen to 59,000; by 1846, when the blight destroyed Ireland's potato crop, that number had reached 98,000, and two years later it was 160,000. The Alien Tax Cases revealed each state's income from the bond-surety and commutation system favoring admission of immigrants, despite social welfare costs, which in New York involved political corruption. Lawyers' appellate arguments channeled social welfare problems and politics into issues testing the respective limits of state police powers versus an exclusive commerce power. The arguments directly addressed white immigrants, but also implicitly, free blacks and slavery. The first section considers Webster's engagement with the U.S. passenger bill, as well as divisive anti-immigrant and slavery politics that reinforced advocacy of the exclusive commerce power enabling admission of immigrants. The second section considers New York attorney general Van Buren's argument for concurrent police powers amid the state's endorsement of the commerce power sustaining the U.S. passenger bill. He also supported stronger immigrant regulations favoring admission of immigrants amid antislavery politics. In the third section the appellant arguments within the adversarial process are examined. The License Cases (1847) providing uncertain precedent for the Alien Tax Cases is the subject of the fourth section.

Famine Relief, the Passenger Bill, and Daniel Webster's Exclusive Commerce Power Arguments

During his alien tax appellate arguments from 1845 to 1848, Webster held the perspective of a Massachusetts U.S. senator involved in bipartisan congressional Irish-famine relief. The September 1846 *London Times* reported that the failure of the potato crop brought famine throughout Ireland. By January 20, 1847, the *Boston Pilot* began publishing reports of the famine's terrible progress, including "coffin" ships reaching American ports overloaded with destitute and diseased people, often in violation of the spatial regulations stipulated in U.S. and British Passenger Acts. In 1842, despite the economic depression, Chief Justice Shaw's *Norris* opinion had suggested that the state's "small" alien tax paid by nineteen foreign immigrants shipped from New Brunswick to Boston had modest financial effect. By the late 1840s, however, Boston and Massachusetts confronted escalating poor-law demands from foreign immigrants. Also during the famine the numbers of Irish immigrants arriving in Northern states increased because, despite having contracted to remain in British North America, about 60 percent removed to Irish American communities such as Boston. Political demands governing the legal status of "persons" converged with a U.S. passenger bill. These pressures shaped Webster's argument that the alien taxes violated an exclusive commerce power that resisted excluding immigrants and free blacks despite political contention over ambivalent police powers advocated by Know-Nothings and slavery supporters.

During U.S. Senate debates Whigs such as Webster supported various Irish relief measures, including special grain shipments and expanded spatial regulations in the passenger bill. South Carolina Democrat John C. Calhoun did the same, "present[ing] a petition from the Irish Emigrant Society of New York." Bipartisan congressional famine-relief efforts indicated that the poorly enforced federal spatial regulations on board vessels transporting diseased and destitute immigrants affected state police power regulations of those same immigrants upon arrival in port. Amid debate of the 1847 passenger bill proposed in the House Judiciary Committee, a supporter exclaimed that "it intended to correct one of the most enormous and aggravated abuses which now existed in Christendom. The emigrants from abroad frequently came into the port of New York in such crowded condition on board of ships . . . that they were landed in so diseased a condition as to be unable to walk, and were carried in carts to the almshouse, and sometimes died on the way." On board ship, "[n]umbers died on the passage from the same cause. By this abuse an immense expense was imposed on the city, as well as a crying inhumanity perpetuated." New York or Boston administrators decided whether state police powers, including poor laws, could maintain the preexisting policy favoring admission of immigrants to the state or if it was necessary to impose restrictive exclusions like those targeting free blacks in the South.

Against bipartisan support for the passenger bill including Webster and Calhoun, the Native American or Know-Nothing Party mobilized opposition demanding immigrant exclusion. The passenger bill's supporters insisted its "object . . . was not to check immigration, but to provide by law that sufficient space should be reserved on board the importing ships for comfortable accommodation of passengers, so that they might arrive on our shores in a state of health, instead of presenting a revolting spectacle, which was a disgrace, not only to our laws and our country, but to humanity itself." Prescribed shipboard spatial dimensions for steerage and cabin passengers reflected instrumental and humanitarian justifications that nonetheless required shippers' compliance, which informed observers such as Herman Melville said was unlikely to be forthcoming. By contrast, the Know-Nothings publicized neither their anti-Catholicism nor general resistance to poor immigrants. Instead, they attacked a perceived political-party machination by which weak federal naturalization laws and administration of state poor laws enabled immigrant voters. A more accurate title for the passenger bill, a Know-Nothing critic exclaimed, was "to afford additional facilities to the paupers and criminals of Europe to emigrate to the United States." He expressed "at length . . . opposition to the whole system of importing voters from abroad; attributing it to a party policy, with a view to weaken the Native American Party."

Bipartisan party support for and the Know-Nothings' opposition to the passenger bill obscured conflicted state police powers governing "persons." The Know-Nothings rejected the federal law in part because it enabled poor immigrants to enter Massachusetts, New York, and other states, whereupon federal naturalization within state borders permitted local party officials to recognize them as "persons" entitled to citizenship on the basis of state police powers. Know-Nothings addressed these issues through three constitutional claims. First, as the *Miln* decision affirmed, the Constitution's commerce power did not prevent states from regulating immigrants as "persons," rather than commerce. Second, while state and federal governments shared power to regulate interstate and international commerce, state sovereignty—enforced through the state's police powers—was supreme when it came to protecting the state from external health, morals, and welfare threats identified with poor immigrants. Finally, the supremacy of state police powers meant that each state could establish a regulatory regime that excluded foreign immigrants from its borders and empowered it even to expel those who may have already established residence. Given the weak administration of federal naturalization, the Know-Nothings advocated employing police powers to disrupt party politics that all too often readily conferred citizenship upon recent immigrants in places such as New York and Boston.

Webster's and Calhoun's bipartisanship also obscured that Southern leaders and Know-Nothings were ambivalent about using police powers to admit foreign immigrants as legal "persons." Southerners knew that Irish American immigrants voted Democratic in local, state, and federal elections. Northern and Southern Democrats thus recognized most poor foreign immigrants as legal "persons" subject to state police powers empowering the grant of citizenship. In principle, too, the Know-Nothings agreed with Southerners that foreign immigrants were legal "persons" under state police powers. Know-Nothings endorsed the police power principle over "persons," however, first in order to circumscribe the federal commerce power underlying the passenger bill that facilitated immigrants' admission to states. Know-

Nothings also would employ police powers to exclude from citizenship immigrants who established residency within states, including entry into labor markets, free exercise of religion in public education, and participation in juries. Police powers also could be employed to expel various undesirable immigrants from states, like the Southern states' Negro Seamen Acts and laws targeting free blacks from the West Indies. Thus, Southern and Northern Democrats endorsed state police powers as a basis for admitting and conferring citizenship upon foreign immigrants, whereas Know-Nothings advocated police powers as a regulatory device to exclude immigrants from entry to states and citizenship therein.

Webster's arguments in the Alien Tax Cases also dealt circumspectly with a sovereignty exception in U.S.-British treaties regarding U.S. Southern and Canadian control of legal "persons." As secretary of state from 1841 to 1843, Webster negotiated with Lord Ashburton the 1842 treaty bearing their names that settled the boundary between the United States and British North America. The treaty also sanctioned the phrase "subject always to the laws and statutes of the two countries respectively." This rule authorized legal classifications of "persons" that enabled Southern states to exclude British free black seamen and West Indian émigrés and British North American colonies to free fugitive slaves despite slaveholders' legal protests. The treaty-sovereignty exception authorizing states or colonies authority to admit or exclude free blacks or slaves also had implications for state-federal regulation issues arising from the distinction between "persons" and "commerce" in the Alien Tax Cases. During his appellate arguments Webster understood the implicit constitutional connection between the two Northern states' taxation of immigrants and the state-sovereignty treaty exception permitting Southern state port officials to exclude or imprison free blacks who were British Crown subjects. The same treaty exception also enabled Canadian authorities' refusals to surrender fugitive slaves to Southern slaveholders because doing so went against British imperial policy.

Webster's alien tax arguments also considered federal laws or treaties that some Court members might support as the exercise of an exclusive commerce power. Since *Gibbons*, only a few state-sovereignty absolutists such as Justice Daniel rejected Marshall's reliance upon a federal statute as the primary basis for overturning state laws in conflict with an exclusive congressional commerce power. Also, the 1847 passenger bill Senator Webster supported reaffirmed British-U.S. treaties endorsing the 1819 U.S. Passenger Act, which employed the commerce power; once the new bill passed addressing the "famine ships," it would be sanctioned by both the commerce power and the treaty. Webster's construction of an exclusive federal commerce power regulating transatlantic passengers provided a legal counterargument to the state-sovereignty and police powers proslavery supporters relied on to defend Southern exclusion of free blacks. Indeed, in 1848 Secretary of State James Buchanan in the waning Polk administration said that Southern states' sovereignty exercised in the black-seamen laws defeated British claims of national sovereignty over British subjects. By contrast, even some prominent Southerners such as Alabama's John Campbell criticized the Polk administration's weak enforcement or nonenforcement of the international slave trade ban, despite U.S. participation in several international agreements affirming it, including the Webster-Ashburton Treaty.

Webster also avoided the implication that the exclusive commerce power regulating immigrants in the passenger bill affected the interstate movement of free blacks or slaves classified as "persons." North-South bipartisan party support for the Passenger Act assumed that spatial regulations on board vessels transporting immigrants to U.S. ports did not limit those same immigrants' admission to states under police powers. Still, Webster's challenge was to persuade at least five members of the Supreme Court that the alien tax was an unconstitutional exercise of police powers because it clashed with an exclusive commerce power underpinning the passenger law, treaties, and revenue measures, as Story's dissent contended in *Miln*. Yet Webster's victory in *Groves v. Slaughter* indicated how leery the Supreme Court was concerning an exclusive-commerce-power argument because abolitionists radicalized it in support of the theory that the interstate slave trade was unconstitutional. Calhoun and other Southerners supported, by contrast, the passenger bill promoting entry of white immigrants into states. Evens so, Southerners employed the commerce-person distinction in order to enable police power exclusion of free blacks as "persons" from slave states; but contrary to the Know-Nothings, that same distinction justified *admitting* Irish immigrants into Northern states so that they might become loyal Democrats.

Webster also treaded carefully in the exclusive-commerce-power argument because by 1845 the interstate slave trade divided his own Whig Party. Both nationally and in Massachusetts older "cotton Whigs" favoring the South faced opposition from "conscience Whigs" advocating the abolition of both the interstate slave trade and the slave trade in Washington, D.C. Some conscience Whigs based interstate slave-trade abolition on an exclusive commerce power. Webster's rejection of that argument in *Groves* put him at odds with "conscience Whigs" whose influence might determine the party's choice for presidential nomination in the 1848 convention. Webster also knew, however, that a carefully crafted argument would garner support among divided Massachusetts Whigs if he did not formally deny that an exclusive commerce power protected the state's free black seamen from Southern states' exclusion laws. The issue inflamed Massachusetts merchants because in 1844 the governor sent Samuel Hoar to challenge in South Carolina courts Charleston's imprisonment of Bay State free black seamen. State and city officials ignored Hoar's claims that the exclusion laws violated the commerce power; instead, asserting police powers, these officials simply expelled Hoar and his wife from the state without any formal hearing. Webster's alien tax argument thus carefully balanced an exclusive federal commerce power against state police powers promoting admission of immigrants and free blacks.

At the same time Webster argued the appeals in the Alien Tax Cases, he also litigated state temperance laws in the License Cases. Massachusetts, New Hampshire, and Rhode Island imposed license fees on smaller amounts in liquor sales. The license fees taxed liquor shipped from other states and, after being purchased from importers, foreign nations: did the laws violate the commerce power? Meanwhile, the Massachusetts Whig Party's support of the temperance laws aggravated immigrant communities, including the growing numbers of Famine Irish. State Democrats affiliated with former governor Morton used the anti-temperance issue to mobilize immigrant supporters against not only Whigs, anti-immigrant groups, and the Liberty Party, but also a local Democratic faction that remained loyal to Southern Democrats in national elections. Antislavery and pro-immigrant Massachusetts Democrats also supported Barnburners who in 1848 nominated former president Van Buren as the Free-Soil Party candidate. Thus, at the very time Webster made commerce power arguments in the Alien Tax and License Cases, he confronted the complex party politics impinging on the police powers that linked temperance laws and Know-Nothings targeting white immigrants to Southern exclusion of free blacks. Indicating the necessity for careful argumentation, Webster said, "Everything may be said agt [*sic*] them [the license laws], which Massachusetts says agt [*sic*] South Carolina [exclusion of free blacks]."

John Van Buren's Appellate Arguments amid Famine Immigrants and Expanded Police Powers

From 1845 to 1847, John Van Buren was state attorney general defending New York's alien tax in the U.S. Supreme Court. In 1848 removing to New York City to be a lawyer in private practice, Van Buren continued representing the state in *Smith v. Turner*. Appeal of the case coincided with the state assembly resolution supporting the new U.S. passenger law. During the same period, the assembly conferred upon a New York City commission expanded police powers in order to administer the immigration system, including quarantine and Maritime Hospital located on Staten Island. Law makers also expected that the new Emigrant Commission would overcome the corrupt practices city investigators had exposed from 1842 to 1843. Van Buren's appellate arguments and tenure as state law enforcer coincided with the transatlantic famine that disrupted the state-federal regulations linking new federal passenger legislation and expanded police power administration in New York City. The alien tax funding the Maritime hospital was levied in New York harbor on the same destitute immigrants the federal passenger law regulated aboard ship. Van Buren argued for concurrent police powers over the exclusive commerce power sanctioning collection of the alien tax and nonpayment penalty, as well as general admission and only limited exclusion of immigrants. At the same time, he also wrestled with Barnburner and Free-Soil Party politics that resisted slavery and aided free blacks.

Van Buren's appellate arguments from 1845 to 1847, as well as

New York's support for the federal passenger law, coincided with the onslaught of the famine. The fungus causing the potato blight appeared in 1843 within the New York–Philadelphia area; it spread into the Great Lakes region and British Maritime Provinces by 1845; over the summer of that year, transatlantic trade carried the fungus into Belgium, the southern Netherlands, and German Rhineland. By late August and September the blight reached throughout northern and western Europe, including in Britain, Wales, Scotland, and Ireland. In Ireland dependence upon the potato was most extensive; the entire crop failed during 1846. The British government's slow response to starvation and death increased emigration of the Irish poor. Accelerating immigrant demand on transatlantic vessels exposed the profoundly inadequate spatial regulations governing steerage-class passengers. In 1847, as tens of thousands of destitute Irish and German immigrants poured into New York and other ports, American shippers fearing possible enforcement of new federal passenger-law penalties, temporarily turned their "coffin" ships to Grosse Isle, near Quebec. Although initially 100,000 "destitute and miserable emigrants" overwhelmed colonial authorities, within a year relief measures were relatively effective. As many as 60 percent of the Irish immigrants, however, moved across the border into Irish American communities such as New York City.

From 1845 to 1847 Van Buren's emphasis in the appellate argument shifted. Attorney General Van Buren's tenure began the same year Justice Nelson finally took the "New York" seat on the Supreme Court vacant since Justice Thompson's death. A respected state judge, Nelson had supported his court's decision favoring health officer Turner. Following the state court precedent, Van Buren's initial Supreme Court argument in *Smith v. Turner* focused on the alien tax's police power purpose supporting the physician at the Maritime Hospital on Staten Island. Thus, Van Buren argued that although the tax was levied upon immigrants transported in vessels regulated by the federal Passenger Act, similar British laws, and international treaties, it was not collected as revenue but was instead a police power measure. Also, though the state tax in some form had existed since the U.S. Constitution's early years, neither the initial tax nor the 1829 law establishing it as the funding source for the Maritime Hospital had been challenged until immigration began increasing during the 1840s.

Even so, after 1847 Van Buren shifted his argument to emphasize admission of immigrants, despite the human and poor-law costs resulting from the famine migration. The Court's decision was imperative, he said sarcastically, "especially in reference to the poor devils who are now at Quarantine. The cholera is raging among them with fearful mortality, and it would be a consolation to their friends to know that they are dying constitutionally." Sarcasm aside, Van Buren's argument indicated that the purpose of quarantine was to alleviate the cholera threat until its sufferers either died or were sufficiently recovered to be admitted into the city. At this point there were few if any deportations.

Like Van Buren's appeal, the "disaster of 1847" shaped the New York assembly resolution urging the state's congressional delegation to support the U.S. passenger bill favoring admission of immigrants. The state lawmakers said that the "regulation of commerce between foreign countries and the United States belongs, by virtue of the constitution, to the [U.S.] Congress." Moreover, "from the increase of emigration within the last few years, the transportation of steerage passengers from the nations of Europe to this country has become a large and lucrative branch of commerce, profitable in proportion to the number of persons who can be induced to take passage on board each vessel employed in this trade." Among the shippers, agents, and masters involved in the immigrant trade were "many inhumane persons, careless of the wants, the health, and the comfort of their passengers, and eager only for gain." New Yorkers were keenly aware that "almost weekly, some vessel, swarming with human beings, arrives at our port," exposing "their sufferings, arising from the crowded state of such vessel; the neglect of the master to see secured a sufficiency of provisions, and the water for the voyage, and the conveniencies [*sic*] for preparing food." The shipmaster's "inattention" to the "cleanliness of the steerage, and the comfort and health of the passengers are shocking to our sense of humanity, and disgraceful to any country possessing the power to prevent the recurrence of such enormities."

Knowing the human and police power costs the state incurred because agents and shippers ignored the U.S. passenger law, New York lawmakers urged strengthened federal regulations. The New York assembly and senate thus jointly instructed the two U.S. senators, and "requested" its large House delegation, to "use their best efforts to obtain the passage of a [U.S.] law limiting and defining the number of passengers for each vessel engaged in the transportation of passengers from any foreign country to the United States, according to her burden." These spatial specifications expanded upon those of the 1819 U.S. Passenger Act and the corresponding regulations the British Parliament enacted. The 1847 federal passenger regulations applied the new spatial standards in "determining the quantity of provisions and water for each passenger on the voyage; securing the presence of a physician on shipboard, and prohibiting the stowing of merchandise or other freight between decks when occupied by immigrant passengers." The joint resolution also advocated inclusion in the new federal legislation "such other regulations as may be thought necessary and proper to prevent the great and crying evils which at present so often occur, and which" were "so contrary to the controlling and benevolent spirit of the age." Although informed observers such as Herman Melville doubted that the new regulations would be enforced, shippers' fear of complying with them facilitated the "disaster of 1847."

Van Buren argued, as did the legislature's resolution promoting the U.S. passenger law, that the alien tax was concurrent, rather than in conflict, with the federal commerce power. The New York legislature urged its congressional delegation to support stronger federal regulation of steerage-class passengers because shippers' and masters' noncompliance with the 1819 U.S. Passenger Act fostered disease and destitution, increasing state and local social welfare costs once those same passengers disembarked from vessels. More directly, the state resolution suggested that stronger federal regulation would alleviate the growing costs of the Maritime Hospital and Quarantine, which operated together on Staten Island. While the U.S. passenger law and state alien tax were within the state-federal regulatory system, Van Buren said, the constitutional issue was how to determine where the federal commerce power ended and the state police powers began. Van Buren's appellate argument comported with the assumption that the police power function of the tax did not conflict with the U.S. passenger law. The "tax in question" was, argued Van Buren, "an indispensible part of a health and quarantine system," that U.S. Supreme Court precedents and decades of New York policies affirmed were the "exclusive subject of state jurisdiction." The tax operated like the "rates of pilotage" or "wharf and harbor charges," which also did not clash with the congressional power.

Such polices operating coincidently as state and federal regulations, said Van Buren, "would seem to show a concurrent power in the states over foreign commerce." Following *The Federalist* and Chief Justice Marshall in *Gibbons*, Van Buren stressed, "every argument and decision in favor of the exclusive power . . . except[ed] from its operation pilot, health, and inspections laws," including "quarantines." The scope of the latter concurrent powers was left an open question in *Miln*, but in the License Cases decided in 1847 "a majority of the judges expressly hold the power to be concurrent." The "commerce-person" distinction established in *Miln* remained "within the unquestionable power of States," as was true of "pilot, inspections, quarantine, and slave laws." Moreover, the argument that the state alien tax violated an exclusive commerce power underlying treaties should recognize the treaty exception, without which "no tariff law, and certainly no law prohibiting the entry of colored persons into States, could be upheld." Echoing the Know-Nothings' and Democrats' limited agreement regarding police powers, Van Buren emphasized that "the State had the power altogether to forbid the landing on her shores of such persons as she chose to forbid, or to expel those who entered," or to "dictate the terms on which they should be permitted to enter. This was vital to her self-preservation." The alien tax exemplified the "exercise" of that "right," which "must of necessity, be left to her discretion."

As the state assembly supported the new U.S. passenger law in 1847 it also enacted a new system of immigrant regulation for New York City, which also engaged John Van Buren. The 98,000 immigrants disembarking into the city in 1846 greatly increased the social costs resulting from the famine-driven migration. These demands mobilized a self-described "citizens" group including the city's Irish, German, Welsh, Scotch, and English immigrant societies, the Catholic Church's Archbishop John Hughes, prominent merchants such as William F. Havemeyer, and newspaper publisher and Whig Party boss Thurlow Weed. In opposition were agents, shippers, masters, and Democratic Party bosses who had exploited the failure to account for income from the bond-surety and commutation system authorized by the mayor's office. Although the opposition group advocated a commutation tax in order to fund poor laws, Quarantine, and Maritime Hospital, it rejected the "citizens'" proposal for an independent, state-funded commission charged with administration of the whole police power system governing immigrants. In 1847 Attorney General Van Buren helped Weed and Lieutenant Governor Addison Gardiner to break a deadlock between the two groups in the state senate. By a single vote the law passed funding six commissioners of emigration, which included representatives of major immigrant societies such as Andrew Carrigan, merchant Havemeyer, and Whig Party boss Weed.

Van Buren's concurrent-powers argument in the Alien Tax Cases was consistent with the authority of the immigrant commission and New York's 1848 personal liberty law. Van Buren's concurrent-powers argument reinforced the immigrant commission's police powers governing admission or exclusion of foreign immigrants as legal "persons." While the exclusive commerce power sustained the federal passenger laws' spatial regulations on board vessels transporting those same "persons," state police powers nonetheless also enforced New York's sovereign right of self-preservation. Similarly, Van Buren's concurrent-power argument was consistent with New York's 1848 personal liberty law barring local authorities from aiding masters seeking to enforce the 1793 U.S. Fugitive Slave Act. Although the state and federal laws applied to the same black "persons," the personal liberty law took precedence because it enforced state sovereignty. Thus, state sovereignty conferred upon the immigrant commission precedence in exercising police powers enforcing admission over exclusion of white immigrants, despite the concurrently operating federal passenger laws regulating those same persons aboard ship. In the same way, notwithstanding possible interference with the U.S. fugitive slave law, New York's right of self-preservation empowered local courts and officials under the personal liberty law against slave catchers and kidnappers threatening the state's sovereignty.

Divisive state politics further connected Van Buren's alien tax appellate arguments, the immigrant commission, and the 1848 personal liberty law. During the years Van Buren argued the Alien Tax Cases, he promoted Barnburner support for New York's Free-Soil Party, culminating in his father's nomination as its 1848 presidential candidate. Although Van Buren carried no state, father and son were credited with dividing New York's crucial Democratic support sufficiently that Whig Zachary Taylor won the national election. In addition, John Van Buren was aligned with a Democratic faction that along with Whigs passed in the state senate the Emigrant Commission by a single vote. By contrast, New York Whig cotton merchants and pro-Southern Democrats blocked stronger personal liberty laws. Other Whig and Democratic factions, however, enacted the state's 1848 personal liberty law that did ensure blacks most of the same rights and due process in state courts guaranteed white New Yorkers, including new immigrants. The emerging legal equality based on state police powers enabled free blacks, fugitive slaves, and white abolitionists to defy the U.S. Fugitive Slave Act. Thus, Van Buren's divided party politics reinforced his appellate argument for state sovereignty, which in turn sanctioned the commission's police powers generally admitting rather than excluding white immigrants, as well as greater rights claims for free blacks and fugitive slaves. Van Buren engaged Webster within an adversarial process.

Lawyers' Appellate Arguments in Adversarial Process

Each side in the appellate process addressed whether the federal commerce power was exclusive from or concurrent with state police powers. Webster, David B. Ogden, and J. Prescott Hall argued that *Miln* applied only to passengers subject to police power regulations once they disembarked from vessels. The manifests the state required detailing passengers' condition were minor state-authorized regulations that neither burdened nor otherwise interfered with the U.S. commerce power. Webster and his colleagues also argued that *Miln* was consistent with *Groves v. Slaughter*, in which the Court held that state regulations governing the interstate slave trade did not impinge upon the exclusive federal commerce power unless a federal statute or treaty imposed a direct conflict. Webster said also that New York City authorities proposed the 1847 U.S. passenger bill resting on the exclusive commerce power in order to address problems of admitting immigrants that were beyond the constitutional capacities of state police powers. The states' counsel John Van Buren, Willis Hall, and

John Davis focused on the few U.S. enactments: the Jay Treaty of 1794, the 1799 General Collections Act (authorizing customs duties), and the 1819 Passenger Act prescribing shipboard spatial requirements based on tonnage. The states' alien taxes were police regulations of "persons" conflicting directly with none of these federal commercial regulations, which followed the *Miln* precedent.

Webster's reported argument for the ship captains and the shippers expressed the "hop[e] that this court would preserve with sedulous care all the rights that belonged to the State of Massachusetts as well as to the national government." Striking such a balance within the existing American federal polity was difficult. It was *Miln*, Webster said, "which gave rise to the idea that a door had been opened thereby to the States, to enable them to raise revenue out of the exercise of the commercial power." The resulting "law" establishing the alien tax and the system for its collection was "a pure commercial regulation," and it shared nothing "in common with any police law. . . . A tax on goods, on tonnage, or on any of the operations of commerce, cannot be construed into a poor tax or a police tax." He conceded that "it [was] yet to be proved that a tax on the importation of persons is not a tax on imports." Ogden asserted that based on "principle" and "authority" the "power to regulate commerce with foreign nations is vested in Congress *exclusively*; that the States have no power to interfere with it." The "passengers" in the case were "as much part of commerce and intercourse as goods or merchandise," and "no State has the power of making any regulations upon the subject, and most assuredly not of laying and collecting an import duty upon passengers imported or brought into the United States."

J. P. Hall observed that the constitutional clause that delayed Congress imposing the slave trade ban until 1808 did not distinguish among "persons," embracing their general migration and importation. "The Constitution and the Laws of Congress encourage and protect emigration. The condition of mankind solicits it: ships are given up entirely to the importation of passengers, their decks being loaded with responsible beings instead of merchandise." American "institutions and laws" drew immigrants: "Can the maritime States, then, by their own legislation, restrain or destroy that commerce which relates to the importation of passengers, and their migration to other States open for their reception?" Webster argued the Constitution and federal laws promoted "importation of all foreigners free, untaxed." Massachusetts, however, "claims the right to tax these foreigners at her discretion, for the benefit of her exchequer." Massachusetts also "claims the right . . . to exclude all foreigners from her soil; for if she can tax them two dollars she can tax them any amount." Accordingly, were "not the objects and ends of the Massachusetts law repugnant to the objects, and ends of the laws and Constitution?" If the Court upheld the alien tax, other states "in the exercise of [their] sovereign discretion" would declare all such laws "a pauper law" that "Congress cannot repeal," whereupon "all the States will replenish their treasuries by a tax on aliens arriving in the United States!"

The "great truth" was that the federal government possessed "jurisdiction over" the nation's "commerce" and "ports" regarding "strictly commercial purposes," said Webster. He countered the claim that "if the State has not a right to tax alien passengers, it will have no power to redress the evils of foreign pauperism." Instead, "it belongs to Congress to redress evils of this kind . . . at its discretion." Thus, in response to New York City "authorities" Congress had before it a bill, soon enacted as the 1847 Passenger Act, "to regulate the admission of alien passengers. It goes back to the point of embarkation in the foreign country, and requires the alien to prove his character before the American consul." Webster again distinguished *Miln*, as a constitutional exercise of the police power over persons, from the two states' alien taxes, which violated the "exclusive" federal power over commerce. Webster cited the Court's holdings in *Groves v. Slaughter* that the state's slavery regulations did not trench upon this exclusive federal power. "Some powers were granted by the States to Congress, and some were retained. This tribunal was constituted as the surveyors of the boundary line between the two governments: and whenever either Government gets on the wrong side of the line," it was the Court's duty" to "adjudge accordingly."

Representing the states, Van Buren, Davis, and W. Hall focused on police powers over "persons" as concurrent with federal laws or constitutional provisions regulating "commerce." Like other lawyers on both sides, Van Buren cited Madison's published convention papers construing the 1808 international slave trade for the proposition that although it granted "Congress power to tax the admission of whites, it would not destroy the concurrent power of State taxation" over those same "persons." Davis conceded that the states' police powers addressing the massive influx of immigrants might "affect" U.S. commerce power. The "fact" that the alien taxes did "affect commerce does not make them unlawful, though the influence amounts to regulation, because they are made for other lawful purposes, and are as indispensable to the public welfare as foreign commerce." Moreover, Hall claimed, the Court's 1847 decision in the License Cases upheld state temperance laws as having no impact on interstate commerce unless there was a direct conflict with a federal law. The states' alien taxes regulating persons for state police power purposes did not clash with the 1799 customs or 1819 passenger laws, nor the 1794 U.S.-British treaty, which were clearly commercial regulations enacted pursuant to the federal commerce power. Even though the alien taxes slightly affected federal commerce, the intent and result embraced legal "persons" who clearly came within the "jurisdiction" of each state's "sovereignty."

The state's sovereignty to tax "alien persons" was consistent with state police power regulations of free blacks, which did not conflict with a federal commerce power. Following the Court's decision in *Groves* affirming that the state's police power controls over the interstate slave trade did not clash with the exclusive federal commerce power, Webster and his colleagues made only inferential reference to Southern states' Negro Seamen Acts and certain Northern free states' black laws. Davis, however, more expressly compared police powers underlying those race-based laws to police powers applied to regulating immigrants as legal "persons." "If we cannot meet and control by suitable regulations the introduction of such persons [poor immigrant aliens classified as paupers, vagabonds, insane, or criminals]," Davis queried, "on what principle can the laws expelling or forbidding the introduction of free Negros be sustained? Such laws exist, and I apprehend it will be found difficult to sustain them on the ground of color alone." Indeed, Van Buren said, at least fifteen free and slave states excluded or regulated free blacks seeking admission to their borders, consistent with the Court's finding in *Groves* that slaves and free blacks were "persons" outside the federal commerce power.

These considerations recognized that legal "persons" were not commodities within the federal commerce power. The Supreme Court affirmed in *McCulloch v. Maryland* (1819) and the License Cases

(1847), said Davis, that the taxing "power" was "vital, essential to the existence of the State, unabridged, concurrent, coextensive with the sovereignty of the State, applies both to persons and property, knows no supreme law over it, may reach any object within the jurisdiction, and may be carried in its application to any extent the government chooses." A famous limitation was the national second Bank of the United States; since 1836, of course, it ceased to exist. Also, the Constitution's Article I, Section 10, stated that "[n]o State shall, without the consent of Congress, lay any Imposts or Duties on Imports or Exports. . . . No State shall, without Consent of Congress, lay any duty of tonnage." For the alien taxes to be contrary to these express provisions they would have to be taxes on "imports" or "tonnage." Applying the reasoning in *Miln*, however, passengers were "persons," not "cargo," placing them in either commercial category. In addition, the 1808 international slave-trade provision taxed slaves, said Hall, not free (white) immigrants.

The states' lawyers argued that state police powers and the commerce power were concurrent. Hall noted that Congress passed laws in 1796, 1799, and 1832 authorizing federal revenue officials to cooperate with state authorities in the implementation of the state quarantine laws. State and federal laws thus "sanction the whole system of State quarantines, and everything appurtenant to quarantines, such as hospitals, and the means of purifications, and the preventing the spreading of contagion." Even so, he declared, the states' "possession of the power to establish embraces the power to support." Also, Congress recognized that like quarantine, "pilotage" of vessels entering state ports was not a federal commercial regulation, which reinforced the holding in *Miln* that "passengers are not the subjects of commerce, and are not imported goods." Hall rejected the idea that the alien taxes could violate a dormant-commerce power: "This rule of construction will be found oppressive in the extreme, and impossible. Oppressive, because it requires men to obey laws which they cannot know; impossible because the courts cannot apply it." Moreover, Van Buren concluded, the alien tax was part of the quarantine system whereby New York "may arrest and purify the stream before it enters her veins, that the blood of life to the rest of the Union may not be infection and death to her." These arguments occurred amid the Court's divided and uncertain commerce power precedent.

Uncertain Precedent: the License Cases (1847)

During the appeals of Alien Tax Cases, the License Cases revealed the Supreme Court's internal divisions. Between the fragmented opinions in *Groves v. Slaughter* (1841) and the initial hearing of both the License Cases and the Alien Tax Cases during 1845–1846, Daniel, Nelson, Woodbury, and Grier joined the Court. After two hearings and despite Justice John McKinley's nonparticipation due to illness and onerous circuit riding, the Court finally decided the License Cases in 1847. The single opinions Daniel, Woodbury, and Grier each wrote covering the three New England states' License Cases were their initial formulations of commerce power doctrines expressed from the Court. The same was true of Nelson, though his few lines simply expressed agreement with Taney's single and Catron's two opinions. Restating his exclusive-commerce-power position, McLean wrote a separate opinion for each of the three cases. Wayne said simply that he voted for the result. The ten cryptic or full opinions established unclear precedent, leaving the outcome in the alien tax appeals more uncertain than ever.

The three states' temperance laws enacted during the 1830s reflected a Protestant reform impulse reaching across New England, upstate New York, Ohio, and beyond. The laws enabled county officials to impose the licenses fee on retail liquor sales in varying small amounts. The legislative policy assumed that local officials could enforce a virtual prohibition in retail liquor sales; some commentators claimed that as many as half of Massachusetts counties had indeed implemented prohibition. Given the deep religious support for the temperance movement throughout New England and the so-called burned over district reaching westward, the constitutional question was not whether the fee-tax was in principle a legitimate exercise of states' police powers. The question was instead whether the local tax conflicted with a particular state constitutional provision, a congressional regulation of interstate commerce, or a treaty involving international trade. In *Commonwealth v. Blackington* (1837) upholding the temperance law under the Massachusetts constitution, Chief Justice Shaw stated the general rule: "A large discretion is thus given to the legislature to judge what the welfare of the Commonwealth may require; and this power is restrained only so far, as not to be expressly or by necessary implication, repugnant to the constitution. The power is the general rule: the restraint of it the specific exception."

In *Commonwealth v. Kimball* (1837), Shaw used the general rule to affirm the Massachusetts temperance law over the federal commerce power. Shaw recognized that some enumerated federal powers were exclusive, while others coincided with a state's "collateral . . . implied powers." Despite such "complexity," Shaw said, "[a]ll other powers of sovereign government necessary and proper, to provide for the peace, safety, health, morals and general welfare of the community, remain entire and uncontrolled, to the State government." Applying the general rule, Shaw said, in the "exercise" of police powers, state governments "have the right and power to resort to all adequate and appropriate means, for carrying these powers into effect, unless they happen, in any particular instance, to come directly, in conflict with the *operation* of some law of the United States made in pursuance of its enumerated powers" (emphasis in original). Thus, only to the extent that a conflict arose between state and federal laws or regulations implementing enumerated federal powers would the state police power yield, but "no further." According to historian Leonard Levy, Shaw followed the general rule in affirming the temperance law as an exercise of police powers, suggesting a concurrent commerce power. He also distinguished Marshall's "original-package" doctrine in *Brown v. Maryland*, which invalidated a state license tax on "unbroken" packages of international imports.

After the three New England state high courts affirmed the license tax, the Supreme Court's review under section 25 of the 1789 Judiciary Act required a showing of legal errors regarding the commerce power. Lawyers and judges agreed that arguments concerning express legal "errors" limited the issues reviewable by the Court, its holdings, and precedential uses. The Marshall Court's three commerce power decisions were comparatively straightforward, given Marshall's own three opinions, one published dissent, and a single concurring opinion. Under the Taney Court, however, in *Miln* alone there were a majority opinion, two concurring opinions, and one dissent. Following the majority opinion in *Groves*, there were one full dissent, three full concurring opinions, and further concurring statements from the participating justices supporting or dissenting from the decision. In the License Cases, the Court unanimously affirmed the three New England states' license fee on liquor sales, but it did so in ten brief or full opinions.

The Court's diverse opinions owed partially to the divergent fact-situations of the three states' license tax cases. The Massachusetts and Rhode Island cases involved retail sales of liquor that when imported had been subject to international tariffs. But since the license tax regulated retail sales within the domestic market, it did not violate the "original package" doctrine, which struck down state interference with goods regulated under international tariffs. The New Hampshire case, by contrast, involved the license tax in wholesale purchases affecting interstate commerce; still, the Supreme Court could reason that there was no conflict with any federal law then being enforced. Neither did these domestic sales conflict with an international treaty or tariff under the original-package doctrine. In addition, during the License Cases Wayne gave a public speech espousing temperance, which was consistent with his silent concurrence in the result of the Court's opinions. Since the Court's other members did not share Wayne's temperance beliefs, their unanimous holding for the same result probably owed little or nothing to those particular moral convictions.

In support of the three states' license taxes, Taney applied the original-package doctrine to uphold a concurrent power. As counsel, he admitted arguing against Marshall's doctrine in *Brown v. Maryland*. Like Shaw's carful affirmation of the same doctrine, however, Taney said, "It appears to me to be very clear that the mere grant of power to the general government cannot, upon any just principles of construction, be construed to be an absolute prohibition to the exercise of any power over the same subject by the States." Taney also agreed with Marshall's limitations on an exclusive commerce power in *Gibbons*, and the broad police powers affirmed in *Willson* that "quarantines" or pilotage regulations exemplified "a State's execution of its powers of internal police." Those same police powers enabled the state to "make regulations, of foreign commerce" that were "valid, unless they come into collision with a law of Congress." While Taney implied a state-federal concurrent power, like Shaw he did not prescribe explicit limits beyond the operation of the temperance law that presented no express conflict with a federal law regulating interstate or international trade.

Catron's Massachusetts opinion agreed with Taney's and Shaw's construction of the temperance laws, suggesting a concurrent power that permitted county officials to impose license fees on retail liquor sales no longer bound by treaties. Also, treaties with Holland and France governing imports did not apply in the New Hampshire case, said Catron, because the "spirits sold were not foreign, but American gin." Moreover, even though the New Hampshire law clearly "was a regulation of commerce among the states," it "constitutionally passed, because" there was "no regulation of Congress, special or general, in existence to which the State law was repugnant." He added that the "States have power to regulate their own mode of commerce among the States, during the time the power of Congress lies dormant, and has not been exercised in regard to such commerce." Catron left unsettled whether the Court's precedents prescribed only the limited exclusive commerce power Marshall set out in *Gibbons* or that which Thompson disputed in *Brown*, beyond the lawfulness of quarantines, pilotage, and limited inspection or revenue laws. Finally, the *U.S. Reports* stated that Justice Nelson "concurred in the opinions delivered by the Chief Justice and Mr. Justice Catron." These three members of the Court thus endorsed a concurrent power, though Catron also favored the commerce power supporting treaties.

McLean and Grier generally agreed. McLean upheld police powers supporting the temperance laws as a "great moral reform." Congress possessed an exclusive commerce power to regulate foreign commerce, McLean said, but states could still regulate quarantines, pilotage, and temperance practices. More so than Taney or Shaw, McLean grounded constitutional legitimacy on separate "sovereign powers," whereby the "federal government" was "supreme within the scope of its delegated powers, and the State governments" were "equally supreme in the exercise of those powers not delegated by them nor inhibited to them." Where a conflict arose, the resolution "must depend on the supremacy of the power by which it was enacted." Applying this principle consistent with the original-package doctrine, the temperance policies either lawfully taxed retail liquor sales or affected interstate trade unregulated by Congress. Justice Grier's brief opinion concurred in McLean's formulation of separate "sovereign powers." Suggesting issues in the Alien Tax Cases, Grier also equated temperance regulations with "quarantine laws," which "restrain the liberty of the passenger" and "operate on the ship." This was so, he said, not "from any power which the States assume to regulate commerce or to interfere with the regulations of Congress, but because police laws for the preservation of health, prevention of crime, and protection of the public welfare, must of necessity have full and free operation."

Woodbury supported the temperance laws as police powers equivalent to regulations excluding paupers or slaves through a partially concurrent power. The three states' liquor-sales regulations did not "direct how" foreign commerce "shall be carried on," or "under what duties or penalties," nor affect it "on shipboard, or between ship and shore." The license fees did not operate until the goods "came within the limits of the State, and out of the possession and jurisdiction of the general government." For similar reasons, he said, the temperance laws did not violate interstate commerce. He then went beyond other members of the Court, stating that the police "power to forbid sales of *things*" was "surely as extensive, and rests on as broad principles of public security and sound morals, as that to exclude *persons*" (emphasis in original). Moreover, suggesting the explosive issues entwined in the Alien Tax cases, Woodbury asked, "[W]ho does not know that slaves have been prohibited admittance by many of our States, whether coming from their neighbors or abroad? And which of them cannot forbid their soil from being polluted by incendiaries and felons from any quarter?" Unlike McLean, Woodbury did not base state or federal regulation on separate "sovereign" powers, but instead on concurrent federal-state powers that for some purposes were exclusive to Congress but for other purposes were not exclusive. Yet Woodbury did not say how to distinguish between these separate purposes.

Daniel agreed that his colleagues correctly upheld the three states' temperance laws, but in so doing the "majority of judges" wrongly relied on Marshall's original-package doctrine. Daniel "believed" that the "principles" that should have decided *Brown v. Maryland* were those in Thompson's "able dissent," which held that the distinction between goods within or "broken-up" from original packages denied economic reality, leaving the state import tax a valid exercise of police powers. Daniel aimed to preserve the property holder taxed by the state "whether he shall have imported that property, or purchased it at home." He opposed the original-package doctrine because it virtually "deemed void" any "State laws which may remotely or incidentally affect foreign commerce," including federal revenue regulations fixed under international treaties. Daniel warned that construing the Supremacy Clause so expansively "involves a great fallacy," undermining enumerated powers. Unlike his colleagues' use of Marshall's "false" doctrines to uphold the three states' license taxes, Daniel's expansive police powers and limited federal commerce power reached the same result, finding they "impose no exaction on foreign commerce. They are laws simply determining the mode in which a particular commodity may be circulated within the respective jurisdictions of those States."

The opinions in the License Cases provided uncertain precedent for the Alien Tax Cases. Van Buren's view that the Court's majority supported a concurrent commerce power suggested some justices' willingness to equate police powers underpinning the retail liquor license fee with the alien taxes supporting New York City's Maritime Hospital and Massachusetts' poor law. New York's sanction of the 1847 U.S. passenger bill and the state Emigrant Commission's expanded police powers further indicated that state authorities perceived no conflict between state-police and federal laws regulating foreign immigrants disembarking from foreign vessels in ports. Webster's side, however, could hope that the Court's insistence on finding an express conflict with federal laws and treaties enabled a majority to accept that the states' alien taxes interfered with the operation of U.S. passenger laws, sustained by an exclusive commerce power. Both Webster and Van Buren could take heart that proslavery, Know-Nothing, and Whig politics divided rather than united the Taney Court Democrats who promoted admission of immigrants and exclusion of free blacks. Van Buren's side was confident in having the support of Taney, Nelson, Woodbury, and Daniel. Catron's regard for treaties made his vote doubtful. Webster could count on McLean and hope that Grier, Catron, and Wayne were persuadable. Assuming McKinley's participation in the Alien Tax Cases, his fifth vote would decide the result.

CHAPTER 4

Passenger Cases

Divided Decision and Opinions, 1848–1849

Once arguments ended on December 22, 1848, the Taney Court grappled with opinions in the consolidated Passenger Cases. Since 1845 the Court's unsettled membership had interrupted the appellate arguments in what the *U.S. Reports* described were two "kindred cases . . . argued together" and "brought up to this court by writs of error issued under" section 25 of the 1789 Judiciary Act. Overturning the two state courts' decisions required finding errors that Daniel Webster's side contended for in police powers versus the federal commerce power, before a full Court. As a state judge Nelson had participated in the New York case; he was now the Taney Court justice most familiar with the state's enormous burdens resulting from the famine migration. A pro-Southern New Hampshire Democrat, Woodbury was the Supreme Court justice for the New England U.S. Circuit Court confronting the social welfare costs and party politics at issue in the Massachusetts case. Announced February 7, 1849, eight opinions reshaped the famine-immigrant crisis, sectional struggle over slavery in the Mexican Cession, and Northern states' defiance of the federal fugitive slave law into the Taney Court's 5–4 decision affirming the commerce power. Justice McKinley, participating in his first commerce power case since *Groves*, determined the outcome that upheld admission of immigrants and, indirectly, free-black citizenship.

The eight opinions and closely divided decision overturning the alien taxes were conflicted. The first section examines the process whereby Daniel Webster learned from Chief Justice Taney and Justice McLean that Justice McKinley would provide the fifth vote ending a 4–4 deadlock, amid sectional and anti-immigrant politics impinging on the Court's opinion making. The second section discusses the Wayne, McLean, Catron, Grier, and McKinley majority opinions that upheld U.S. treaties and passenger regulations following Marshall's reasoning in *Gibbons*. The majority also affirmed police powers promoting admission of white immigrants and limited free black citizenship, revealed Wayne' s claim that the "commerce-person" distinction lacked majority support in *Miln*, and depended upon McKinley's unique dormant commerce power. The third section considers the Taney, Woodbury, Daniel, and Nelson dissents favoring Southern and Northern states' exclusion of, respectively, free blacks and poor white immigrants, as well as Taney's rebuttal of Wayne. The fourth section considers the public response to the Court's decision in February 1849, whereby the two states addressed the lost tax revenue, while the Northern and Southern press adopted the dissenters' fears regarding immigrants, free blacks, and slavery. The conclusion confirms Webster's assessment that the 5–4 vote upholding federal regulation of foreign immigrants in the Passenger Cases was the most significant commerce power decision since *Gibbons*.

The Fifth Vote: The Taney Court's Public and Private Decisional Process

Private contacts revealed Daniel Webster's growing understanding of the Court's likely votes in the Passenger Cases. "When I consider the state of things on the Bench, & the known differences of opinion among the Judges, on all Constitutional Questions, I am constrained to regard the result as doubtful," Webster wrote his son Daniel Fletcher at the end of 1847. "There are eight Judges present; & it would not surprise me, if, on this case, they stand four & four." By March 1848 Webster wrote Robert Brown Minturn, New York merchant and commissioner of immigration: "I suppose it very likely that the state of opinion on the Bench, in the questions involved in these cases, is exactly what it was last year . . . the eight Judges equally divided, four & four. But of this, of course, I cannot speak with certainty. If this be so, our chance depends on the presence of the ninth Judge [the unnamed McKinley]." There was "reason to think the opinion of the absent Judge would be in our favor: & there is some hope he may be present at the next meeting of the Court. I wish I had a better account to give, of this tedious & laborious case. You and your friends must be impatient . . . for myself I am nearly worn out with it." Taney and McLean opened to Webster the status of the fifth vote, amid the Court's internal and external politics embracing famine migration, Northern free blacks, and slavery in Western territories.

Prior to the final argument Taney responded to Webster's requests for information, as did McLean. "I am very sensible of the importance of having a full Bench in the New York and Boston passenger cases," Taney wrote Webster on October 11, 1848. "I have today written to Judge McKinley and hope he will be able to attend. Gentlemen who have seen him tell me that he is much better than he was when he was last at Washington." McKinley indeed was present for the final argument on December 22. Five days later Webster wrote McLean, "I took cold in the Court room, on friday [*sic*] & have been so much threatened with rheumatism, that I have not left for the North. Since I have now staid so long, I would stay for the *decision*, if it be likely to come soon, & *to be worth waiting for*" (emphasis in original). He continued: "I send this note for the purpose [of] a little inquiry of you. If you have nothing to say today, but think you may have tomorrow, I will in that case, wait at least till tomorrow. If that be so, you need only say, in answer to this, that I had better wait till tomorrow. I pray you excuse this trouble." On December 29 Webster wrote cocounsel J. P. Hall, "I was in Court yesterday, & have heard from those regions today. No conference has yet been had, & none will be had this week. I keep eyes & ears open, but as yet hear nothing important. Opinion *off the Bench* is certainly with us. I feel it to be my duty to stay till something transpires; & shall keep you informed, daily for the benefit of our clients."

Uncertainty about the fifth vote came to an end. On December 26 Webster wrote his son: "I argued my cause well enough, & if I were not always lucky, now days, in such cases, I should think I saw a glimm[er]ing of success. But tho' we shall get 4 judges, I fear we may not a 5th." On January 3, 1849, however, McLean wrote Webster, "We had no consultation last night. But rest easy. I think there will be a right decision." McLean's note was all Webster needed. The same day, seeking "an augmentation of my contingent fee," he wrote to New York lawyer and one-time port collector Edward Curtis, who in 1845 had brought Webster into the *Turner* case. Webster went right "to the point. *We shall succeed in the cause*, as I now believe. If no Judge dies, or is obliged to leave the Bench, within 15 days, the New York judgment will be reversed" (emphasis in original). The frank private commentary indicated Webster's facility in linking his own and his clients' interests to the information procured from Taney and McLean regarding the outcome of the Passenger Cases, weeks before the Court announced its decision. Taney's helpful notice that McKinley would participate in the Passenger Cases undoubtedly encouraged Webster to approach McLean once arguments had ended.

The initial contact with Webster during appellate arguments in October 1848 *followed* McLean's withdrawing his name from consideration in both the Whig and Free-Soil presidential conventions. Thus, possible immediate connections between newspaper reports concerning delays in the Court's decisions such as the Passenger Cases and McLean's persistent hopes for presidential nomination had passed by the point Webster solicited information. At the time he told Webster to "rest easy" about the vote in the two cases, however, McLean's involvement with Ohio's Whig and Free-Soil parties coincided with Salmon Chase's "breathtaking example of backroom maneuvering," said historian Jonathan H. Earle. "Chase traded Free Soil support for Democratic control in the state's lower house, for the Jacksonians' support of Chase for the [U.S.] Senate seat and the repeal of Ohio's repressive black laws." Coinciding with Whig and Barnburner Democrat support of the New York personal liberty law, Ohio's repeal of black laws established near legal equality in court between free blacks and whites, including recent Irish and German immigrants. Amid these political shifts McLean said publically that his exclusive-commerce-power theory was consistent with the "sovereignty" principle affirmed in *Groves*. He also supported state police powers enabling both free blacks and white immigrants to gain state citizenship, and Western states emerging from the Mexican Cession to exclude slavery.

Coincidentally, newspapers publicized accounts consistent with those Taney and McLean had given Webster. On January 25, 1849, the *Boston Post* quoted the "Washington correspondent of the *New York Commercial Advertiser*," stating that as a result of delays regarding the "New York case" the Court had earlier "concluded to postpone judgment, until after another argument before a full Bench. Since then, the Judges have stood four to four, and upon arrival of Judge McKinley, it was found that his opinion was adverse to the claims of the States." These news accounts revealed how well-informed the press was concerning the Court's opinion-making progress in the Passenger Cases weeks before the 5–4 vote and the separate opinions addressing it were read from the bench on February 7.

Justice Wayne seized the opportunity publicity presented. Ever since *Miln*, Wayne was critical of Taney's refusal to address Baldwin's opposition to the "commerce-person" distinction Barbour incorporated into the majority opinion without his colleagues' consent. In 1837, the same year the *U.S. Reports* published Barbour's majority opinion including the doctrine, Baldwin, of course, had separately published his opinion rejecting it. By 1849, from the Court deciding *Miln* only Taney, McLean, and Wayne remained aware that the Chief Justice had declined to address the concern that a majority had not supported Barbour's statement. Wayne had concurred in *Groves* with the majority decision in only a few cryptic lines. He also formally concurred without opinion with the Court's unanimous result in the License Cases; the *U.S. Reports*, however, printed Wayne's strong reply to lawyers' arguments relying on Barbour's phrase to support the precedential authority of *Miln*. Wayne, the *U.S. Reports* stated, "declare[d] his entire dissent from the general opinions expressed in the language in question." Accordingly, as members of the Court prepared opinions in the Passenger Cases, Wayne incorporated an extensive "narrative" denouncing Taney's actions in *Miln*. "An unfortunate collision has occurred between Wayne and the Chief Justice," Daniel wrote his sister, "in which there is some approach even to bitterness." In open Court on February 7 Wayne revealed the depth of his feelings.

As the Taney Court wrestled with the Passenger Cases, its constitutional role was politicized. Since summer 1848, congressional party leaders had considered extending Supreme Court jurisdiction over the conflicted status of slavery in the Western territories acquired in the war with Mexico. The plan Delaware Whig senator John M. Clayton proposed "leaves the entire question in the dispute to the [federal] Judiciary," ultimately the Supreme Court. Although Clayton's proposal had some bipartisan support, it did not pass amid congressional consideration of Calhoun's February 1848 Senate resolution, declaring that Congress lacked constitutional authority to prohibit slavery in the Mexican Cession. In early 1849, as the Congress debated Oregon's statehood without slavery, Calhoun asserted that the Constitution itself guaranteed opening the Western territories to the institution. During the period party politics defeated Clayton's proposal, the Boston *Daily Atlas* disputed whether the Taney Court could effectively address controversial police power issues embracing white immigrants and free backs in Rhode Island's Dorr Rebellion. The paper blamed Chief Justice Taney for repeated delays, urging his retirement so that "a *progressive* Democrat" could "be appointed" to handle the Court's troubled docket; it also suggested sarcastically that "Judge McKinley would not insist on living so long, or would at least resign on account of ill health."

Public scrutiny of the Taney Court's delayed decisions and defeated Clayton proposals was the context for internal and external politics influencing the opinion-making process in the Passenger Cases. Taney's and McLean's private responses to Webster's solicitations revealed that the five-vote majority finally was present after years of delay, a fact that newspaper accounts readily confirmed. By early 1849 Taney had reason to favor publicity regarding his view that state police powers enabled the states to exclude both destitute white immigrants and free blacks, whereas the federal government—contrary to repeated abolitionist agitation—could not regulate the interstate slave trade. Taney's reasoning was consistent with Calhoun's insistence that the federal government could not exclude slavery from the Western states. McLean's "sovereignty" principle sustaining an exclusive commerce power, however, granted voters in the Western states the authority to admit or exclude slavery. His "sovereignty" principle also supported personal liberty laws that since the *Prigg* decision had increasingly enabled Northern states' defiance of the U.S. Fugitive Slave Act. The same principle also permitted abolition of discriminatory black laws, whereby state police powers promoted equality of free blacks and white immigrants as legal "persons." The Court's eight opinions in the Passenger Cases reshaped this political contestation into doctrines pitting police powers against the federal commerce power.

Five Opinions Overturning the State's Alien Tax Announced February 7, 1849

The majority agreed that the states' alien tax unconstitutionally disrupted foreign commerce. The master in the New York suit commanded a British vessel; in the Massachusetts case the captain and his schooner were from St John's, New Brunswick, a British North American colony. Both captains legally protested paying the taxes, whereupon state authorities compelled compliance. Each state's policy on its face arguably violated the 1794 commercial treaty between the United States and Great Britain, which permitted taxes only under limited reciprocal conditions, subject to exceptions permitted by either nation's domestic laws. Did the state alien taxes come within the exceptions? Justices Catron and Grier held that the state taxes conflicted with treaties and federal regulations enacted by Congress that were therefore the "supreme law of the land." Justices McLean and Wayne held that congressional foreign and interstate commerce powers were exclusive; it was sufficient that the state taxes violated that power, though the commercial treaties and regulations were enacted pursuant to the Constitution as supreme law. McKinley's opinion supporting the same result uniquely rested on a dormant commerce power. Read on February 7, the majority's interlocking concurring opinions agreed upon Marshall's doctrine that a proven direct conflict with a "supreme" federal law or treaty was the surest affirmation of the commerce power; it was a position that avoided direct political conflicts.

Confirming the consensus regarding the 1794 treaty and its successor agreements, Wayne identified eight holdings concurred in by the majority of five. These justices agreed that the state taxes were commercial regulations violating powers the Constitution *expressly* conferred upon Congress to regulate commerce with foreign nations. Moreover, the states unconstitutionally taxed international and interstate commerce—which included the transportation of alien passengers—in order to implement the execution and operation of their own police powers. The taxes also violated federal authority over passengers entering U.S. ports, such as the Passenger Acts, as well as federal naturalization laws, which distinguished white immigrants and blacks, though both were objects of commerce refuting the "commerce-person" minority holding in *Miln*. Congressional authority was sufficient also to ensure that through taxes and other means, states did not destroy their own commercial equality. The states violated the mandate in Article I, Section 8, that duties, imposts, and excises should be uniform throughout the United States. The taxes also unconstitutionally burdened the federal commerce power regulating navigation on waterways. Still, the states possessed sufficient police powers to fund "essential inspections," quarantine, health laws excluding the insane, immoral, or criminals, and pilotage that only indirectly affected merchandise and persons entering U.S. ports.

By different paths, three justices accepted Catron's holding requiring conflict with "supreme" federal laws and treaties. Unlike Wayne and McLean, Catron declined to address the exclusive commerce power, arguing that the fundamental "question" the alien taxes raised was "whether a State can regulate foreign commerce by 'a revenue measure,' for the purpose of its own treasury." Still, Wayne and Grier accepted Catron's application of Marshall's reliance on federal laws and treaties as "supreme" in such cases. The 1794 treaty stated that "the inhabitants of Great Britain shall have liberty freely and securely to come with their ships and cargoes to our ports, to enter the same, and to remain and reside in any part of our territories" and that "no higher or other duties should be imposed on British vessels than that were by our laws imposed on American vessels." Applying Marshall's reasoning, McLean held that the treaty's reciprocal revenue provisions rested on the exclusive commerce power. In order to collect the taxes, Catron said, state law also clashed with property protections in the 1819 Passenger Act and U.S. general collections regulations, by "forbid[ding] the owner to land; they hold him out of the courts, and separate him from his property, until, by coercion, he pays to the master for the use of the State any amount of tax the State may at its discretion set upon him and his family; and this on the assumption that Congress has not regulated in respect to his free admission."

McLean and Grier considered implications invalidating the alien taxes might have for state police powers governing white immigrants or free blacks. "Except to guard against disease and paupers," McLean said that "a State cannot prohibit the introduction of foreigners. It may deny them residence unless they shall give security to indemnify the public should they become paupers." McLean's comments embraced the bond-surety system, the early status of free blacks in Ohio, and the idea that by 1849 white immigrants and free blacks possessed the same right as all free "persons" to establish residence in McLean's home state. By contrast, Grier said the taxes interfered with the express policy affirmed in federal naturalization laws and, implicitly, the Passenger Acts that healthy white foreigners were "persons" free to enter ports and to travel across all states and territories. The "cherished policy of the general government" was "to encourage and invite Christian foreigners of our own race to seek an asylum within our borders, and to convert these waste lands into productive farms, and thus add to the wealth, population, and power of the nation." Although the states claimed that the alien taxes extended police powers aiding health and safety, they interfered with the operation of U.S. naturalization and passenger laws. The "just and well-settled doctrine established by this court," said Grier was "that a State cannot do that indirectly which she is forbidden by the Constitution to do directly."

Grier and Wayne noted the distinct purposes for which Congress exercised international and interstate commerce powers over white passengers but not free blacks. Grier indicated that the alien taxes levied on board vessels conflicted with the federal-passenger spatial regulations tied to tonnage: "If she [the state] cannot levy a duty or tax from the master or owner of a vessel engaged in commerce [based] on tonnage . . . of the vessel," the state "cannot effect the same purpose by merely changing the ratio, and [basing] it on the . . . number of passengers which she carries. We have to deal with things, and cannot change them by changing their names." Wayne most directly addressed free blacks as legal "persons." The "fear" the dissenters ascribed to the majority's decision "has no foundation," Wayne said, that "if the States have not the discretion to determine who may come and live in them, the United States may introduce into the Southern States emancipated Negros from the West Indies and elsewhere." Suggesting McLean's "sovereignty" principle, Wayne said, "All the political sovereignty of the United States, within the States, must be exercised according to the subject-matter upon which it may be brought to bear. . . . The Constitution was formed by States in which slavery existed[,] . . . and States in which slavery . . . was abolished." The "continuance of that difference between the States at that time" was the "recognized condition in the Constitution for the national Union."

Concurring in McLean's and Catron's opinions, McKinley's opinion alone rested on Article I, Section 9, which authorized Congress to ban the international slave trade in 1808. McKinley, however, distinguished between white "migration" as international travel and "importation" of "persons [slaves]" with "no exercise of volition in their transportation," which states controlled through "[m]igration or Importation" laws up to 1808. Congress already controlled all other immigration in the four states not covered by the clause, because these states had not existed when the Constitution was ratified. After 1808, McKinley argued, the "power of Congress over the whole subject of migration and importation was complete throughout the United States." The "great question" was: "Where does" the federal "power . . . over this subject end, and where does the State power begin?" It was "one of the most perplexing questions ever submitted to the consideration of this court," he said; and Marshall's reasoning in *Brown v. Maryland* provided the best guide. McKinley's unique solution suggested modern applications of the dormant Commerce Clause formulated as "field pre-emption." Still, he concurred in Catron's opinion recognizing that the Necessary and Proper Clause in tandem with the Supremacy Clause and Article I, Section 9, even "in the absence of Legislation by Congress on this subject," already established the "whole ground . . . occupied by Congress before" the New York tax "act had passed."

Overturning the states' alien taxes, the majority thus employed diverse reasoning. Four justices applied Marshall's "supremacy" doctrine in *Gibbons*, while McKinley rested his fifth vote on *Brown v. Maryland*. Also, Wayne, McLean, and McKinley said that federal supremacy derived from the exclusive commerce power, and only Catron endorsed McKinley's expansive construction of "immigration" in the clause giving Congress power to ban the international slave trade. Directly or indirectly, however, four justices accepted Catron's reliance upon federal treaties and the Passenger Act as the basis for overturning the states' alien tax as a revenue measure, which followed Marshall's holding in *Gibbons* supporting the supremacy of federal law. Wayne's opinion also showed that the majority carefully distinguished between federal supremacy promoting admissions more than exclusion of white immigrants and Southern states' police powers excluding free blacks. Wayne's opinion repeated the earlier admonition that the dissenters' fears of federal compulsion driving free blacks into the South were groundless. "It will be found, too, should this matter of introducing free negroes [*sic*] into the Southern States ever become the subject of judicial inquiry," Wayne said, "that they have a guard against it in the Constitution, making it altogether unnecessary for them to resort to" the extreme law of nations implicating secession "for their protection and preservation."

Moreover, Wayne targeted the "commerce-person" distinction stated in *Miln*. On February 7, and in rejoinders exchanged after Taney's continued rebuttals the morning after, Wayne explained why "I will now do what I have long wished to do," and for which the majority in the Passenger Cases offered "a proper opportunity." Wayne then presented the details developed in chapter 2 of this study, revealing that Justice Barbour's "declaration that persons were not the subjects of commerce . . . had not the assent of a . . . majority of the judges who concurred in the judgment" deciding *Miln*. Defending individual recollections, Taney and Wayne noted the fluid circumstances that confused the vote in *Miln*, while they disputed whether a majority of the Court ever expressly concurred in Barbour's phrase that "persons" were not "commerce" subject to congressional regulation. Taney said that Wayne should not have raised the matter so long after it occurred. But Wayne said that he repudiated the phrase from *Miln* because Taney, Daniel, and others—including lawyers' arguments in *Groves*, the License Cases, and the Passenger Cases—applied it in order to reject possible inclusion of free blacks and slaves within Marshall's federal-supremacy doctrine established in *Gibbons*. Wayne indicated, however, that by resting their decision on Marshall's "supremacy" doctrine, the Passenger Cases majority—like Marshall himself in three commerce power cases—threatened state control of neither slavery nor free blacks.

The key points linking these opinions were Wayne's revelation about *Miln* and divergent support for Catron's and McKinley's reasoning. More significant than the revelation that the "commerce-person" distinction lacked authority in *Miln* was Wayne's use of it to reinforce Marshall's supremacy doctrine in *Gibbons* as controlling the result in the Passenger Cases. Wayne followed Marshall, showing that while congressional regulations embraced the widest commercial "intercourse" of persons and merchandise—including steerage passengers escaping famine—it did not abridge police powers protecting states from disease, the insane, criminals, or free blacks. Applying similar reasoning, Catron's opinion clearly articulated the problem with the alien tax: it was collected on board vessels as a condition for disembarkation in order to provide revenue supporting one state's poor law generally and another state's Maritime Hospital in particular. Catron and Grier emphasized that the primary purpose of the tax was revenue, not protection from undesirables. Notwithstanding attachment to an underlying exclusive-commerce-power doctrine, McLean and Wayne agreed with Catron and Grier on these points. McKinley's unique reasoning, by contrast, endorsed what Catron identified as a dormant commerce power, but did so following Marshall's separation between a police and a commerce power in *Brown v. Maryland*, which provided sufficient federal supremacy to reach the result in the Passenger Cases.

Dissenting Opinions in the Passenger Cases

The dissenting opinions read on February 7, and Taney's amended rebuttal to Wayne's revelation presented the following morning, supported state over federal authority. Nelson said only that he had "examined particularly" Taney's opinion for both the New York and Massachusetts cases and "concurred, not only in its conclusions, but in the grounds and principles upon which" it rested. Nelson's cryptic yet complete endorsement reinforced the dissenters' opinions, given that as a state judge and federal circuit justice he knew most intimately the regulatory burden the famine immigration imposed on New York's police powers. Woodbury's involvement in the Massachusetts alien tax case as federal circuit justice began after the state high court's decision and the initial federal appeal. The lengthy opinion he read reflected state and federal immigration policies embraced by the Know-Nothings and proslavery Democrats. Like his first commerce power opinion in the License Cases, Woodbury's dissent in the Passenger Cases suggested a concurrent commerce power that firmly defended the states' police powers to exclude undesirable white immigrants and free blacks. Since joining the Court in 1842 Justice Daniel had become the leading advocate of states' rights, slavery, and quite limited federal power. In the License Cases Daniel rejected a fully concurrent or exclusive commerce power, as well as Marshall's original-package doctrine; his dissent was even more vigorous in the Passenger Cases.

Taney's dissenting opinion asserted confident but beleaguered leadership. Since becoming Marshall's successor in 1836, Taney had been on the majority side in five commerce power cases that affirmed state police powers regulating immigrants, slave traders, and license fees on local alcohol sales. Unlike Marshall's commerce power decisions, however, dissension from within characterized Taney's leadership in these cases: Baldwin privately challenged the "commerce-person" distinction in *Miln*, McLean surprisingly announced a concurring opinion that splintered the Court in *Groves*, and in the License Cases ten opinions supported only a unanimous result. The 5–4 decision and eight opinions in the Passenger Cases conflicted further the Taney Court's mixed and unsettled record constructing timely commerce power doctrines that shaped policies toward white immigrants and free blacks as legal "persons." Although Taney's own tightly focused dissenting opinion excoriated the majority's reasoning and holdings that overturned the two states' alien taxes, it fostered rather than alleviated doctrinal uncertainty. Moreover, the years of delay and deadlock preceding the announcement of opinions on February 7, 1849, occurred amid radicalized antislavery politics that polarized the public image of both the Supreme Court and its chief justice, which the dissenting opinions reinforced.

Defending state police powers, the dissenters endorsed only the narrowest U.S. commerce power. Daniel said that "a reasonable interpretation" was "that the powers so granted" to Congress were "never exclusive of similar powers existing in the States, unless where the Constitution has expressly in terms given an exclusive power to Congress, or the exercise of a like power is prohibited to the States, or there is a direct repugnancy or incompatibility in the exercise [there]of by the States." Thus, he asserted, "In all other cases it seems unquestionable that the States retain concurrent authority with Congress." Since in the Passenger Cases the regulations of foreign immigrants coexisted within a state-federal system, there were no grounds to invalidate the alien tax as an improper exercise of police powers. Woodbury was still more explicit that states could not surrender to Congress their sovereign authority to tax alien immigrants. Indeed, "notwithstanding that a grant to Congress is explicit, if the States are not directly forbidden to act, it does not give to Congress exclusive authority over the matter, but the States may exercise a power in several respects relating to it, unless, from the nature of the subject and their relations to the general government, a prohibition is fairly implied." A concurrent regulation of commerce could "be exclusive as to some matters and not to others, and everything can in that respect be reconciled and harmonious, and accord . . . with the nature and reason of each."

Taney flatly denied that any federal law or treaty deprived the "people of the several States of this Union" the "power of expelling from their borders any person, or class of persons . . . deem[ed] dangerous to its peace, or likely to produce a physical or moral evil among its citizens." The assumption shaped Taney's reaction to Wayne's revelation that a majority never supported the "commerce-person" distinction in *Miln*. The phrase meant, he believed, that poor white immigrants and free blacks were "persons" governed by state police powers and not merchandise subject to the U.S. commerce power. Thus, the alien taxes were police regulations safeguarding the two states from the "evils of pauperism." Moreover, Taney said, these same police powers protected Southerners from the "emancipated slaves of the West Indies [should they] have at this hour the absolute right to reside, hire houses, and traffic and trade throughout the Southern States, in spite of any State law to the contrary; inevitably, producing the most serious discontent, and ultimately leading to the most painful consequences." Taney noted that the License Cases upheld state retail liquor-sale fees affecting foreign and interstate trade. The "grant of power to Congress was not a prohibition to the States to make such regulations as they deem necessary, in their own ports and harbours, for the convenience of trade or security of health; and that such regulations were valid, unless they came in conflict with an Act of Congress."

Like Taney, Woodbury focused on the need to preserve the "commerce-person" distinction. Congressional regulations of imports and exports embraced merchandise but not "persons," said Woodbury. The states' "power" was "manifestly as great in a harbor within her limits to tax men and property as it" was "on shore, and can no more be abused there than on shore, and can no more conflict there than on shore with any authority of Congress as a taxing power not on imports as imports," because "imports" referred to goods or property. Woodbury rejected McKinley's unique opinion that "importation" referred to two separate classes of "persons" identified as free white immigrants and slaves, over both of which Congress had the exclusive power to regulate. Such an exclusive commerce power undermining the "commerce-person" distinction had catastrophic implications. "If Congress, without a coordinate or concurrent power in the States, can prohibit other persons as well as slaves from coming into States," Woodbury warned, federal authorities "can permit and demand the admission of slaves, as well as any kind of free person, convicts or paupers, into any State, and enforce the demand by all the overwhelming powers of the Union, however, obnoxious to the habits and wishes of the people of a particular State." Federal jurisdiction displacing state control over expulsion could "force upon the States slaves or criminals, or political incendiaries of the most dangerous character."

Protecting state police powers over "persons," Taney and Woodbury refuted the majority's claim that the alien taxes violated the 1794 or other treaties and the U.S.-British Passenger Acts. For the dissenters, the immediate issue was whether the federal government possessed under an international treaty an exclusive power to regulate the right of alien passengers to enter a state of the Union. Reading selectively reciprocal commercial treaties, as well as the 1819 Passenger Act, Taney emphasized that ultimately, the municipal laws of separate U.S. states and British colonies governed enforcement of the particular provisions of "foreign" law. Taney did not state, however, that such treaty stipulations were exceptions recognizing slavery or temperance laws coexisting with all the other objects to which reciprocal trade applied. Though unmentioned, Taney's argument followed the U.S. government defense of the South's Negro Seamen Acts, which was consistent with what he had used as attorney general, defending proslavery laws as state-exemptions stipulated in U.S.-British treaties. Taney nonetheless did say that the revenue exemptions in the treaties and Passenger Acts—coinciding with transnational reciprocity—could not "subject [the state's] domestic concerns and social relations to the power of the Federal government." Indeed, Woodbury queried, "who ever thought that these treaties were meant to empower, or could in any moral or political view empower, Great Britain to ship her paupers to Massachusetts, or send her free blacks from the West Indies into the Southern States or into Ohio, in contravention of their local laws."

Taney addressed carefully Wayne's revelation regarding the "commerce-person" distinction. As Daniel's letter to his sister suggested, Taney was embittered that Wayne exposed the dissatisfaction Baldwin and others had felt in 1837 about not removing the phrase from *Miln*. Unlike Wayne, Taney disclaimed having precise recollections of factual circumstances. Yet he was so concerned about preserving the precedential legitimacy of the phrase within *Miln* that Taney defended it not only on February 7 but in further comments the next morning. Relying on the phrase, Taney disputed Wayne's and McLean's citation in the Passenger Cases to Marshall's expansive definition in *Gibbons* defining commerce as "intercourse" sustaining an exclusive congressional power, as well as McKinley's unusual cite to *Brown v. Maryland* supporting state police powers. Taney argued that since white passengers were "persons" not classifiable as "imports," the alien tax was outside the constitutional prohibition regulating imports, Marshall's and McKinley's holdings to the contrary notwithstanding. Applying the "commerce-person" distinction, Taney thus held that passengers were not taxable imports, since the well-settled meaning of the word was that "imports" and "importation" referred to property and not persons. Paradoxically, since the same section permitted "absolutely necessary . . . inspections," *Miln* enabled state examination of passengers in order to levy and collect the alien tax.

Daniel supported Taney against Wayne and went further defending the "commerce-person" distinction. Daniel implied that revelations about past decisions were inappropriate given that evidence offered as proof usually was mere opinion. More aggressively than Taney, he argued that alien taxes were not regulations of "imports," asserting that "alien passengers, rational beings, freemen carrying into executions their deliberate intentions, never can, without singular perversions be classed with subjects of sale, barter, or traffic [like slaves]; or, in other words, imports." Daniel also declared that treaty exemptions governed the status of "persons," while the general reciprocity provisions regulated merchandise. The latter provision sustaining a discriminatory state tax on goods, Daniel conceded, would be unconstitutional. Since alien passengers were "persons," not merchandise, however, the treaty exemptions embraced the states' alien taxes. "Admitting," said Daniel, the reciprocity provision "of the treaty to be in full force, and that it purported to take from the State of New York the right to tax aliens coming . . . within her territory, it would be certainly incompetent for such a purpose, because there is not, and never could have been any right in any other agent than her [New York's] own government to bind her by such a stipulation." Daniel concluded that if the majority's "cherished policy" of admitting aliens required "uniformity" under an exclusive commerce power, it violated state sovereignty.

Taney stressed the dangers undesirable white immigrants and free blacks unleashed into the states because of the majority's decision. He hammered Wayne's admonition that neither international treaties nor the 1819 Passenger Act regulating transatlantic passenger traffic threatened the states' police powers governing free blacks. Indeed, Taney insisted, the "fundamental question is: Has the Federal Government power to compel States to receive, and suffer to mingle with its citizens, any person or class of persons?" Taney believed that *Groves*, *Prigg*, and other precedents upheld the idea that "the States have the power to expel and exclude." While "[t]here can be no concurrent [federal-state] power respecting such a matter," the state's exercise of police powers was "necessarily discretionary. Massachusetts fears foreign paupers; Mississippi, free Negros." The Constitution empowered neither the federal government nor the states to "distinguish between different grades of aliens." The Massachusetts law "only exact[ed] security against pauperism. We [Taney and his fellow Southerners] cannot admit emancipated slaves." The New York law was "a quarantine law, and no more. The provisions for making it self-supporting are legitimate incidents." The immediate public response to the Passenger Cases indicated that the majority and dissenting opinions reflected polarized party and racial politics within the states and the nation.

Assessment: Public Response to the Passenger Cases in Early 1849

The Court's 5–4 decision and eight opinions in the Passenger Cases vindicated the shippers' many years of litigation. Following the announcement of the decision Webster wrote one correspondent that the Court had overturned the "judgments" concerning the two states' "passenger laws . . . declaring those laws null & void. Of course, there will be such things as *draw-backs*, and repayments." His associate in Boston, John Plummer Healy, wrote at the same time, "I have been busy notifying the parties interested, & getting matters into shape to commence the necessary suits [for recovery from the city]." Meanwhile, after learning from Justice McLean that victory was likely, Webster had written Richard Milford Blatchford that the Court's decision upholding the federal commerce power, like the years of argument preceding it, "has been made under great discouragements and evil auspices." Webster's characterization of the past and current struggles over the alien tax was consistent with the public commentary during the weeks and months immediately following the Court's narrow majority decision. The ambivalent commentary reflected not only the conflicted legal and constitutional reasoning the justices employed for or against the shippers and the states, but also the polarized state and national party politics contesting the legal status of impoverished immigrants, free blacks, and Southern slavery.

The lawsuits Webster began to recover his clients' taxed money coincided with publication of Robert C. Manners's central role in the lengthy litigation. "I should now be pleased to learn, whether suits have been brought, or what progress has been made, in these matters," Webster wrote Healy. "When the City is sued, I suppose it will represent the case to the Legislature; and the sooner this is done the better. I take it, that interest is running, on all the sums." Some weeks later the March *Niles' National Register* reprinted a notice from the *New York Journal of Commerce* revealing that British vice consul at Boston Manners "obtained through perseverance" and "expense" the Supreme Court's "recent decision . . . against the constitutionality of the Alien Passenger Tax" levied by Massachusetts and New York. The news report stated Manners's "protest" campaign was based on the claim that the tax was unconstitutional, "contrary to existing treaties." Manners's efforts began in 1837 with the Massachusetts legislature and continued in the state's courts, after ensuring that the plaintiff Captain Norris "should be protected against all cost and charges to which the suit might give rise." Manners's efforts finally achieved victory in the Supreme Court after "nearly twelve years." During this time, "most owners and consignees of emigrant vessels paid the tax under protest, and the consequence is," echoing Webster, "that a large amount of money is to be returned to them."

The Court's decision in the Passenger Cases altered the states' funding sources. Both states confronted the immediate loss of tax revenue collected on board vessels and the legal obligation to cover the protests accumulated over the years during which the alien taxes were enforced. Shortly after the Court's decision, both states increased the fees and penalties collected from the bond-sureties and the commutation fee that shipmasters and shippers paid to local officials. All parties and the Supreme Court's opinions acknowledged that this system rested on the legitimate exercise of police powers enforced, administrated, or litigated in court within the state's onshore jurisdiction. The loss of the Massachusetts alien tax effectively was dispersed throughout the state's general poor-law revenues; ending the New York alien tax had a proportionally larger impact, however, since it funded the Maritime Hospital. The Emigrant Commission responsible for administering New York City's entire immigration system initially reduced the numbers of people whose physical condition upon arrival in Quarantine qualified for admission to the Maritime Hospital on Staten Island. The administration of the more limited selection criteria heightened the commissioner's attention to corruption and abuse resulting from private bond agents and hospitals, which in turn increased demands for more regulation funded through higher returns from the bond-surety and commutation system.

Shippers and shipmasters circumvented increased federal regulation in the 1849 U.S. Passenger Act. The Supreme Court's decision eliminating the alien tax coincided with persistent demands from the state assembly for federal regulation of the deplorable conditions steerage passengers suffered upon vessels arriving in New York City from foreign ports. By 1849 the British Parliament also addressed increased lobbying for stronger regulation and enforcement from Liverpool immigration commissioners, who argued that avoidance of regulations imposed in the 1847 Passenger Act aided the Americans' competitive advantage. Moreover, the Supreme Court's overturning of the alien tax reduced the American shippers' costs compared with the British shippers obligated to pay the same tax upon entering British North American ports. Amid conflicting demands Congress passed with bipartisan and North-South support the 1849 Passenger Act; formally, it improved the spatial and ventilation conditions on board American vessels transporting immigrants, including for the first time Chinese laborers arriving in Gold Rush California. Herman Melville was quoted saying that implementing the regulations would improve steerage-class passengers' welfare, but it was quite unlikely that effective enforcement of either the American or British laws would occur. Abuse resulting from active police powers and weak enforcement of the 1849 Passenger Act soon proved Melville right.

The Court's decision in the Passenger Cases temporarily stymied the Know-Nothings. The self-described "American Party" had opposed the 1847 Passenger Act, emphasizing the franchise advantage other parties gained from federal naturalization policies and the states' enforcement of immigrants' admission over exclusion. The eight opinions in the Passenger Cases, by contrast, agreed that police powers enforcing exclusion of most undesirables from states was legitimate; but Grier and McLean vigorously urged the traditional "cherished policy" favoring state admission. Once the Court's opinions accepted the restrictive police powers, the Know-Nothings and other anti-immigrant groups advocated the state exclusion policy in order to support increased commutation and bond fees targeting the transportation of variously defined "defectives." Still, in Massachusetts the shippers avoided the state's higher fee by shifting "defectives" admitted from transatlantic trade into Portland and New York. The shippers then used coastal commerce—which even Taney's opinion acknowledged required freer trade involving white immigrants—thereby gaining their admission at a lower fee in Boston harbor. An anti-immigrant U.S. senator noted the "constitutional difficulty": given that the "states had authority and had acted . . . [w]here was the jurisdiction in Congress? He was opposed to immigration, but did not know how to frame a bill not in conflict with state authority, state rights, and state jurisdiction."

The press publicized federal-state constitutional conflicts arising from immigrants and free blacks confronting Northern and Southern states' rights. Opposing the five-vote majority that overturned the alien taxes, the Boston *Daily Atlas* declared, "These laws have been adjudged to be constitutional by the unanimous opinion of the highest Courts of Massachusetts and New York; and now they are to be to be destroyed by the casting vote of Judge McKinley, of Alabama, whose mind, it is said, has been long in a balanced and vacillating condition." The danger was that "[i]f the laws of the Northern States which assume to regulate the introduction of aliens, whether white or black, are to be destroyed by the judgments of Southern Judges, while the laws of the Southern States regulating the introduction of free blacks are to stand, it will awaken reflections of no pleasant character [a Southern sectional threat]." The *Charleston Mercury* warned of the Northern danger: "If we correctly understand the points decided, they sweep away our inspection laws enacted to prevent the abduction of our slaves in Northern vessels [by abolitionists]. They sweep away also all our laws enacted to prevent free colored persons—citizens of Massachusetts—or whatever abolition region, from entering our ports and cities." The "Union" was "to be so administered as to strip the South of all power of self-protection and to make submission of its rule equivalent to ruin and degradation."

Illinois congressman Thomas J. Turner indicated that the Passenger Cases facilitated conflict between Northern and Southern states. During February 1849 amid congressional debate over slavery in the Mexican Cession, Northern states' personal liberty laws defying enforcement of the U.S. Fugitive Slave Act, and abolitionist attacks on the interstate slave trade, Turner addressed the House, "speaking . . . for the people of the North." He wrestled with the same multifaceted antislavery sentiment among his constituents that fellow Democrats Morton and Van Buren faced, respectively, in Massachusetts and New York as a result of the Free-Soil and Liberty parties. The "Supreme Court, in the celebrated [passenger] case which has lately been adjudicated within this Capitol, says in effect that the law of South Carolina is unconstitutional" because, Turner said, it "forbid[s] the colored citizens of Massachusetts from going into that state [and] even imprisoning them when they go there aboard their vessels." This law was the "most flagrant violation of the Constitution ever perpetrated in" America. Turner suggested Justice McLean's sovereignty principle supporting divergent police powers conferring citizenship in Ohio while denying it in the South. Rejecting Southerners' arguments that "Massachusetts has no right to make negroes [*sic*] citizens," Turner asserted that the Bay Sate was exercising the same state sovereignty to establish citizenship for blacks "that South Carolina [enforced] . . . to make them slaves."

The decision of the Passenger Cases also coincided with McLean's exclusive commerce power becoming more politicized. McLean defended the voters of Ohio's Western Reserve after Georgian Alexander H. Stephens "cursed" them for electing in 1848 abolitionist Joshua R. Giddings. In part, Giddings received such criticism for advocating a commerce power that McLean had told McKinley was "entirely orthodox." By January 1849, a Mississippi senator attacked McLean for claiming that police powers enabled states to exclude slavery from the Mexican Cession, though the justice said also that those same powers prevented Congress from interfering with the interstate slave trade. Ohio abolitionist Joel Tiffany's 1849 treatise declaring slavery unconstitutional further agitated McLean's exclusive commerce power. Like Giddings, Tiffany advocated Lord Mansfield's 1772 *Somerset* Doctrine, which held that slavery required express legislation in order to exist. Employing the "absolutely" exclusive commerce power, Tiffany said further that since Congress used the power to regulate commerce to abolish the international slave trade after 1808, "they have the same power to annihilate the domestic slave trade." Moreover, the same reasoning enabled Congress to exclude slavery from the Mexican Cession, including California. Although McLean's views did not comport exactly with those of Tiffany and Giddings, for Southerners they came close enough to justify condemnation.

The ambivalent public responses to the Passenger Cases revealed how politicized the state-federal regulatory system had become by early 1849. The Court narrowly affirmed that state alien taxes collected on board vessels as a condition for passenger disembarkation violated treaties and federal commerce regulations. The Know-Nothings and other anti-immigrant groups lobbied Congress and state legislatures advocating stronger regulations targeting undesirable immigrants. Shippers maneuvered within federal-state regulations, avoiding both the states' exclusion policy and the improved conditions U.S.-British passenger laws mandated aboard vessels. Anti-immigrant groups did not stop. Grier's "cherished" immigrant-admission policy encountered counterdemands for exclusion, while the Northern and Southern press questioned the implications the Passenger Cases had for the police power status of white immigrants, free blacks, and slaves as legal "persons." Despite the Supreme Court majority's contrary assertions, the Northern and Southern press pronounced the dissenters' claim that the Court had unleashed upon the states undesirable white immigrants and free blacks. Southern attacks on Justice

McLean further politicized his advocacy of state police powers versus an exclusive commerce power affecting slavery in the Mexican Cession, the interstate slave trade, and free blacks' citizenship in certain Northern states.

Ambiguous Significance of the Passenger Cases in Early 1849

Commenting on the Passenger Cases as precedent, Webster wrote prominent New York lawyer Richard M. Blatchford that the "decision will be more important to the country, than any decision since that in the steamboat cause [*Gibbons*]." On the winning side in both, despite periodic travails, he believed these "two cases have done something towards, explaining and upholding the just powers of the government of the United States, on the great subject of commerce." His letter to J. P. Hall indicated that the decision enabled shippers to limit costs states imposed on the immigrant trade; but it was silent about his clients' likely noncompliance with the improved health regulations imposed by the Passenger Acts. He noted the state police powers in *Miln*, notwithstanding Story's dissent with which Marshall had agreed, upholding the 1819 Passenger Act based on the exclusive commerce power. Webster concluded that the "weight of Chief-Justice Marshall's opinion, as well as that of Judge Story's, is to be added to the opinions of the five now concurring in" the decision of Passenger Cases. Finally, Webster said, Taney's dissent "admitted . . . that the New-York law must be regarded as clearly unconstitutional and void, so far as it purported to tax passengers coming to New York from other States," which followed Marshall's reasoning in *Gibbons*. Webster did not comment regarding how tenuous was the five-vote majority, given that McKinley, absent because of ill health, had Catron read his opinion.

Consistent with Marshall's reasoning in *Gibbons*, the majority opinions in the Passenger Cases affirmed federal regulation of international commerce as "intercourse." Unlike Marshall's silence on slavery, however, Wayne joined McLean in suggesting Webster's argument since *Groves* that the commerce power did not reach the interstate slave trade because slavery was a special case recognized by the Constitution's framers. Although state jurisdiction generally prescribed police powers regulating admission or exclusion of free blacks, slaves, and white immigrants, states only partially governed immigrants when there was an express clash with a federal law or treaty. Although Wayne revealed that the "commerce-person" distinction in *Miln* lacked precedential force, the majority and dissenters agreed that the states regulated the movement or abolition of slaves, except for federal enforcement of the international slave trade ban. While Catron and McLean diverged on whether to address the exclusive commerce power, they agreed that the framers granted slavery a special status, meaning Congress could not regulate the interstate slave trade, despite abolitionists' contrary arguments. Whether a concurrent or dormant commerce power enabled shared or exclusive regulation remained an open question regarding white foreign immigrants; but states dominated slavery and controlled exclusion or admission of free blacks, including in certain Northern states conferral of limited citizenship.

From outside and inside the Supreme Court, Webster and Wayne appreciated the national importance of the Passenger Cases. Although Webster had prevailed in *Gibbons*, he understood that Marshall upheld a narrow federal-supremacy doctrine in order to avoid suggesting that an exclusive commerce power might invalidate the states' powers over slavery or free blacks. Wayne also embraced Marshall's limited supremacy doctrine once state police power regulation of foreign immigrants in *Miln* coincided with Southerners' fears that West Indian emancipated blacks propagated abolitionism and slave revolts. Wayne's commitment to Marshall's doctrine explained his private and public rebuff of Taney's support for the "commerce-person" distinction that shielded from federal regulation state control of free blacks, slaves, and white foreign immigrants. While Webster's winning argument in *Groves* defended slavery and free blacks from congressional commerce power regulation, the opinions of Taney, McLean, and Baldwin divided amid abolitionist attacks on the interstate slave trade. Webster's and Wayne's vindication of Marshall's supremacy doctrine in the Passenger Cases encouraged the hope that the Court and the nation might disentangle the legal status of foreign white immigrants, free blacks embracing personal liberty laws that conferred limited citizenship, and slavery's penetration into the Western territories.

CHAPTER 5

Passenger Cases

Precedential Significance, 1849–1870

As a result of the Passenger Cases, the conflicted legal status of immigrants and blacks as legal "persons" evolved through three phases from 1849 to 1870. The first section locates within anti-immigrant and antislavery politics the first phase of the decision's precedential significance supporting the 1850 Compromise. In early 1849 Congress funded publication and distribution of the Court's eight opinions. The multiple opinions addressed immigrants and blacks under police powers and the commerce power; they also reflected contested admission of slavery into the Western territories, Northern states' personal liberty laws defying the U.S. fugitive slave law, and abolition of the slave trade in Washington. The Court's majority opinions sustaining police powers that conferred citizenship on white immigrants and free blacks supported a compromise, which left to voters the decision whether to admit or exclude slavery in the Western territories based on the principle of "popular sovereignty." The dissenters' insistence that police powers enabled exclusion of free blacks reinforced a Southern congressional address condemning Northern states' personal liberty laws, which, based on state sovereignty, often freed fugitive slaves. Accordingly, the 1850 Compromise included a draconian U.S. Fugitive Slave Act. The majority's and dissenters' agreement that states primarily controlled slavery justified a compromise permitting Congress to exclude the slave trade beyond state jurisdiction in Washington, D.C.

The first phase ended after a new majority of the Supreme Court reinterpreted police powers and the commerce power in the *Cooley* Case (1852), discussed the second section. A second phase of immigrants' and blacks' evolving legal status, examined in the third section, occurred amid anti-immigrant and antislavery struggles over state and federal exclusion policies during the 1850s. By 1860 Southerners justified secession in part based on the perceived evil of blacks' citizenship upheld in Northern state personal liberty laws affirmed in the Passenger Cases. In the third phase of immigrants' and blacks' contested legal status during the Civil War and Reconstruction, examined in the fourth section, the precedential significance of the Passenger Cases was reasserted amid California's exclusion of the Chinese and New York's promotion of the transatlantic immigrant trade. The federal citizenship granted "persons" in the Fourteenth Amendment comported with the California Supreme Court's reliance on the Passenger Cases to uphold Chinese aliens' opposition to state exclusion policies. By 1870 Commissioner Friedrich Kapp also analyzed the U.S. Supreme Court precedent in support of New York regulations promoting admission of immigrants against "Western" states' demanding a federal alien tax. Until the last two justices participating in the Passenger Cases were gone in 1870, the Court disputed the precedential meaning of the decision that distinguished state police powers and the federal commerce power.

Publicizing the Passenger Cases and the Compromise of 1850

After contentious congressional debate during 1849–1850 the compromise concerning slavery finally became law in September; meanwhile, Congress publicized the Passenger Cases. Senators Daniel Webster, William H. Seward, John C. Calhoun, George E. Badger, and others supported a special congressional appropriation to publish and distribute 5,000 copies of the Supreme Court's eight opinions. The publicity signaled continued bipartisan support for another U.S. passenger bill, which Know-Nothings nonetheless impeded. Whig senator Seward promoted the mixed results of the Court's eight opinions amid Know-Nothing agitation against growing numbers of immigrants, which from 1849 to 1850 totaled 434,000 in New York alone. Seward drew upon the multiple opinions to justify balanced state and federal admission and exclusion of immigrants, which was distinct from exclusion of slavery in Western territories and state sovereignty defending New York's personal liberty law over the U.S. Fugitive Slave Act. For Webster, the eight opinions supported "popular sovereignty" in the Western territories, enforcement of the Fugitive Slave Act, and resistance to immigrant exclusion. Calhoun and Badger of South and North Carolina, respectively, joined the Southern congressional delegation in publicizing the Court's opinions in order to facilitate Irish immigrants becoming Northern Democrats, admission of slavery into the Mexican Cession, and a stronger Fugitive Slave Act.

Seward's support for federal publicizing of the Passenger Cases reflected state immigrant and racial politics. A powerful New York Whig, Seward aided complex compromise politics that enacted the Emigrant Commission and the personal liberty law with the support of Democrat factions in 1848. Seward also maintained an antislavery stance during 1849–50, resisting Southern demands for a new U.S. Fugitive Slave Act and the admission of slavery into Western states, especially California. These state politics also enabled the Emigrant Commission to redress the invalidation of the alien tax. By 1849 the lost funding for the Maritime Hospital accentuated the commissioners' understanding of the need to "reach the emigrant before he fell into the hands of the plunderers who stood ready to deceive him." Accordingly, the commission lobbied the legislature and litigated in order to purchase landing facilities in New York City where a state-operated immigrant-processing center could be built. The facility known as Castle Garden was not completed until 1855 because of Know-Nothing agitation. Still, a major step was the Labor Exchange, established in 1850 at Canal Street, where after just one year, the number of immigrants "provided with opportunities for self-support in such kind of labor as their previous habits best qualified them to perform" jumped from about 8,000 to 18,204. Seward thus promoted admission of immigrants, limited equality of immigrants and blacks as legal "persons," and opposition to slavery.

Diverse motivations also facilitated Webster's support for dispersing the 5,000 copies of the Passenger Cases opinions. After the Court's favorable decision, Webster turned to Boston lawyer Benjamin R. Curtis to lobby the Massachusetts legislature to appropriate the moneys and interest accumulated since Robert Manners's protest strategy began in 1837. Some state officials, however, resisted the appropriation; publicizing the Court's opinions thus accentuated the state's and the city's unpaid obligation. Moreover, after leaving the

Senate and accompanying new Whig president Millard Fillmore on tour in 1851, Webster spoke at Buffalo supporting new immigrants despite Know-Nothing demands for exclusionary legislation. Webster also defended the new Fugitive Slave Act he had helped pass as part of the 1850 Compromise. Contrary to Seward's antislavery stance, Webster's defense of the federal law received a cool reception as New York antislavery advocates urged its defiance based on state sovereignty embodied in the 1848 personal liberty law. Webster felt sorely the shifting antislavery and anti-immigrant politics in 1851 as a coalition of Free-Soil and disaffected pro-immigrant Democrats, along with conscience Whigs, voted in radical Charles Sumner to fill the Senate seat Webster vacated in 1850 in order to become secretary of state. Sumner supported a new Massachusetts personal liberty law enabling resistance to the U.S. Fugitive Slave Act and improved legal equality of free blacks.

Badger and Calhoun voted to publicize the Court's opinions for two primary reasons. It was, Badger said, "important that the community" understood the "precise position of constitutional law which the majority of the Supreme Court has assumed." Implicitly, the majority encouraged admission of Irish immigrants into Northern cities where they became reliable Democrats. The Court's decision also coincided with the Address to the Southern States' Congressional Delegation's Constituents denouncing Northern states and abolitionists. This was the "most important subject ever presented" to Southern voters, grounded on the "conflict between two great sections of the Union, growing out of a difference of feeling and opinion . . . existing between the two races, the European and African, which inhabit the Southern section, and the acts of aggression and encroachment to which it has led." Since the Missouri Compromise separated free and slave states and territories, the "North" pursued "hostility to that portion of the Constitution which provides for delivering up of fugitive slaves." In many Northern states "hostile acts" attained such "progress" and "success" that the fugitive slave clause "may be regarded now as practically expunged from the Constitution." In the states bordering British North America—the fugitive slave's frequent destination—the resistance had "brought the South, the Union, and our system of Government to their most perilous condition," endangering Southerners' "property, prosperity, equality, liberty, and safety."

As Congress debated the status of slavery in the West and North amid the Passenger Cases decision, the address exclaimed that Southerners must grasp just how serious were the dangers. The Framers inserted the Fugitive Slave Clause into the Constitution assuming that the Northern states would readily assist in its enforcement. The Supreme Court affirmed that obligation in *Prigg* and other cases. In the states bordering British North America, however, Southern masters, "in their attempt to recover their slaves, now meet, instead of aid and co-operation, resistance in every form; resistance from hostile acts of legislation, intended to baffle and defeat their claims by all sorts of devices, and by interposing every description of impediment—resistance from judges and magistrates—and finally, when these fail from mobs composed of *whites* and *blacks*, which, by threats or force rescue the fugitive slave" (emphasis added). As a result, recovering fugitive slaves in the Northern states subjected masters to "the hazards of insult, heavy pecuniary loss, imprisonment, and even life itself." Moreover, Northern state officials countenanced "secret combinations" known as the Underground Railroad, which aided slaves to "escape" and "to pass . . . secretly and rapidly, by means organized for the purpose into Canada, where they will be beyond the reach of" U.S. law and the Constitution.

The chief perpetrators of these attacks, the address proclaimed, were abolitionists. Their "systematic agitation" since 1835 in the press, pulpits, election campaigns, and other "means" made "the South and the relation between the races there, odious and hateful to the North." As a "domestic institution" slavery was dependent upon state sovereignty and states' rights underpinning police powers for either its existence or abolition. "And yet," the "Abolitionists . . . openly avowing their intention, and resorting to the most efficient means for the purpose, have been attempting . . . to force the Southern States to emancipate their slaves," with little opposition from, and the implicit or direct assistance by, "Northern" states. Moreover, rejecting the Missouri Compromise 36°30' line separating slave and free states or territories, certain Northern politicians supported applying the abolitionists' agenda to the Mexican territorial cession and California, urging the Free-Soil platform. Thus, the address asserted, "All, whether savage, barbarian, or civilized, may enter and remain, we [white Southern slaveholders] only being excluded." In addition, Northern officials further endorsed the abolitionists' cause, actively pursuing the end to the slave trade in the nation's capital and abolition of the long-contested interstate slave trade.

Northern defiance of the fugitive slave law, exclusion of slavery from the Mexican Cession, and abolition of the domestic slave trade would have "depressing effects . . . on the white race at the South." These outcomes would encourage the "hope . . . in the black of a speedy emancipation." Under the influence of abolitionist "fanatics" the "great body of the North is united against our peculiar institution. Many believe it to be sinful, and the residue . . . believe it to be wrong." Some Northerners also talked of "prohibit[ing] what the abolitionists call the internal slave trade, meaning thereby the transfer of slaves from one State to another," which would "render them worthless by crowding them together" in the present Southern states, "and thus hasten the work of emancipation." The "result" was "certain," the address affirmed, unless Southerners united against the "aggression . . . promptly." Indeed, "[t]o destroy the existing relation between the free and servile races at the South would lead to consequences [without parallel] in history." White and black racial subordination "cannot be separated, and cannot live together in peace, or harmony, or to their mutual advantage, except in their present relation." Thus, should American abolitionists succeed, as had their British counterparts in ending West Indian slavery, "wretchedness, and misery, and desolation, would over spread the whole South."

The ultimate danger was that a free-interracial "combination" would dominate Southern whites. American abolitionists could prevail only "through the agency of the Federal Government, controlled by the dominant power of the Northern States of the Confederacy, against the resistance and struggle of the Southern. It can then only be effectuated by prostration of the white race." Concerning the "blacks of the South," however, "[o]wing their emancipation to" Northerners, the freedmen "would regard them as friends, guardians, and patrons." Such a free interracial combination "impelled by fanaticism and the love of power . . . would not stop at emancipation," but would "raise" the freedmen "to a political and social equality with their former owners, by giving them the right of voting and holding offices under the Federal Government." Moreover, the interracial "political union" would impose "complete subjection" upon the "white race at the South." Gaining federal political patronage and offices, the "blacks and the profligate whites" would "be raised above the whites of the South in the political and social scale. We would . . . change conditions with them—a degradation greater than has ever yet fallen to the lot of a free and enlightened people, and from which we could not escape, should emancipation take place."

Racial conflicts the address predicted shaped Southerners' public stance toward the Passenger Cases and the 1850 Compromise. The Southern Rights Association repudiated abolitionists, helping to *defeat* Henry Clay's compromise proposal, which would have guaranteed the interstate slave trade in the 1850 Compromise. Alabama senator Jeremiah Clemens noted that despite passing references in *Groves* and the License Cases, the Supreme Court never formally ruled on the issue whether Congress might "interfere with the transport of slaves from State to State." But the "opinions declared by some of the judges, in the 'passenger cases,' raise very painful apprehensions on this subject. . . . Petitions to Congress to prevent the transmission of slaves from State to State, for sale, and denunciations of the internal slave trade, will now become a staple of anti-slavery agitation." The 1850 Compromise endorsing the more stringent U.S. Fugitive Slave Act and admission of slavery in Western territories based on "popular sovereignty" temporarily diffused Southern fears, despite exclusion of the slave trade from the nation's capital. Harriet Beecher Stowe's *Uncle Tom's Cabin* (1852) and Frederick Douglass's famous 1852 speech, "The Meaning of the Fourth of July for the Negro," fired anew, however, the abolitionist cause. The Supreme Court attempted to ameliorate tensions that the Passenger Cases reflected with a compromise commerce power doctrine fashioned by a new justice, Benjamin Curtis.

Commerce Power Compromise: *Cooley v. Philadelphia Board of Wardens* (1852)

Rounding out the first phase of the Passenger Cases' precedential significance, the Court formulated a compromise commerce power. During the early 1850s Northern states defied the Fugitive Slave Act based on state sovereignty, abolitionists claimed that an exclusive commerce power enabled abolition of the interstate slave trade, and anti-immigrant groups demanded exclusion employing police powers and a limited commerce power. Amid these struggles Justice Woodbury died in 1851. At Webster's suggestion, Fillmore appointed to the Court Benjamin Curtis, who fashioned a commerce power compromise that sought to avoid the controversies associated with the Passenger Cases. Curtis addressed access of the immigrant trade to the nation's ports and harbors in the *Cooley* decision. Drawing upon state and federal powers that prescribed localized regulation of pilots, Curtis fashioned what became known as the doctrine of selective exclusiveness; it sanctioned a seemingly concurrent state and congressional power over the interstate slave trade and exclusion of immigrants. The Passenger Cases upheld international commerce resting on a limited exclusive commerce power, consistent with Marshall's federal supremacy doctrine in *Gibbons*. Justice Curtis held, by contrast, that the commerce power was "selectively" exclusive with state police powers, depending on whether the "subject" was state or federal regulation; how to distinguish between the two, however, was unclear.

The background Curtis brought to the Supreme Court in 1851 included experience in Boston's maritime industry and the more conservative Whig politics identified with Webster. From Taney's perspective, Woodbury's sudden death involved both the loss of a close colleague friendly to the South and the grim political reality that for the first time since Jackson's presidency a strong Whig filled a seat on the Court. Webster's influence in the appointment aggravated Taney's concerns that Curtis might not appreciate the North-South political exigencies following the 1850 Compromise, particularly contention over the new Fugitive Slave Act and the commerce power. Curtis ameliorated Taney's concerns by effectively enforcing the Fugitive Slave Act in the New England circuit consistent with Webster's pro-Southern stance, which nonetheless was unpopular with Seward and other prominent Whigs. Regarding commerce power issues Curtis proved most capable. The death of his sea-captain father when Curtis was a child undoubtedly encouraged his legal work with Boston's shippers; it was also an expertise originally encouraged during the 1830s when he studied commercial law at Harvard Law School, led by Joseph Story. By the 1840s Curtis established himself among the finest commercial and patent lawyers in Boston and the state. Webster had solicited Curtis's assistance in the settlement litigation resulting from the success of Manners's protest strategy in the Passenger Cases

Curtis joined the Court at the point surging transatlantic immigration tested long-standing precedents governing pilot regulations in ports and harbors. Since colonial times, American ports had followed the traditional practice that left government regulation of pilots to local market and political pressures. The unique federal system created in the Constitution raised a possibility that federal commerce powers might disrupt local governance of pilots. In one of its first laws enacted at the start of the national government in 1789, however, Congress exercised federal authority merely in order to continue the localized-pilot system. The 1789 Pilot Act included the provision: "That all pilots in the bays, inlets, rivers, harbors and ports of the United States, shall continue to be regulated in conformity with the existing laws of the States respectively wherein such pilots may be, or with such laws as the States may respectively hereafter enact for the purpose, until further provision shall be made by Congress." The 1789 law maintained sufficient authority that Webster's argument in *Gibbons* affirmed that regulation of pilots rested on police powers representing no conflict with major or "higher branches" of commerce subject to an exclusive commerce power. Marshall essentially agreed, holding: "The acknowledged power of a State to regulate its police, its domestic trade, and to govern its own citizens, may enable it to legislate on this subject [of pilots] to a considerable extent."

Curtis knew, of course, that emerging and established precedents were contestable. Thus during the appeals of Alien Tax Cases, Chief Justice Shaw and the Supreme Judicial Court of Massachusetts decided new precedents that construed state laws defining the jurisdiction of Boston pilot regulations from the city's inner harbor to as far as Martha's Vineyard and beyond. A key issue involved state statutes conferring upon a pilot partial or "half" fees for hailing and offering services to an incoming vessel, even if the shipmaster did not hire that particular pilot. The Shaw Court (Supreme Judicial Court of Massachusetts) developed rules of provable "facts" for the jury showing that the shipmaster had acknowledged the pilot's offering of services. The rules assumed that pilots possessed such extensive local knowledge that they could offer evidence proving to the judge and jury where, and therefore whether, a shipmaster encountered the pilot and accepted or rejected an offer of services. The presumption followed that the 1789 Pilot Act endorsed state policy until Congress altered it. In 1848 interstate competition with New Jersey became so intense that New York City authorities hired John A. Dix to lobby Congress for repeal of the 1789 law. Five thousand petitions claimed that the federal law sanctioned overly "active competition" between the two states' shippers and pilots, rather than supporting the "half-pilotage" fees maintained by the City's "best system" of "most rigid regulation." Dix failed, however, leaving the federal law unchanged.

This contestation was little recognized at the time or later, but it resonated with the facts confronting Curtis in *Cooley v. Philadelphia Board of Wardens* (1852). Aaron B. Cooley was the consignee for the vessels *Consul* and *Undine* plying coastal waters from Philadelphia to New York and other ports. Since colonial times the Pennsylvania legislature had delegated to local officials the regulation and governance of Philadelphia pilots; the 1789 U.S. pilot law reinforced the traditional practice. In 1803, however, the state further empowered the city's Board of Wardens to collect "half-pilotage, due by a vessel which sailed from Philadelphia without a pilot, when one might have been had." The law authorized suit by a city alderman for collection of the unpaid fee from the offending captain or consignee. The money won from the debt judgment went to the Board of Wardens, which regulated services for pilots and their families. Though the system varied in particulars, the purpose was like that operating in Boston, New York, and other ports in America and abroad: it provided compensation in order to ensure qualified pilots operating safely in the risky entry into and departure from harbors. Once Cooley refused to pay the pilot fee, the alderman sued for recovery of the debt before the municipal magistrate who awarded the wardens judgment. On appeal in 1850, the Pennsylvania Supreme Court affirmed the award and upheld the 1803 law as constitutional, thus finding no conflict with federal law.

Like the appeals in the License and Alien Tax Cases, Cooley alleged state court errors in applying state and federal laws. His counsel contended that the 1803 law establishing the pilot fee was "not an act to regulate pilots," but instead its purpose was "to raise a fund for the support of decayed pilots." The law thus did not represent concurrent powers like those Woodbury suggested in the License Cases, but was a revenue measure like the alien tax overturned in the Passenger Cases. Classified as a revenue measure, the 1803 law interfered with commerce defined as "intercourse," and as such violated the federal coasting statute upheld in *Gibbons*; it was also not an ordinary state pilot regulation like that Congress authorized in the 1789 act. The 1803 law also granted unconstitutional duty preferences to vessels operating on the Delaware River from Philadelphia to New Jersey and Delaware ports. The state's lawyers stressed that *Gibbons*, *Miln*, and the License and Passenger Cases all designated pilot regulations as within police powers adaptable to local circumstances, which Congress authorized in the 1789 act. International law and new state precedents, including *Commonwealth v. Ricketson* (1843) from Massachusetts, held that a pilot fee was not a tax, but instead was a duty like the lawful local retail fee affirmed in *Brown v. Maryland*, though the "half-duty" ensured qualified pilots and safe harbors. Similarly, the local duties preferring vessels that operated in the Delaware River were lawful regulations.

As the only member of the Court without a publicized position regarding these issues, Curtis was assigned writing the *Cooley* opinion. McKinley's poor health prevented participation, McLean and Wayne dissented, and Daniel concurred only in the result. Curtis thus led four votes supporting the holding that the pilot system required such extensive "local knowledge" that Congress in the 1789 act had properly left regulation to state control. Beyond that, Curtis innovated: federal commerce *power* as such did not sustain a given regulation, but rather the *subject* governed whether the regulation was constitutionally left to state or federal authority. "The power to regulate commerce embraces a vast field, containing not only many, but exceedingly various subjects, quite unlike in their nature; some imperatively demanding a single uniform rule, operating equally on the commerce of the United States in every port; some like the subject now in question, imperatively demanding that diversity which alone can meet the local necessities of navigation," said Curtis. "Either absolutely to affirm, or deny, that the nature of this power requires exclusive legislation by Congress," neglected the "nature of the subjects of this power, and to assert concerning all of them, what is really applicable but to a part. Whatever subjects of this power are in their nature National, or admit only of one uniform system, or plan of regulation, may justly be said to be of such a nature, as to require exclusive regulation by Congress."

Curtis wrote for a majority of five supporting a compromise commerce power doctrine eventually termed "selective" exclusiveness. McLean, joined by Wayne, agreed that although as a practical state policy "half-pilotage" was "correct," state officials should have asked Congress, "to whom the subject peculiarly belongs," for extended authorization under the 1789 act. "If this [Curtis] doctrine be sound," however, "the passenger cases were erroneously decided," because, McLean claimed, the conflict between state alien taxes and federal treaties and passenger laws would not have been found to be "direct." But McLean ignored that Catron and Grier had indeed found an express conflict between state and federal law in their Passenger Cases opinions. Even so, Catron and Grier endorsed Curtis's construction in *Cooley*, holding that the 1789 act conferred upon the states "power to regulate pilots," and "although Congress has legislated on this subject, its legislation manifests an intention . . . not to regulate this subject, but to leave its regulation to the several States." Curtis's compromise was also close enough to the partially concurrent, state-federal powers Taney and Nelson affirmed in the License Cases. Finally, Curtis cited *Federalist* 32 in support of concurrent state-federal powers, in order to rebut Daniel's claim that since state pilot regulations existed prior to the Constitution, they—like slavery—rested on state sovereignty, with which Congress could never legitimately interfere.

Curtis's compromise doctrine of "selective" exclusiveness contrasted with the tensions emanating from the Passenger Cases. Catron informed James Buchanan that he had "not doubted" the "truth of the doctrine" Curtis enunciated in *Cooley*. Catron also suggested that the commerce power "question" was "now settled" because "Curtis is a first rate lawyer—exceedingly fair minded—and writes smoother than any man on the Bench." Indeed, Curtis blended new state pilot rules the Shaw Court fashioned in *Ricketson*, the concurrent state-federal powers Woodbury stated in his License and Passenger Cases opinions, and the shared sovereignty underlying the 1789 Pilot Act. Admittedly, Curtis's doctrine left vague the basis for determining when the commerce power was exclusive because the subject matter was expressly national and where, because the subject matter was primarily local, it enabled the states' concurrent regulation. The doctrine's flexibility supported, however, the state-federal regulations evolved from *Gibbons*, *Brown v. Maryland*, and *Willson v. Black Bird Creek* to *Miln* and the License Cases, through the contentious Passenger Cases, to *Cooley* itself. The doctrine also reinforced Webster's claim in *Groves*, that because the Constitution exceptionally guaranteed slavery, Congress lacked power to overturn the interstate slave trade, despite the abolitionists' contrary assertions. By the mid-1850s antislavery and anti-immigrant crises subsumed these arguments.

The Commerce Power in Anti-immigrant and Antislavery Crises to 1860

The *Cooley* doctrine had little effect before the impact of the multiple opinions in the Passenger Cases entered a second phase agitating anti-immigrant and antislavery crises. Upholding an exclusive commerce power, the Court promoted federal regulation of the international immigrant trade, enabling Congress to institute more effective enforcement provisions in the 1855 Passenger Act. Although American captains continued to evade American and British regulations, informed observers agreed that within a short period the 1855 law "has been as effective as any measure of that kind can be." Unlike the British system subject to Parliamentary supremacy, however, the Passenger Cases and *Cooley* alike accentuated that dual sovereignty made difficult a determination of legal boundaries separating state and federal jurisdictions. Following the Court's invalidation of the alien taxes, the New York Assembly allotted to the Emigrant Commission funding to establish the Immigrant Receiving Station at Castle Garden. The Emigrant Commission thus began a course of regulation that gradually ameliorated abuses that various private hotels, hospitals, and transportation agents perpetrated upon newly arrived, often destitute, immigrants. Know-Nothings achieved further state and federal regulations excluding "undesirable" immigrants. These immigrant regulations reinforced Northern states' defending free blacks and fugitive slaves, which, Southern states contended, justified secession.

The Know-Nothings won impressive election victories. In 1854, wrote historian David Potter, Illinois Democratic senator Stephen A. Douglas observed "that the Catholic or immigrant question might replace the slavery question as the focal issue in American political life." Alarmed that the issue might undermine President Franklin Pierce's electoral gains won following the 1850 Compromise, Douglas "began assailing the Know-Nothings, rather than the anti-slavery groups, as the principal danger to the Democratic [P]arty." Douglas' fears were well-founded. The Know-Nothings' surge in 1854 elections occurred in the same year the Republican Party formed, drawing from Conscience Whigs, disaffected Free-Soil Democrats who were also pro-immigrant, and the pro-abolitionist Liberty Party. Over a few months, Know-Nothing party membership soared nationally from 50,000 to 1 million. The same year in New York local and statewide elections, Know-Nothings won 25 percent of the vote; by the next year they numbered 150,000 spread among 1,000 chapters. During the same period Massachusetts Know-Nothings won 63 percent of the popular vote, further isolating the Irish Catholic minority that voted Democrat. Amid such compelling victories, Know-Nothings, known as the American Party in Congress, won incorporation into the 1855 Passenger Act a provision that denied giving federal duties to local assistance societies like those aiding Irish and German immigrants in New York City and other ports.

Despite the Know-Nothings' growing political clout, they encountered difficulties with the ambiguous legal status of "persons" prescribed in the Passenger Cases. The Know-Nothing victory ending federal aid for immigrant assistance societies clashed with Southern Democrats' rejection of a broad federal commerce power, which potentially could be construed to aid abolitionists' attacks on the interstate slave trade and the Negro Seamen Acts. Aware that Irish immigrants in particular usually voted Democrat, Northern and Southern wings of the party preserved weak federal naturalization policies. In the states, by contrast, Know-Nothings urged deploying police powers in order to impose a fourteen-year residency requirement—which the federal government dominated by Federalists had instituted in 1798 only to be repealed in 1802—before immigrants qualified for the franchise, jury service, or militia membership. While Democrats generally preserved shorter over longer residency requirements,

Know-Nothings briefly prevailed in the use of police powers to deport unemployed, destitute, or physically disabled immigrants. The deportations agitated the ambiguous status of white immigrants as legal "persons" suggested in Justice Grier's "cherished policy" and the dissenters' criticisms in the Passenger Cases. Ultimately, the Know-Nothings confronted not only the difficult problem of distinguishing desirable from undesirable immigrants; their efforts also became entangled in distinguishing the legal status of white immigrants versus free blacks and fugitive slaves.

The Know-Nothing political gains began dissolving at the point antislavery and race issues regained prominence. Employing police powers, Massachusetts deported as many as thirty immigrants; in conjunction with instituting Castle Garden, New York's Emigrant Committee also engaged in some deportations. But ultimately, New York officials implemented only a two-year residency requirement in order for a foreign immigrant to attain state citizenship, and no further deportations occurred. As Know-Nothing influence abated shortly after reaching its height in 1854–1855, Massachusetts followed New York's compromise course, including the termination of deportations. In 1858, by contrast, federal restrictions of Chinese indentured "coolie" labor on the West Coast maintained an aggressive exclusion policy. Nevertheless, by the Civil War state immigrant regulations generally did not implement the Know-Nothings' strictest exclusionary goals. The fears expressed by the dissenters in the Passenger Cases and the Southern congressional "Address," however, came to pass. Faced with mounting public furor, Northern-state elected officials increasingly endorsed local defense of runaway slaves by employing personal liberty laws against enforcement of the 1850 Fugitive Slave Act. Also, New York and Massachusetts used the same police powers to permit modest public school desegregation, in the latter state overturning the "equal-but-separate" doctrine affirmed in *Roberts v. Boston* (1849).

The anti-immigrant and antislavery conflicts were more entwined by the later 1850s. Increased agricultural production and labor demands attending the Crimean War influenced the precipitous drop in Europeans arriving in U.S. ports: in 1855 European immigrants numbered 197,337, a nearly 50 percent decline compared to the 1854 season. Among the two largest immigrant groups from 1854 to 1855, the number of Irish dropped from 101,606 to 49,627 whereas the numbers of Germans declined from 215,209 to 71,918. Over the same period, some blacks and whites collaborated throughout the Northern states' borderland to resist the 1850 Fugitive Slave Act. Although masters won most federal court cases, effective local opposition enabled even more fugitive slaves and free blacks (who faced kidnapping), to establish residence and conditional citizenship in the border free states, or to escape into British North America. In addition, the Republican Party in Ohio's Western Reserve, upstate New York, Massachusetts, and other New England states welcomed Protestant black voters, who had favored temperance, over Catholic immigrants. In these free-state locales interracial collaboration sometimes was both antislavery and anti-immigrant, benefiting Republicans; but Republicans also received support from disaffected Free-Soil Democrats and Whigs like Seward who were antislavery and pro-immigrant.

By the mid-1850s limitations of Know-Nothings' policies converged with the state police powers supporting Northern personal liberty laws benefiting free blacks. Advocating police powers and state sovereignty regulating the status of legal "persons," free states increasingly applied the personal liberty laws to blunt or defeat enforcement of the 1850 Fugitive Slave Act. In addition, the Massachusetts legislature overturned the "equal-but-separate" doctrine for schools in 1855; small numbers of blacks also fought for and won some integrated schools in New York and Ohio. Blacks in several free states also voted on and otherwise controlled public funding for segregated schools not unlike Catholic immigrants seeking authority over public school curriculum shaped by Protestant leaders. In addition, Northern and Southern bipartisan party politics defeated Know-Nothing attempts to impose the fourteen-year residency requirement on immigrants as a condition for citizenship. Meanwhile, some Northern courts narrowly interpreted racially discriminatory franchise provisions enabling thousands of blacks to vote. Know-Nothing efforts to exclude immigrants from the franchise using lengthy residency requirements also generally failed as Democrats and Republicans promoted, respectively, new Irish and German voters. The formal legal equality courts instituted under personal liberty laws also benefited Protestant and Catholic immigrants, undercutting Know-Nothing attempts to exclude.

Congress had published 5,000 copies of the eight opinions in the Passenger Cases in response to converging anti-immigrant and antislavery crises. Addressing the Know-Nothing exclusionary demands, Whigs, Democrats, and Republicans ultimately supported less restrictive policies, which prevailed as the American Party and numbers of immigrants declined after 1855. Bipartisanship embraced state police powers governing legal "persons" and an exclusive commerce power applied to the international immigrant trade, which by the late-1850s included the Chinese. Despite different reasoning, the majority in the Passenger Cases had sanctioned these same state and federal powers. Publication of the eight opinions also followed shortly after the Southern delegation circulated its address and the Southern Rights Association published pamphlets echoing the dangers the dissenters pronounced. Fundamentally, Southern leaders envisioned a free-state interracial "combination" threatening white supremacy through Northern states' defiance of the Fugitive Slave Act and slaveholders' exclusion from California and the Mexican Cession on the basis of state-centered popular sovereignty. Interracial abolitionists also insisted that the commerce power enabled ending the interstate slave trade just as Congress had abolished the slave trade in Washington, D.C., in the 1850 Compromise. But the Supreme Court's 1857 *Dred Scott* decision affirmed Southern slavery, reinforcing the dissenters' views in the Passenger Cases.

By 1860, the regulatory process New York and other free states exercised to admit immigrants rested on the same state sovereignty principle sustaining personal liberty laws. Following the notorious *Dred Scott* decision, in which Chief Justice Taney said blacks possessed no rights a "white man" was "bound" to "respect," Wisconsin employed state sovereignty in order to resist the 1850 Fugitive Slave Act and the Taney Court's adverse decision in *Ableman v. Booth* (1859). The next year New York's highest court affirmed state sovereignty upholding the state's personal liberty law, thereby freeing Mrs. Juliet Lemmon's eight slaves as she briefly passed through New York City en route to New Orleans and Texas. New York merchants compensated Lemmon, but Virginia appealed. Reviewing all relevant precedents including the Passenger Cases, a divided New York Court of Appeals upheld the personal liberty law, declaring that the "question is one affecting the State in her sovereignty. As a sovereign she may determine and regulate the *status* or social and civil condition of her citizens, and every description of persons within her territory. This power she possesses exclusively; and when she has declared or expressed her will in this respect, no authority or power from without can interfere." Therefore, "neither an African negro nor any other person, white or black, can be held within her limits for any moment of time, in a condition of bondage."

From the Passenger Cases to the *Lemmon* decision, state sovereignty and the status of blacks and white immigrants as legal "persons" were contested. Finally, citing *Lemmon* and the images of free personhood it embodied, South Carolina's 1860 Declaration of Causes of Secession named Northern states' defiance of the 1850 Fugitive Slave Act, conferral of citizenship on blacks, and sanction of abolitionists' radical Christian beliefs as causes for secession. Southern states joined the Union, the declaration declared, only because the Constitution secured slavery. But since 1845 "an increasing hostility on the part of non-slave holding States to the institution of slavery, has led to a disregard of their obligations." The free states "denied the rights of property established in fifteen" slave states, "denounced as sinful the institution of slavery," allowed the formation of radical abolition societies, "encouraged and assisted thousands of our slaves to leave their homes; and those who remain have been incited by emissaries, books and pictures, to servile insurrection." Finally, a "sectional combination" named the Republican Party arose, "aided in some of the States by elevating to citizenship, [black]persons, who," under the Constitution "are incapable of becoming citizens; and their votes have been used to inaugurate a new policy" and to elect a president "hostile to the South." Secession was therefore essential because the Northern states "invested a great political error with the sanctions of a more erroneous religious belief."

Shifting Significance of the Passenger Cases by 1870

Defeat of Southern slavery in the Civil War vindicated Northern personal liberty laws governing blacks and immigrants, but altered the influence of the Passenger Cases. Disputed federal citizenship established in the Civil Rights Acts and the Fourteenth Amendment as applied to legal "persons," ended the prewar conflict over the Northern states' personal liberty laws. California's discrimination against Chinese immigrants and Nevada's attempt to tax passengers leaving the state strengthened the exclusive commerce power through reinterpretation of the Passenger Cases. These precedents supported German émigré commissioner Kapp's argument for state regulation of immigrants. During the 1850s he critiqued European immigration and Southern slavery and mobilized German immigrants in support of the Republican Party. Appointed to the state Emigrant Commission in 1867, Kapp in an 1870 book documented that although immigration was "undoubtedly a matter of national importance," it was a leading "State concern also," especially in New York, the "principal port of entry for" at least 70 percent of all immigrants arriving in America. Kapp explained how New York lawmakers gradually established the regulatory system—including the innovative receiving station at Castle Garden—that accommodated the doubling of immigrants from 1,427,337 during 1839–1849 to 2,968,194 during 1849–1860. Kapp's evidence revealed the shifting precedential uses of the Passenger Cases amid Reconstruction.

The California Supreme Court decision *Lin Sing v. Washburn* (1862) supported Kapp's assessment. The 1858 Treaty of Tientsin empowered federal and state officials to exclude "Coolie" indentured contract labor—which smacked of slavery—from entering U.S. ports. The treaty also, however, recognized the federal government's exclusive authority to admit "voluntary" Chinese labor, especially for work on Western railroads. In California, the competition between "free white" and Chinese labor nonetheless reached the point that the assembly passed in 1862 "An Act to Protect Free White Labor against Competition with Chinese Coolie Labor, and Discourage the Immigration of the Chinese." In order to implement its frankly discriminatory purpose, the law levied each month a $2.50 "Chinese Police Tax" on individual laborers residing in California and their "Caucasian" employers. The tax did not apply to self-employed Chinese and those involved in manufacture or production of tea, coffee, sugar, or rice, as well as others licensed as mine workers. The police tax was yet another example of anti-Chinese xenophobia arising in California since the 1850s. Like other discriminatory laws, it mobilized opposition primarily from well-organized resident Chinese associations supported by Christian missionary groups, and also some white employers. Following an earlier moderately successful strategy targeting such discrimination, the Chinese hired a lawyer to initiate a court test of the police tax.

Lin Sing sued for recovery of a $5.00 police tax paid to the tax collector of San Francisco City and County. The state's attorney general and cooperating business counsel argued the tax was a valid police power measure supported by dissenting opinions in the Passenger Cases and Marshall's original-package doctrine in *Brown v. Maryland*. The California Supreme Court voted 2–1, however, construing both precedents to hold that the tax clashed with the commerce power and the treaty guaranteeing free immigrant trade between the United States and China. The majority noted Justice Wayne's assertion that the *Miln* case and Passenger Cases majorities rejected the "commerce-person" distinction. Even so, California's general right to tax resident "persons" within its jurisdiction could not enable discriminatory taxation that interfered with what Justice Catron and the rest of majority had said was the federal "policy [which] has always been to cultivate intercourse with foreign nations." The California Supreme Court majority went somewhat further, holding that regarding the "former [alien tax] the person was met at the time of his arrival and taxed for the privilege of landing, and in the latter [police tax] he is permitted to land and the tax levied as a condition of his residence." Since the police tax was "limited in its terms to Chinese residing in the State," the "immigration from China will necessarily be affected by it," making the tax invalid under the exclusive commerce power and the treaty between the United States and China.

The precedential influence of the Passenger Cases shifted in *Crandall v. Nevada* (1868). In 1865 the Nevada legislature levied a "capitation tax of one dollar upon every person leaving the State by any railroad, stage coach, or other vehicle engaged or employed in the business of transporting passengers for hire." The law required individual or corporate owners of these carriers both to pay the tax and to file a monthly report with local officials showing the number of passengers upon whom it was levied. Crandall, the Carson City agent for the Pioneer Stage Co. and Wells, Fargo, & Co., refused to comply with the law; according to the local paper he was then "constructively" jailed for one day. Although technical legal issues permitted a magistrate to "release" Crandall, the underlying constitutional question was whether the tax violated an exclusive commerce power. On appeal the Nevada Supreme Court upheld the tax, finding a conflict with neither an exclusive law Congress could have expressly enacted addressing the issue nor a dormant commerce power. The transport company appealed to the U.S. Supreme Court, asserting errors in the construction of the federal commerce power; but, surprisingly, it neither filed supporting briefs nor was represented by counsel. Until 1864–1865 Taney, Catron, Nelson, Wayne, and Grier were left from the Court that had decided the Passenger Cases; but by February 1868 when the Court handed down its *Crandall* decision, only Nelson and Grier remained.

The Court decided 6–2 in favor of Justice Samuel F. Miller's opinion, which applied novel reasoning to strike down the tax. Like the state's counsel, Miller distinguished the Nevada tax from the state alien tax levied on "persons" subject to international commerce in the Passenger Cases, and the state license duty voided by the original-package doctrine preserving international trade in *Brown v. Maryland*. But neither precedent, Miller said, governed the "question before us." Instead, Nevada's tax was like that the Marshall Court struck down in *McCulloch v. Maryland* (1819). That decision was "not based . . . on any express grant of power, but was claimed to be necessary and proper to enable the government to carry out its authority to raise revenue, and to transfer and disburse the same." Miller reasoned, accordingly, that the Nevada tax could have burdened the U.S. government's railroad transport of troops during the Civil War, or passengers crossing the nation on interstate railroads. In addition, Miller relied on the Marshall Court's *Brown* decision declaring Maryland's import duty void "because it interfered with the exercise of a right derived by the importer from [U.S.] laws." Thus, Miller said, "the right of passing through a state by a [U.S.] citizen" in *Crandall* was "one guaranteed to him by the Constitution," and was "as sacred from State taxation as the right derived from the importer from payment of duties to sell goods on which the duties were paid."

Miller's *Crandall* opinion and Justice Nathan Clifford's dissent suggested the Passenger Cases' shifting precedential significance. Miller acknowledged that the Court's abandonment of the "commerce-person" distinction meant that the alien tax on "persons" actually was paid by the business carrier, which in turn clashed with international tariffs and U.S. Passenger Acts resting on an exclusive commerce power. Nevada's "capitation" tax on in-state passengers, however, violated no express federal law. Though Miller praised the *Cooley* doctrine of selective exclusiveness, he rejected its application to the state tax where Congress had not acted. While Clifford's dissent, joined by Chief Justice Salmon P. Chase, concurred in the result of the *Crandall* decision, it rejected Miller's reliance on the necessary-and-proper clause and implied constitutional "rights" derived from *McCulloch*. "On the contrary," Clifford said, "I hold that" the Nevada tax law was "inconsistent with the power conferred upon Congress to regulate commerce among the several States, and I think the judgment of the court should have been placed exclusively upon that ground." Indeed, "I am clear that the State legislature cannot impose any such burden upon commerce among the several states," which, consistent with a dormant commerce power, was the policy "irrespective of any Congressional action." Thus, both Miller and Clifford supported overturning the tax, relying on neither *Cooley* nor the Passenger Cases.

Friedrich Kapp addressed the "legal questions" emerging from the "financial interests connected with" immigration, especially the merits of state versus federal regulation. Overturning the alien tax in the Passenger Cases, the Supreme Court settled part of the question "whether a single State has or has not the right to tax the immigrant on his arrival for sanitary purposes and for his protection," employing police powers. During the Civil War the financial-legal issues arose again regarding New York City's immigrant regulations that authorized a "tax, or commutation money, of $2.50 . . . levied on each immigrant [after] landing at New York," providing an average annual revenue of between $500,000 and $750,000. "Western newspapers" and "some Western members of Congress" insisted that the "commutation money" the "immigrants pa[id] at the several ports of entry be distributed, *pro rata*, among the States where they settle." In order to implement this purpose Western interests urged that the "United States Government should take the whole business of immigration in its own hands; that the Secretary of the Treasury make all needful rules and regulations, and appoint the proper officers in the same manner" as "Custom House offices" were "appointed." Such federalization, Kapp warned, would end "all State institutions which have been established in the course of years for the protection of immigrants" in New York City or other leading ports such as San Francisco.

Kapp argued that maintaining New York's "exclusive control over immigrants" served America's "real interest." Consistent with the holdings in the Passenger Cases, Kapp agreed, Congress "not only" had "the right, but [was] absolutely bound, in the interests of humanity, to protect the immigrant on the high seas, in his transit from foreign countries, and to make for that purpose international treaties, which Congress alone can do." Once immigrants landed, however, they became subject to "police" regulations governing a "boarding-house" license, the "policeman who protects him," and "transportation" to the "railway depots." By contrast, federalization would require as many as a "dozen" receiving stations like Castle Garden, ineffectually administered by the "clumsy machinery of a central [federal] board." Funding such extensive national operations would also necessitate either "quadruple the present tax" ensuring practical "prohibition," or a general federal tax, making the "immigrant the nation's pauper." A national system also would only compound existing corruption in federal customs collections, which already "costs . . . millions in bribes, theft, and embezzlement to collect" $300,000 "in revenues." Finally, New York's regulations constituted a "contract" guaranteeing poor-law protection during a five-year federal naturalization period, until an immigrant qualified for citizenship.

The Passenger Cases, *Miln*, *Lin Sing*, and *Crandall* left "unsettled," Kapp said, whether the "power to regulate foreign and inter-State commerce" was "vested in Congress to the exclusion of the States." Also, were import duties or otherwise lawful state taxes constitutional that "incidentally" regulated foreign or interstate commerce? Moreover, despite Justice Wayne's revelation that the majority in *Miln* never accepted the "commerce-person" distinction, litigants continued to argue that "passengers" were not taxable as "commerce" prior to their disembarkation from "foreign" vessels. Most significantly for Kapp's purposes, given the "Western" demands for the federalization of New York's commutation tax, it remained unclear by 1870 "[w]hether States may circuitously impose a tax, by first exacting bonds, and then permitting them to be commuted for a specified sum of money." A state could, however, exclude "foreign paupers, or foreigners likely to become paupers" and tax "foreigners" within its "jurisdiction" for purposes of supporting "paupers" who were not "imports or subjects of commerce." Moreover, the "Federal Government" had "no power to maintain paupers, foreign or domestic, or to levy taxes for that purpose." In addition, any "law of Congress" exercising proper commerce powers was "paramount to any State law purporting or pretending" to share those same powers. Finally, states could not tax passengers coming from ports or towns in other states.

Conclusions

The precedential significance of the Passenger Cases concerning legal "persons" shifted from 1849 to 1870. Before and during the 1850 Compromise, bipartisan congressional support for publicizing the Court's eight opinions reflected converging antislavery and anti-immigrant crises. Webster, Calhoun, and other leaders promoted an exclusive commerce power supporting stronger U.S. Passenger Acts against Know-Nothings' demands to exclude immigrants. The most restrictive anti-immigrant policies did not pass, however, because Southern Democrats blocked any federal legislation that might possibly justify abolitionist claims that the commerce power permitted ending the interstate slave trade or even slavery itself. The agitation also disrupted the status of white immigrants and free blacks as legal "persons" under Northern states' personal liberty laws. The abolition of slavery redefined state and federal status of legal "persons." During Reconstruction the Freedmen fought for rights under civil rights laws and the Fourteenth Amendment that conferred ambiguous federal citizenship upon all "persons." An exclusive commerce power, by contrast, defined both promotional state-immigrant policies Kapp described and stronger protections for the Chinese in the Burlingame Treaty of 1868. The Court also applied the *Cooley* doctrine of selective exclusiveness in state-federal regulation of railroads, the telegraph, and other national business; but the doctrine little influenced immigration policies.

An expanded exclusive commerce power reflected changing reliance on the Passenger Cases. From Marshall Court decisions in

Gibbons, *Brown*, and *Willson*, to the divided Taney Court opinions from *Miln* through the Passenger Cases, state control of slavery and free blacks was preserved. The same policy also supported limited exclusive federal regulation of white immigrants under treaties and other federal laws. In order to restrict the exclusive commerce power, Taney and a few colleagues pronounced the distinction between "commerce," subject to limited federal regulation, and "persons," governed only by state police powers. Justice Wayne's Passenger Cases opinion exposed the Court's minority support for the "commerce-person" distinction; in response, Taney's dissent insisted that states could not tax white "citizens" moving across state lines. Kapp's book, the California Supreme Court in *Lin Sing*, and Clifford's *Crandall* dissent endorsing a dormant commerce power, accepted Wayne's position sustaining an exclusive commerce power. Miller's *Crandall* majority opinion rejecting the commerce power, however, quoted Taney's Passenger Cases dissent: "[A] tax imposed by a State, for entering its territories or harbors, is inconsistent with the rights which belong to [the white] citizens of other States, as members of the Union. . . . Such a power in the States could produce nothing but discord," and "they very clearly do not posses it."

Secession and Civil War altered the relative legal status of immigrants and free blacks. Southern states partly justified secession on the ground that Northern states' personal liberty laws conferred citizenship on blacks. During Reconstruction, the Freedmen fought for federal citizenship established in federal laws and the Fourteenth Amendment against discriminatory Southern states' black codes. The discrimination the Chinese challenged in California's *Lin Sing* case paralleled what the Freedmen experienced under the black codes during and after Reconstruction. The difference was that California's Chinese police law fell before the California Supreme Court's expansive reading of the Passenger Cases, upholding the U.S. treaty with China based on an exclusive federal commerce power. The problem was, however, that the California Supreme Court's decision left Chinese rights claims dependent upon a Congress buffeted by growing demands for exclusion. Moreover, Justice Miller's unusual reasoning that distinguished away the Passenger Cases in order to invalidate Nevada's tax in *Crandall* left uncertain implied congressional regulation of immigrants through an exclusive commerce power. Kapp's

1870 book skillfully construed the Passenger Cases and other commerce power precedents to promote the New York Emigrant Commission's effective care for immigrants; but it also accepted an exclusive commerce power that, as the Chinese understood, ultimately was vulnerable to the politics of exclusion.

CHAPTER 6

Federal Supremacy and a Mixed Legacy of the Passenger Cases

While the precedential significance of the Passenger Cases declined after the Civil War, the precedent suggested the state-federal balance of power governing immigration regulation that eventually prevailed. The Court's divided majority in the Passenger Cases affirmed a federal regulation of immigrants aboard vessels arriving within state ports that limited state police powers governing those very same legal "persons." Before the Civil War, the balance between federal and state powers in commerce power decisions nonetheless favored the states—*Gibbons* and the Passenger Cases being the most significant exceptions—because slavery, free blacks, and white immigrants politicized the legal status of "persons." After the Civil War, the Fourteenth Amendment extended rights claims to "persons" that embraced not only citizens, but also, to a certain extent, aliens as well. Meanwhile, federal supremacy based on naturalization, treaty powers, and federal-state cooperation displaced commerce power regulation of immigrants. Justice Scalia's dissent in *Arizona II* (2012), by contrast, presented a commerce power analysis enabling states to exclude illegal immigrants. From World War II on the Passenger Cases offered a right of travel based on the commerce power or the Fourteenth Amendment that was more inclusive of legal and illegal immigrants alike.

Justice Samuel Miller's opinions in 1875 in cases from New York, San Francisco, and New Orleans prompted Congress to create a federal regulatory system enabling decades of exclusionary policies. The first section examines Miller's three opinions for a unanimous Court instituting a new doctrine that promoted federal immigration regulation and curbed state police powers. The doctrine undercut the decades-old connection between state poor-law regulation and the bond-commutation system. Miller's *Henderson* opinions also began limiting the influence of the Passenger Cases, which steadily recede in importance in the second section. From the 1880s to the 1920s, federal supremacy resting on naturalization and treaty powers promoted a policy of exclusion that extended beyond the Chinese to include many other immigrant groups. During the same period, however, the Court partially extended rights under the Fourteenth Amendment that aliens shared with U.S. citizens. The politics of preferential racial exclusion driving Congress and the Court also fostered resistance from resident Chinese aliens allied with elite lawyers, winning a victory that benefited future generations of immigrants.

The third section attempts to summarize the historic shift from racial and national preferences Congress instituted in 1924 to the gradual limitation of quotas between World War II and their end in the 1965 Immigration Act. The commerce power and the Passenger Cases regained influence amid the emergence of inclusive immigration. Although based on federal supremacy, inclusive immigration regulation incorporated the right of travel the Court announced in the *Edwards* (1941) and *Graham* (1971) decisions. Aliens and American migrants alike possessed the right of travel under the dormant commerce power and the Passenger Cases, as well as the Fourteenth Amendment. The fourth section considers federal and state policing of undocumented or "illegal" immigrants since the 1970s. The *De Canas* decision (1975) drew upon the commerce power and the Passenger Cases to support state regulation of illegal immigrants that was consistent with federal supremacy, preemption, and federal-state cooperation. The Court's decisions in *Arizona I* and *II* relied on the latter principles without reference to commerce power precedents. Justice Scalia's dissent in the latter case nonetheless adhered to commerce power analysis in order to affirm a state's power to exclude illegal immigrants. Renewed attention to the Passenger Cases and the precedent's incorporation into the right of travel and commerce power analysis could foster, however, greater admission than exclusion of immigrants.

Turning Point: Justice Miller Promotes Federal Immigration Regulation in 1875

Justice Miller's three opinions for a unanimous Court decided three related cases within a transformed global-trade order. In *Miln* (1837) the Court upheld state reports providing data about foreign immigrants; the Passenger Cases (1849) overturned state "alien" taxes levied on the same class of immigrants. Miller's opinions undercut, however, the states' bond and commutation systems that had operated for decades within these commerce power precedents. In New York, New Orleans, San Francisco, and other ports the bond and commutation systems funded state Emigrant Commissions and the administration of social services; some private immigrant associations also received funds. By 1873 the United States entered its first industrial depression, giving rise to the worst labor unrest to that point in the nation's history. Competition increased between established and immigrant workers. Also, by the 1860s steamships had increasingly displaced sail, enabling shippers to transport ever-growing volumes of immigrants from Europe and Asia, including Chinese arriving in California. Amid these developments, the Court decided together in 1875 *Henderson v. The Mayor of the City of New York* and, from New Orleans, the *Commissioners of Immigration v. North German Lloyd*; it separately decided the California case, *Chy Lung v. Freeman*. Justice Miller's opinions established a new doctrine that ended the federal-state balance of power affirmed in the Passenger Cases, promoting national supremacy in the federal regulation of immigrants.

All three appeals originated soon after the 1873 depression began, testing the bond-commutation systems that for decades the states had imposed and the shippers had generally accepted. Basically, the system required foreign owners or consignees to provide for each "emigrant passenger" upon arrival in New York, New Orleans, or San Francisco within a stipulated period (usually twenty-four hours), a bond carrying a nonpayment penalty of on average $300. The bonds also required "two sureties" who were state residents. The bond and penalty indemnified the "Commissioners of Emigration, and every county [or parish], city, and town in the State, against any expense for the relief or support of the person named in the bond for four years thereafter." The vessel owners or consignees could commute the bond, however, by paying $1.50 for each passenger after disembarkation. The nonpayment penalty for each passenger's commutation was $500, which was "made a lien on, and may be enforced against, the vessel, at the suit of the Commissioners of Emigration." In New York and Louisiana the commutation income was apportioned between "counties" or "parishes" and the commissioners of emigration "for general purposes, and particularly to be used in erecting wharves and buildings, and in paying salaries and clerk hire." California's system differed in that it clothed the commissioner with extraordinary discretion enabling him to target a certain class of Chinese women.

The lawyers' arguments suggested the difference between the Court's earlier precedents and the New York and Louisiana cases. For the shippers' lawyers the issues concerned neither the lawful state reports in *Miln* nor the unconstitutional tax in the Passenger Cases. Instead, they reinterpreted the leading precedent in *Gibbons* to mean that the bond-commutation system violated unstipulated "acts of Congress and our treaties with foreign nations," the Commerce Clause, and the prohibition against states, without congressional consent, enacting any duties or imposts except those "actually necessary for executing inspection laws." The lawyers defending the states' bond-commutation system argued, by contrast, that it was consistent with provisions in *Miln* and the Passenger Cases upholding police powers protecting states from paupers and other undesirables. There was "no practical mode in which the State can correctly decide which of these alien strangers is self-supporting. Hence it may rightfully exact indemnity from all." The state offered the "owner or consignee" the "option" to "commute by paying a small sum instead of giving a bond of indemnity for each" passenger; and it "cannot be tortured into an indirect mode of imposing a tax or duty upon the passenger as such. The option is allowed as a favor to the owner or consignee of the vessel." Still, the commutation was less secure than "a bond on behalf of each indigent person landed."

Though the facts in the New York and Louisiana cases differed somewhat, the issues were essentially the same. In *Henderson*, the British-owned and -operated steamship *Ethiopia* transported immigrant passengers between Glasgow, Scotland, and New York City during summer 1875. When the Emigrant Commission enforced the regulatory system upon passengers disembarked from the vessel, the owners, "in order to test the validity of the provisions of the acts requiring the bond or commutation," sued in the U.S. Circuit Court for the Southern District of New York, which dismissed the case. The owners appealed to the Supreme Court. Also in summer 1875 the steamship company North German Lloyd offered direct immigrant transport between Bremen and New Orleans in competition with the Hamburg-American Transport Association. In addition to the competition costs, the North German Lloyd Company confronted the option presented by the state commissioners of immigration to "exact the bonds or pay . . . the commutation money on all passengers." The shipper declined to do either, seeking an injunction in the U.S. Circuit Court for the District of Louisiana on the ground that the system violated federal laws and treaties. The federal Circuit Court granted the injunction, and the commission appealed to the Supreme Court. The two cases demonstrated the burden the bond-commutation system placed on shippers during the Depression.

"Very similar" New York and Louisiana laws, said Justice Miller, concerned changed economic conditions. By the mid-1870s, "absurd" costs the bond-commutation system imposed upon shippers far exceeded those incurred decades earlier from the reports upheld in *Miln* and the tax overturned in the Passenger Cases. In the latter New York case in 1849 the shipper paid the city health official about $300 for disembarking all passengers from a single voyage. A quarter-century later a steamship entering New York with immigrants "once a month lands from 300 to one thousand passengers," Miller said, "or from three thousand to twelve thousand per annum." Given such volumes, the "small" commutation tax was in fact too much, but payment of the "bonds would amount in many instances, for every voyage, to more than the value of the vessel." Although the expressed "purpose" of the law was "to protect the State against the consequences of the flood of pauperism immigrating from Europe, and first landing in that city," in "effect" it "impose[d] a tax on the owner of the vessel for the privilege of landing in New York passengers transported from foreign countries." Moreover, the "man who is perfectly free from disease, and brings to aid the industry of the country a stout heart and a strong arm," was "as much the subject of the tax as the diseased pauper who may become the object of the" city's "charity" the "day after he lands from the vessel."

Miller established a new doctrine. The reports the Court upheld on the basis of police powers in *Miln* were lawful in order to protect the state from verifiable hygienic or criminal dangers. The divided, narrow majority in the Passenger Cases, however, provided authority only for the point that a tax on immigrants in direct conflict with an international treaty or law was invalid under Marshall's holding in *Gibbons*. Miller listed the majority and minority Court members in the Passenger Cases; none remained by 1875. These considerations encouraged the Court's "hope of attaining a unanimity not found in" previous opinions. Assuming Marshall's premise that the widest economic "intercourse" was "commerce," the "regulation of this great system" of transporting immigrants to America was "a regulation of commerce." The *Cooley* doctrine suggested that some "loosely called . . . police powers" might affect this transport, but the "line between" state and federal regulation was "not easily distinguishable." The Passenger Cases, *Cooley*, and *Crandall* precedents also suggested "a kind of neutral ground" where state law could be "valid so long as it interferes with no act of Congress, or [U.S.] treaty." Miller's new doctrine invalidated a state regulation that effectively "imposes onerous, perhaps impossible, conditions on those engaged in active commerce with foreign nations," which was not just "national" but "*international*" in "character." Valid "commerce" regulations also should constitute "a uniform system" like that established in treaties.

The Court's unanimous decision overturning New York's and Louisiana's bond-commutation system ended with a call for congressional regulation and limits on state police powers. The bond-commutation system violated treaties and federal regulations governing ship owners and operators transporting immigrants from foreign to American ports, including the period shortly after the passengers disembarked when moneys and nonpayment penalties were assessed. "We are of the opinion that this whole subject has been confided to Congress by the Constitution," said Miller, and "Congress can more appropriately and with more acceptance exercise" such power "than any other body known to our law, state or national." In addition, "by providing a system of laws in these matters, applicable to all ports and to all vessels," Congress would effectively resolve "a serious question, which has long been matter of contest and complaint." Miller's opinion also left undecided whether a "neutral ground" existed where "in the absence" of congressional "action," the states might "protect themselves against *actual* paupers, vagrants, criminals, and diseased persons." Nevertheless, the Court had addressed the basic constitutional problem: the bond-commutation system indiscriminately taxed all foreign immigrant passengers because it was impractical to distinguish between those who might or might not threaten the health and welfare of the states' citizens.

In *Chy Lung v. Freeman* Justice Miller said the California law was distinguishable from the other two states' "in two very important points." First, the female plaintiff was a "subject of the Emperor of China" removed by the state immigrant commissioner from the vessel *Japan* and incarcerated. Secondly, the two other states' laws "require[d] a bond for *all* passengers landing from a foreign country," but the California law imposed that stipulation on the shipper "only for classes of passengers specifically described," including "lewd and debauched women." Upon the refusal to pay the bond, the commissioner imprisoned twenty-two Chinese women pending deportation. In the state courts the women sought release by writ of habeas corpus, which on appeal the California Supreme Court denied. The case then went to the U.S. Circuit Court in San Francisco, where Justice Stephen Field wrote the opinion for his two colleagues releasing all but Chy Lung, who appealed to the U.S. Supreme Court. The case was so important for U.S.-China relations concerning the Burlingame Treaty that the U.S. attorney general personally argued for overturning the law; but there was no counsel or brief from California authorities. Justice Miller found the state law "most extraordinary," so "skillfully framed, to place in the hands of a single man the power to prevent entirely vessels engaged in a foreign trade, say with China, from carrying passengers, or to compel them to submit to systematic extortion of the grossest kind."

Miller decided that the detention of the Chinese national under California's law violated international treaty obligations. He emphasized that the "opinion in the previous cases" established that the Court was "at liberty to look to the *effect* of a statute for the test of its constitutionality" (emphasis added). He graphically described how the state commissioner's use of the bond-commutation system extracted from shipper and passenger alike "twenty per cent of all I can get out of you" for "my own pocket" with the "remainder [going] into the treasury of California." The state law's "purpose" was "not to obtain indemnity, but money." And worse, "Whether a young woman's manners are such as to justify the commissioner in calling her lewd may be made to depend on the sum she will pay for the privilege of landing in San Francisco." More ominously, "if citizens of our own government were treated by any foreign nation as subjects of the Emperor of China have been actually treated under this law, no administration could withstand the call for a demand on such government for redress." Even so, should a great power like the "Queen of Great Britain" make such a demand, it was not California but the "government of the United States" that was constitutionally bound to reply. Accordingly, these "effects" placed the California law in violation of the nation's international agreements such as the Burlingame Treaty, amplifying the call in the New York and Louisiana cases for federal regulation.

The unanimous majority deciding together the New York, Louisiana, and California cases limited both police powers and the commerce power, signaling new federal legislation. Miller's opinions maintained the *Miln* precedent in support of state authority to collect data from foreign immigrants arriving on vessels that also were regulated by international agreements and federal law. Although for federal regulatory and state police power purposes these immigrants were lawfully commercial subjects, they nonetheless possessed an ambiguous status as both "commerce" and "persons." Miller's opinion left it an open question how far the combined "commerce-person" category still enabled police powers protecting states from hygienic or criminal dangers within the federal-state regulatory system including "essential" state inspection laws. The extent to which the *Cooley* doctrine permitted or a dormant commerce power denied state regulation in the absence of federal action also was undecided. Miller's new doctrine, by contrast, extended the scope of *Gibbons* and diminished the precedential uses of the Passenger Cases. He formulated an exclusive commerce power identified with international agreements having uniform operation across the nation that the Court would uphold over broader "effects" of state police powers. Over the coming decades the federal government gradually evolved the implications of Miller's doctrine, limiting the commerce power until a federal-exclusion policy prevailed.

Federal Alien Exclusion Displaces the Commerce Power and the Passenger Cases

The Court's three opinions in *Henderson* limited the balance struck in the Passenger Cases between the commerce power and state police powers, favoring federal supremacy. Louisiana responded to the loss of the bond-commutation moneys by abandoning plans to fund an immigration station in New Orleans like the Castle Garden facility that had effectively served New York City. The state's immigration commission no longer assisted the private German American association, which cut aid to German immigrants; the North German Lloyd steamship line, in turn, discontinued service between Bremen and New Orleans. The *Henderson* decision had a more protracted impact on ever-growing immigration to New York and other ports that reached a historic annual record of 1.3 million in 1907. New York authorities revised the commutation system addressing the unsettled issue whether police powers permitted excluding immigrant paupers, criminals, radicals, or disease. President Chester Arthur's 1881 message to Congress urged federal legislation but also accepted some state regulation. Congress enacted a tax on foreign immigrants entering U.S. ports, enabling Treasury funding of a growing federal regulatory system. The Court, however, also upheld limited constitutional rights aliens shared with U.S. citizens. During the 1890s federal regulatory supremacy eclipsed the state-federal balance of the commerce power, reversing the outcome in *Chy Lung* by enforcing Chinese exclusion. Many other immigrant groups were excluded by the 1920s.

In 1882 Justice Miller authored another commerce power decision upholding federal over state regulation of immigrants. New York officials sued French-shipper Compagnie Générale Transatlantique for recovery of state taxes levied on passengers inspectors had determined were "criminals, lunatics, orphans, or infirm persons, without means or capacity to support themselves and subject to become a public charge." On appeal, Miller's opinion for the unanimous Court rebuffed New York's attempted use of purportedly essential "inspections" under Article I, Section 10. Instead, Miller held, the state tax clashed with the 1882 act of Congress establishing the fifty-cent "duty" paid into the U.S. Treasury supporting the "immigrant fund, for the care of immigrants arriving in the United States, and the relief of such as are in distress." The fund enabled a federal system of immigrant regulation within the Treasury Department, Miller said, that "covers the same ground as the New York statute, and they cannot coexist." Miller's opinion expressly invalidated the state's claim of essential "inspections" left unsettled in *Henderson*; it also declared that passengers, being "free men," were not taxable merchandise. Nevertheless, citing the Passenger Cases, Miller held that such "persons" were subject to federal "regulation" under the Commerce Clause. Suggesting the issue that had long troubled Justice Wayne until his death in 1867, Miller narrowly preserved the precedential value of the Passenger Cases.

New York's police powers governing the immigrant trade steadily gave way to growing federal regulation. In the early 1880s New Yorkers lobbying President Arthur threatened to close the immigrant receiving station at Castle Garden unless federal funds defrayed its operating costs; after the Court's decision in *Compagnie Générale Transatlantique* federal funding was forthcoming. The Court then upheld federal exclusion based on federal supremacy in the Chinese Exclusion Cases (1889). During the depression of the early 1890s, New York finally closed Castle Garden. Employing the tax and regulatory system lodged in the U.S. Treasury, the government opened the federal immigrant receiving station at Ellis Island in 1892. First- and second-class passengers moved through the federal facility easily. Federal inspectors subjected steerage-class passengers to close and lengthy scrutiny, however, which enabled exclusion through deportation reminiscent of the state process Justice Miller had condemned in *Chy Lung*. As noted above, New York commissioner Friedrich Kapp in 1870 predicted that federal administration of immigration at least initially was troubled by corruption; also, once immigrants departed Ellis Island they faced the sort of private "swindlers" the Castle Garden facility had circumvented. Still, in 1910 the federal government opened its western immigrant receiving station at Angel Island in San Francisco.

The *Henderson* and *Chy Lung* decisions facilitated restriction, beginning with an 1875 federal law designating foreign convicts and immoral women as two classes subject to exclusion. In 1882 other federal legislation expanded these "excluded" classes expressly to include most Chinese, mentally unstable individuals, "idiots," "lunatics," and other individuals who might be expected to "become a public charge" (known thereafter as "LPCs"). The shippers who brought such persons to U.S. ports were required to pay for their transport back "to the countries from which they came." As noted above, the 1882 law also created a new federal fifty-cent tax on "foreign passengers," which supported their transport to and care upon arrival in U.S. ports. The federal facilities handling arrivals were administered by state and local agents working under federal contract. The act establishing the federal "immigrant fund" also paid for deportation of excluded individuals and others who after disembarkation were identified as a "public charge." Other significant innovations included the federal "head tax" imposed on each individual immigrant rather than the shipper; for the first time since the 1798 Aliens Act, federal legislation reinstituted deportation proceedings; and the federal immigrant receiving stations were established at Ellis Island and Angel Island. By contrast, after the New York U.S. Circuit Court invalidated the 1855 Passenger Act, Congress reenacted a weaker version that shippers preferred.

As the historic "new immigration" prevailed during the turn of the century, regulation relying on other federal powers displaced commerce power regulation of immigration. In the Head Money Cases (1884) a British and a Dutch shipping company challenged the 1882 federal passenger tax, arguing that it was contrary to treaties and related laws based upon commerce power regulations. For a unanimous Court, Justice Miller applied the reasoning in the Passenger Cases and *Henderson*, *Chy Lung*, and *Campagnie Générale Transatlantique* to uphold the federal tax as a "regulation" of commerce consistent with the Constitution's treaty-making power, enforceable by the courts. Shortly before his death in 1890, Miller's *Lectures on Constitutional Law* considered precedents supporting commerce power regulation of immigrants. He indicated that the dormant commerce power established in *Welton v. Missouri* (1875), which overturned a state license-tax on interstate retailers, had little bearing on immigration regulation. The *Cooley* selective-exclusiveness doctrine allowed state regulations of pilots, wharves, and bridges, which indirectly affected the immigrant trade. Miller's death, however, coincided with the Supreme Court's expanded federal regulation based on federal supremacy of naturalization and treaty powers established in the "head" tax, weaker passenger law, and the system of inspections, admission, or exclusion administered at Ellis Island and other ports and along international borders.

Exclusion based on federal supremacy triumphed in the Chinese Exclusion Cases (1889). In 1888 Congress excluded Chinese laborers from the United States, including aliens permitted residence under U.S.-China treaties who had temporarily departed and then sought readmission to the United States. On behalf of one such migrant worker, the Chinese American community sued, arguing that Congress lacked authority to abrogate treaties. The Court's unanimous 1889 decision, however, upheld the law implementing federal exclusion as "an incident of sovereignty, which cannot be surrendered by the treaty making power." Justice Stephen Field's opinion also held that the exclusion policies did not affect the property rights that Chinese aliens acquired during the operation of the Burlingame and other treaties affirmed in the Head Money Cases. The Court's primary holding based on national sovereignty encouraged exclusionists advocating racial and ethnic theories that distinguished between preferable northern European peoples and undesirable immigrants from southern and eastern Europe and Asia. Although Chinese immigration historically began before the Civil War, its growing numbers from the 1860s on enabled West Coast oppositionists to argue that alien culture and race justified exclusion. The exclusionists won from Congress increasingly strict regulation of Chinese laborers; the Court's initial procedural disagreement over the regulations dissolved until Chinese exclusion prevailed in 1893.

Federal supremacy enforcing Chinese exclusion evolved into regulatory policies governing other immigrant groups. In 1891 Congress established a national Bureau of Immigration; it also authorized the Treasury Department to appoint federal inspectors charged with excluding designated "alien" classes from entering the nation. In the same year, California's immigrant commissioner, exercising federal-contract authorization from the U.S. Treasury, refused to admit Mrs. Nishimura Ekiu, a Japanese national, to the port of San Francisco on the ground that she was likely to become a public charge. Shortly after she sued to block exclusion proceedings, a new federal inspector appointed under the 1891 act intervened and implemented the exclusion order. On appeal, the general question before the Supreme Court was whether the 1891 act was constitutional, including its delegation of broad discretionary powers to federal inspectors. Upholding the 1891 act, and Mrs. Ekiu's exclusion, Justice Horace Gray held: "It is an accepted maxim of international law, that every sovereign nation has the power, as inherent in sovereignty, and essential to self-preservation, to forbid the entrance of foreigners within its dominions, or to admit them only in such cases and upon such conditions as it may see fit to prescribe." Only Justice David Brewer silently dissented from the Court's affirmation of the 1891 act and the wide discretionary authority conferred upon federal inspectors.

The discretionary authority the Court upheld in the 1891 law also empowered the U.S. Treasury secretary to "prescribe rules for inspection along the borders of Canada, British Columbia, and Mexico." Historian Erika Lee described the enduring impact of the admission and exclusion system instituted along these borders: it clothed federal inspectors with wide discretion, imposed upon Chinese and other "alien classes" legal documentation equivalent to the passport governing their admission or readmission to the United States, required residence certification that evolved into the "green card," for the first time created a designated criminal offense of "illegal immigrant," and instituted a new general process for deportation. By 1924, Lee said, "Chinese immigration and exclusion along the U.S.-Canadian and U.S.-Mexican borders had transformed immigration policy, the border region, and American border enforcement. Chinese immigrants—racialized as perpetual foreigners—became the first group in the country marked as 'illegal immigrants.' The U.S. Bureau of Immigration's first division to deal primarily with illegal immigration was, after all, called the Chinese Division, making 'Chinese' synonymous with 'illegal.'" Notwithstanding the future imposition of the "illegal" term upon Mexicans discussed below, during the decades preceding 1924, these immigrants were not only admitted but often welcomed throughout the border regions in order to supply cheap agricultural labor.

Exclusion policies divided social-class, business, and labor groups. During and after the 1880s, the influx of southern and eastern Europeans and Asians constituting diverse racial, ethnic, and religious groups clashed with the American Protestant majority and earlier immigrant American communities. Thus, union leader, three-term congressman, lawyer, and state judge Martin Foran won passage of the 1885 act bearing his name, which blocked immigrants from entering the United States under labor contracts signed abroad with American firms. Supporters argued that the act protected American jobs from workers like "degraded, ignorant, brutal, Italians, and Hungarians" that big business recruited in mass from abroad at low wages; after temporarily working in the United States, they returned home. These "sojourner" white workers were classified with Chinese "Coolie" contract laborers excluded from California and other states. Samuel Gompers of the American Federation of Labor urged complete exclusion of the Chinese and "selective restriction" of sojourner white workers, both of whom accepted lower wages and could be strike breakers. Some small business groups fearing unfair competition from rivals' employing "illegal" labor also urged immigration restriction. By 1912, however, the preponderantly Jewish Ladies Garment Workers, though a large AFL affiliate, still opposed policies that closed America to "victims of political, religious, and economic oppressions from finding a place of refuge in the United States."

Immigration quotas eventually triumphed. Congress did not override Grover Cleveland's and William H. Taft's veto of immigration legislation including a literacy test in either 1897 or 1913. But Woodrow Wilson's 1916 veto of this test was overridden in the 1917 act; the more restrictive 1924 Immigration Act also included the literacy test. These restrictive laws levied an $8.00 head tax on all immigrants except children accompanying an adult. The literacy test applied to persons sixteen years and older classified as "illiterate," being all those who were physically capable but who were unable to speak English or certain another languages, including Hebrew or Yiddish. Other excluded persons were: anarchists, "professional beggars," "polygamists," "homosexuals," "idiots," "criminals," "feebleminded persons," "epileptics," "insane persons," alcoholics, and people from an "Asiatic Barred Zone" embracing most of Asia and the Pacific Islands. The 1924 act also added preferential quotas. "We were afraid of foreigners; we distrusted them; we didn't like them," said Brooklyn congressman Emanuel Celler. "Under this Act only some one hundred and fifty odd thousands would be permitted to enter the United States. If you were of Anglo-Saxon origin, you could have over two-thirds of the quota numbers allotted to your people. If you were Japanese, you could not come in at all. That, of course, had been true of the Chinese since 1880. If you were southern or eastern European, you could dribble in and remain on sufferance."

As federal immigration regulation based on national supremacy displaced the commerce power, limited state police powers remained. Once the Civil War abolished slavery, the legal equality guaranteed "persons" in the antebellum personal liberty laws was reconstituted into the ambiguous federal citizenship of Reconstruction civil rights laws and the Fourteenth Amendment. Thus, Justice Field's 1874 *Ah Fong* circuit opinion insisted that California's anti-Chinese laws violated not only treaties based on the commerce power, but also Fourteenth Amendment rights guaranteed all persons—including aliens. As the Court limited the commerce power and expanded federal immigrant regulations, Field joined in the Supreme Court's unanimous decision of *Yick Wo v. Hopkins* (1886); the Court applied the Fourteenth Amendment to protect the property rights of Chinese laundry operators from discriminatory San Francisco license prohibitions based on police powers. The Court upheld rights of "all persons, citizens and aliens alike," as Field had reasoned in *Ah Fong*. While Congress and the Court steadily excluded Chinese from entering the United States, the Fourteenth Amendment property protections were selectively affirmed in some immigrant communities but not others. Operating much like the antebellum state personal liberty laws, these constitutional protections nonetheless acknowledged an alien's formal though limited legal equality, gradually enabling contestation of noncitizenship status.

Miller's *Henderson* decision fostered restrictive federal regulation of immigrants that displaced the federal-state balance established in the Passenger Cases. The Court construed the Fourteenth Amendment to curb state police powers, thereby permitting members of immigrant communities in some states to acquire property rights and political clout, if not federal naturalization and citizenship. More generally, however, federal exclusion resonated with similar *state* restrictions of white immigrants and free blacks disputed under the commerce power in the Passenger Cases. Though the 1849 precedent continued to be cited, it was superseded by decisions supporting federal supremacy. The Court's decision of *Takao Ozawa v. U.S.* (1922) suggested the changes. The issue was whether the Japanese alien's "continuous" twenty-year residence in the U.S. territory of Hawaii and California qualified him for citizenship. The Court "conceded" he was "well qualified by character and education for citizenship." But the Court applied U.S. naturalization laws stating that except for "African descended" people identified with the Civil War Amendments, "only free white persons shall be *included* [original emphasis]" among those the government might grant the "privilege of citizenship." The Court followed federal and state precedents supporting the "determination that the words 'white person' are synonymous with the words 'a person of the Caucasian race.'" Since Mr. Ozawa was "clearly of a race which is not Caucasian" he "belongs entirely outside the zone" of persons qualified to be citizens. This policy was consistent with federal immigration restrictions in the 1924 act, which entered decline during and after World War II.

Inclusive Regulation and the Partial Return of the Passenger Cases: *Edwards* to *Graham*

Two Supreme Court decisions suggested evolving immigration policy from restriction to inclusion. In *Edwards v. California* (1941), the Court cited the Passenger Cases in support of the dormant Commerce Clause, overturning a law that closed the state's borders to unemployed American migrants, using the same police powers that had excluded Asians. As Congressman Celler recalled regarding his struggle for inclusive U.S. immigration policies, under the quotas roughly 70 percent of the preferred groups were from Ireland, Germany, and the United Kingdom. The visas allocated to immigrants from Italy, Greece, Poland, Portugal, and other eastern and southern European nations, however, were so limited that long waiting lists accumulated. The Asian-zone exclusions embraced the Chinese, Japanese, Asian Indians, and residents of U.S. possessions in the Philippines and Pacific Islands. In Alaska the few Russian-descendant whites received a higher preference than Inuit people identified as "Mongolian." In 1943, 1946, and 1952 the preferential quotas were altered; they were eliminated in 1965. Meanwhile, "backdoor" immigration from Mexico and elsewhere in the Western hemisphere continued with inconsistent regulation. By *Graham v. Richardson* (1971), the Court held that states could not block certain welfare benefits aliens shared with U.S. citizens based on the Equal Protection Clause and a right of travel affirmed in *Edwards*, which disputed the precedential standing of the Passenger Cases.

The state's argument in *Edwards* rested on a commerce power construed in *Miln*, the Passenger Cases, and other precedents. Employing police-power language embracing indigent "paupers" like that which had targeted the Chinese, Japanese, and other Asians, the California statute made it "a misdemeanor for anyone knowingly to bring or assist in bringing into the State a nonresident 'indigent person.'" The state's counsel, including Attorney General Earl Warren, cited the Chinese and Japanese immigrants in order to equate them as a "social problem" with Southern "tenants and share croppers . . . [who at the time] swarmed into California." These "poor whites" carried the "various nutritional diseases of the South," imposing on "public relief" the "constant threat of epidemics. Venereal diseases and tuberculosis" also were "common with them" and were "on the increase," as was "rape and incest," and "Petty crime." In "agricultural strikes, they" were "readily led into riots by agitators; although . . . they stubbornly resist all subversive influences, being loyal Americans whose only wish is for a better chance in life." These peoples' arrival in California "has alarmingly increased our taxes and cost of welfare outlays, old age pensions, and the care of the criminal, the indigent sick, the blind, and the insane."

The state court applied the "pauper" law, convicting Edwards for bringing from Texas his "indigent" bother-in-law. For the U.S. Supreme Court, Justice James Byrnes held that California's use of police powers to criminalize travel of unemployed interstate migrants imposed an "unconstitutional barrier to interstate commerce." Byrnes relied on a dormant commerce power. The state, he said, interfered with Social Security and other federal programs that aided "indigent persons" who had "become the common responsibility and concern of the whole nation." Also, the "social phenomenon of large-scale interstate migration" encouraged state "retaliatory measures" against which neither local democratic nor judicial processes provided adequate defense, mandating federal policies. Although Justice William O. Douglas concurred, he cited the *Crandall* precedent to rebut Byrnes's citation of the Passenger Cases and the overturning of the "commerce-person" distinction in *Miln* in order to enforce the dormant Commerce Clause. Douglas urged that the "right of persons to move freely from State to State occupies a more protected position in our constitutional system than does the movement of cattle, fruit, steel, and coal across state lines," regulated by the Commerce Clause. Justice Robert Jackson also argued that the Fourteenth Amendment guaranteed the right of free travel.

The *Edwards* opinions had implications for the legal status of alien immigrants. Before joining the Court, Jackson's tenure as attorney general coincided with Celler's efforts to end exclusion of Chinese, Filipinos, and Asian Indians from Western states and the rest of the nation. During World War II Justice Jackson vigorously condemned the Court's affirmation of Japanese Americans' internment in concentration camps. His concurring opinion in *Edwards* thus implied that new alien groups would be "admitted with the privilege of entering and abiding in the United States, and hence of entering and abiding in any State of the Union." Jackson questioned Byrnes's grounding of the right to travel on the dormant Commerce Clause because it seemed narrower than the rights granted all "persons" under the Fourteenth Amendment. "The world is even more upside down than I had supposed it to be," Jackson wrote in *Edwards*, "if California must accept aliens in deference to their federal privileges but is free to turn back citizens of the United States unless we treat them as subjects of commerce." Even so, following World War II the Court gradually extended to aliens and foreign workers certain Fourteenth Amendment Equal Protection and Due Process Clause protections from education to criminal justice.

More inclusive immigration laws thus coincided with court victories upholding equal protection, due process, and the right of travel. In 1943 Congress repealed the Chinese Exclusion Act. Three years later Connecticut Republican Claire Booth Luce and Brooklyn Democrat Emanuel Celler won passage of a law ending Filipino and Asian Indian exclusions. The Luce-Celler Act established a quota of 100 individuals for each group; once citizenship was attained, they could own property in and petition for family members to enter the

United States. In 1952, overriding President Harry Truman's veto, the Immigration and Nationality Act maintained the basic categories of the preferred national-origins quotas and the annual ceiling of 154,277 persons; but it also ended most Asian immigration exclusions, including the Japanese. The 1952 law extended admission criteria beyond family members to include immigrants with certain education qualifications and skills. Immigration from Mexico, other Latin American nations, and the Caribbean remained free from quotas. From the 1940s on Western-state branches of the NAACP and other groups defended rights of African Americans, the Chinese, Mexicans, Filipinos, Asian Indians, and Japanese Americans. Accordingly, state and federal courts gradually overturned state discrimination against aliens in public education, employment, restrictive covenants in land sales, and anti-miscegenation laws.

The 1965 Immigration Act triggered a new era of mass immigration and alien-rights claims. Proponents of the act expected the total 290, 000 authorized visas would maintain manageable levels of immigrants benefiting from the basic "family reunification" policy. The total number of visas also included "skilled and unskilled workers in occupations for which there was insufficient labor supply," refugees—generally from communist and Middle East nations—granted "conditional entry," and other categories such as tourists. Refuting the positive expectations, 1964 Republican vice presidential candidate William Miller predicted a threefold increase in immigration within a few decades. Myra C. Hacker, vice president of the New Jersey Coalition of Patriotic Societies, also presented to a U.S. Senate subcommittee the likelihood of rising social-welfare rights claims. Given "our 5 percent unemployment rate" and "menacingly mounting welfare costs," she asked, were Americans "prepared to embrace so great a horde of the world's unfortunates? At the very least, the hidden mathematics of the bill should be made clear to the public so that they may tell their Congressman how they feel about providing jobs, schools, homes, security against want, [and] citizen education . . . for an indeterminately enormous number of aliens from underprivileged lands."

Following critics' expressed concerns regarding the 1965 Immigration Act, state challenges to aliens claiming social welfare benefits came before the Supreme Court. In *Graham v. Richardson* (1971), Arizona and Pennsylvania laws refused "welfare benefits to resident aliens or to aliens" living in the United States for a stipulated period of time. Arizona's law conditioned an alien's receipt of certain federal Social Security benefits on a "15-year durational residency requirement." Justice Harry Blackmun's opinion for a unanimous court framed the issue raised by each state's laws to be "whether the Equal Protection Clause of the Fourteenth Amendment prevents a State from conditioning welfare benefits either (a) upon the beneficiary's possession of United States citizenship, or (b) if the beneficiary is an alien, upon his [or her] having resided in this country for a specified number of years." The two states participated in federal Social Security programs enabling benefits the alien residents claimed along with U.S. citizens. The states' argument was, however, that they, "consistent with the Equal Protection Clause, may favor United States citizens over aliens in the distribution of welfare benefits." The states also argued that the "right to travel" established in *Edwards* or the Passenger Cases "extends only to citizens and not to aliens."

Justice Blackmun rejected the states' arguments. He noted that sixty-four-year-old Carmen Richardson was a "lawfully admitted resident alien" from Mexico "residing continuously in Arizona" since 1956. Upon becoming "permanently disabled," she qualified for a federal Social Security "assistance program" Arizona administered; the state, however, "denied relief solely because of the [15-year] residency requirement." The Pennsylvania case concerned Scottish alien resident Elsie Mary Jane Leger, who claimed state assistance based on "a common law marriage with a [U.S.] citizen." This aid was "denied because of her alienage." Blackmun held that "[s]ince an alien as well as a citizen is a 'person' for equal protection purposes, a concern for [state] fiscal integrity is no more compelling a justification for the questioned classification in these [alienage] cases than it was in" precedents in which the Court applied strict scrutiny upholding a U.S. citizen's claim to federal- or state-administered assistance. Blackmun also conceded that the Court had "never decided whether the right" to travel upheld in *Edwards* or the Passenger Cases "applies specifically to aliens." Nevertheless, in cases concerning aliens or U.S. citizens the suspect classification "was subjected to strict scrutiny under the compelling state interest test . . . because it impinged upon the fundamental right of interstate movement."

The *Edwards* and *Graham* decisions reflected the gradual displacement of immigration exclusions by inclusive policies and alien rights claims. During World War II Congress affirmed federal supremacy over immigration policy, ending Chinese exclusions. Congress gradually expanded quota preferences until inclusive admission policies finally prevailed in the 1965 Immigration Act. Within this wider context, the Court in *Edwards* reasoned that a dormant commerce power sustained a right of travel over a California law restricting "indigents" from the American South in the same way it excluded Asians. Justices Douglas and Jackson argued, however, that it was better not to suggest that the right of travel concerned the "commerce-person" distinction disputed in the Passenger Cases. Instead, the California law eviscerated rights "persons" could claim under the Fourteenth Amendment. In *Graham* Blackmun, with Douglas still on the Court, noted that the precedents left unsettled the "source" in "any particular constitutional provision" of the "constitutional right of travel." The Court thus could find that state discrimination depriving alien "persons" of certain federal welfare benefits shared with U.S. citizens violated the Fourteenth Amendment and the "fundamental right of interstate movement." From the 1970s on, the status of "illegal" immigrants in state and federal law agitated inclusive immigration policies and the Court's extension of alien rights claims.

Evolving Federal Supremacy from *De Canas* to *Arizona I* and *II*: Passenger Cases Return?

The Court's decisions in *De Canas v. Bicas* (1975) and *Arizona I* (2011) and *II* (2012) reflected evolving federal supremacy and federal-state cooperation affecting illegal immigrants. In *De Canas* Justice William J. Brennan's opinion for a unanimous Court cited the *Henderson*, Passenger Cases, and *Chy Lung* precedents to support a holding that federal supremacy sustaining federal regulation of illegal immigrants did not preclude state regulations implementing the same policy. By 2012 the Court's 5–3 majorities in the two Arizona cases upheld federal supremacy and preemption prescribing state-federal cooperation in order to police illegal immigrants; but Justice Scalia's dissent argued that early commerce power analysis favored state exclusionary powers. Since the later 1970s the status of undocumented, "illegal" aliens challenged the *De Canas* holding that federal supremacy "contemplate[d] some room for state legislation." The total number of immigrants granted admission into the United States increased from 290,000 in 1978 to 700,000 thousand in 1990 and remained at similar levels despite the War-on-Terror and recurring global recessions. The large proportion of undocumented aliens also entering the nation polarized party politics and media images. Although Congress dominated immigration policy, the Court decided the scope of federal supremacy, federal-state cooperation, and alien rights.

The *De Canas* case arose from Californians' concern that free mobility of "illegal" agricultural workers hurt the local economy experiencing recession in the 1970s. Migrant farm workers registered under state and federal regulations sued in state court to enjoin contractors who had discontinued their employment, hiring instead "illegal" migrants. The question was whether a California law forbidding employment of undocumented, nonresident "aliens" violated federal supremacy under the 1965 Immigration and Nationality Act (INA) and federal prohibitions against farm-labor contractors hiring illegal workers. The state court decided that federal supremacy preempted the state's police power policy of defending employment for lawful resident and alien farm labor. Justice Brennan's opinion for a unanimous Supreme Court reversed, sustaining the "documented" farm workers. Citing the *Henderson*, Passenger Cases, and *Chy Lung* precedents, Brennan noted that immigration regulation was an exclusive federal power. Nevertheless, he said, California "has sought to strengthen its economy by adopting federal standards in imposing criminal sanctions against employers who knowingly employ aliens who have no federal right to employment within the country; even if such local regulation has some purely speculative and indirect impact on immigration, it does not thereby become a constitutionally proscribed regulation of immigration that Congress itself would be powerless to authorize."

While Congress led in immigration policy, the courts selectively expanded alien rights. The 1980 Immigration Act applied United Nations criteria to define refugee status, established a separate maximum refugee total at 50,000, and reduced the global immigrant total to 270,000. The next year an influential select commission reported that shutting the "back door" flow of "undocumented, illegal migration" was a priority, as was giving more attention to providing legal immigrants with "procedures" enabling "fair and efficient adjudication and administration of U.S. immigration laws." The 1986 Immigration Reform and Control Act (IRCA) addressed "illegal immigration" by offering amnesty and "temporary status" to "all illegal aliens" who could prove continuous residence in the United States since 1982. The act also granted farm workers a "separate, more lenient amnesty," enforced legal sanctions against "employers who knowingly hired illegal aliens," and strengthened "inspection and enforcement at U.S. borders." Immigration historian Mae M. Ngai concluded that "even as the courts slowly and spottily expanded aliens' rights of due process, they remained unwilling to challenge the doctrine of [federal] plenary power, so that Congress retains virtually unfettered authority to enact whatever immigration legislation it chooses."

The social and political context influencing the courts' selective expansion of alien rights embraced legal and illegal immigration. By 1988, said economic historian Carol Heim, 840,000 immigrants entering the United States included "an estimated 200,000 undocumented entrants." Among the total number of "new entrants," 67.1 percent resided in California, New York, Texas, Illinois, and Florida. By the 1990s these and other states felt globalization driving formal (legal) and informal (illegal) labor markets. "Many . . . Asian and Middle Eastern immigrants come from middle-class backgrounds, have skills sought by employers, and progress quickly in the United States," Heim concluded. "For many Mexican and Central American immigrants, as well as native born African Americans, moving up [from the 'informal' economy] is more problematic." Economic historian Richard Easterlin noted that from 1980 to 1990, "net legal immigration, accounted for about one-third of the [U.S.] population [growth]." In the early 1980s, estimated "net illegal immigration" was "about 200,000." More than "30 percent" of these "undocumented" workers were from Mexico; primarily "unskilled" and "temporary" labor, they moved back and forth across the international border, though probably the "net flow" ultimately settled in the United States.

Moreover, the economic measurements of immigrant or native labor suggested in *De Canas* or the social welfare costs at issue in cases like *Graham v. Richardson* were contested. "Despite [media] claims to the contrary," said Easterlin, "the evidence indicates that immigration has only a miniscule impact on the employment opportunities of the native labor force." Increased "economic opportunities" resulted from "retention of industries that would otherwise move abroad," improved "aggregate demand for goods," and "new entrepreneurs [added] to the economy." Moreover, "new immigrants compete[d] only to a small extent with native workers, because of deficiencies in language, education, and prior work experience." Immigration had "virtually no impact on general wage levels," though in a weak local market "a high proportion of immigrants," might "adversely affect" the "wages of low skilled workers." In addition, "immigrants, including illegal aliens, rather than being a burden to the American taxpayer," were "a net benefit—they pay more taxes than they receive in the form of government benefits."

By the late 1990s Congress and the courts evolved the federal enforcement regime that eventually rested INS and Homeland Security regulatory structures on the Constitution's Supremacy Clause, federal preemption, and state-federal cooperation in immigration policies. This federal regulatory supremacy impliedly assumed the Court's reliance on the minimal Commerce Clause analysis embracing the Passenger Cases, *Chy Lung*, and *Henderson* precedents Brennan had cited in his *De Canas* opinion. Federal supremacy also accepted the right of travel, whether it rested on the dormant commerce power in *Edwards* or the Fourteenth Amendment in *Graham*. States seeking to exclude undocumented immigrants from employment and social services and to minimize constitutional due process guarantees thus claimed police power exemptions and federal-state cooperation within federal regulatory supremacy and preemption. An Arizona law tested federal supremacy and state cooperation before the Supreme Court in the Arizona Cases of 2011 and 2012.

Arizona's 2010 comprehensive legislation targeted illegal aliens. The law reflected reports that federal and state authorities apprehended "hundreds of thousands of deportable aliens" annually. In the state's leading population center of Maricopa County, which embraced Phoenix, the estimated 8.9 percent of the population considered to be "unauthorized aliens" reportedly were "responsible for 21.8% of the felonies." By another estimate, "Unauthorized aliens who remain in the State comprise[d] . . . almost six percent of the population." Addressing perceived labor-market dimensions related to these problems, the Arizona law imposed civil and criminal sanctions on licensed businesses that employed illegal aliens. Relying upon state-federal cooperation enabled by the federal 1986 IRCA and 1996 Illegal Immigration Reform and Immigrant Responsibility Act (IIRIRA), the state law also exceeded federal voluntary-compliance stipulations: instead, it *mandated* that employers use the federal E-Verify database to ascertain whether prospective workers were documented. If prosecutions resulted, an employer's check of E-Verify data established a defense. The U.S. Chamber of Commerce and "various business and civil rights organizations" filed in federal district court a suit, arguing that the powers granted state officials authorizing "license suspensions and revocation" were "both expressly and impliedly preempted by federal immigration law, and that the mandatory use of E-Verify was impliedly preempted."

The federal district court rejected the federal preemption claims, a decision that the Supreme Court partially affirmed in *Chamber of Commerce v. Whiting* (2011). Chief Justice John Roberts's 5–3 majority opinion compared the Arizona law's licensing and mandated E-Verify provisions to the federal process stipulated in the 1986 IRCA and the verification process of the 1996 IIRIRA. The 1986 IRCA imposed federal civil and criminal penalties on employers who knowingly hired illegal aliens; it also generally preempted possible state prosecutions in such cases. An IRCA "saving clause," however, specifically allowed state prosecutions of illegal aliens under "state licensing and similar laws." The first question was whether the Arizona licensing regulations were within the IRCA saving clause. The second question was whether the state could mandate employer compliance with E-Verify, where the 1996 IIRIRA did no more than require voluntary use. The chief justice's opinion held that Arizona's reliance on business licensing to prosecute illegal aliens was permissible under IRCA's saving clause; it also held that IIRIRA's authorized voluntary use of E-Verify did not preclude making state enforcement contingent upon mandated checks of the same data. In separate dissenting opinions Justices Stephen Breyer and Sonia Sotomayor argued basically that Arizona's regulatory scheme burdened federal enforcement and as such was "preempted."

The federal government challenged four other provisions of the state law in *Arizona v. U.S.* (2012).The government argued that federal immigration legislation established a comprehensive regulatory scheme, including IRCA, based on the Supremacy Clause and powers governing foreign affairs that "preempted" the four provisions. The U.S. district court's injunction enjoined implementation of provisions making it a *state misdemeanor*: (1) for individuals or groups not to "comply with federal-registration requirements," and (2) "for an unauthorized alien to seek or engage in work in the State." The injunction also blocked two provisions that (3) "authorize[d] state and local officers to arrest without a warrant a person 'the officer has probable cause to believe . . . has committed any public offense that makes the person removable from,'" and (4) "require[d] officers conducting a stop, detention, or arrest, to make efforts, in some instances, to verify the person's immigration status with the Federal Government." The Ninth Circuit Court of Appeals affirmed the injunctions, "agreeing" that the Supreme Court could "likely" affirm the federal government's "preemptions claims." Justice Anthony Kennedy's 5–3 majority opinion upheld federal "preemption" preventing implementation of all but the law's last provision, which was left undecided until the state courts determined whether state officials effectively carried out the federal verification process, a view with which the dissenters agreed.

The dissenters in *Arizona v. U.S.* argued that federal "preemption" permitted more state cooperation than the majority allowed. Affirming precedent, Justice Samuel Alito characterized Justice Brennan's *De Canas* opinion as holding that "federal law does not displace state law unless Congress' intent to do so is clear and manifest," especially governing "employment regulation, even of aliens unlawfully present in the [U.S.] . . . an area of traditional state concern." This view omitted that in *De Canas* Brennan cited commerce power precedents of *Henderson*, Passenger Cases, and *Chy Lung* to support a holding that California's immigrant-labor regulations were consistent with federal regulations. Justice Clarence Thomas argued that the *Arizona* majority opinion made the scope of "preemption" simply dependent upon a "free-wheeling judicial inquiry." Justice Antonin Scalia cited *Miln*, but not regarding the Taney Court's dispute over the police and commerce power separating "persons" from "commerce," which had involved slavery and free blacks. Instead, he said, "Arizona has moved to protect its sovereignty—not in contradiction of federal law, but in complete compliance with it. The laws under challenge do not extend or revise federal immigration restrictions, but merely enforce those restrictions more effectively." Assuming federal-state cooperation within federal supremacy, Scalia advocated broader state police power criminal procedures embracing conduct of suspected undocumented aliens.

In the *Arizona* cases the disputed scope of federal "preemption" reflected evolving federal-state cooperation in immigration regulations. Comprehensive federal immigration regulation rested on federal supremacy, naturalization, and treaty powers. Yet Brennan's *De Canas* opinion held that federal supremacy did not preclude state police powers operating in conjunction with federal regulations that enforced the same policy requiring employment of legal rather than undocumented migrant workers. Brennan's reasoning included some commerce power analysis that distinguished state from federal authority in *Henderson*, *Chy Lung*, and Passenger Cases. He also assumed without stating the right of travel inherent in the dormant commerce power and the rights-claims that legal as well as illegal aliens shared with U.S. citizens. The 1986 IRCA and the 1996 IIRIRA laws incorporated these express and implied precedents, instituting the federal regulatory system that endorsed state cooperation within federal preemption. The majority's *Whiting* decision thus rested on a federal statutory-savings clause that regulated state-licensed employers; it also upheld the broader mandated rather than voluntary use of the federal E-Verify data program. In the second *Arizona* decision a different majority affirmed that federal supremacy of federal regulations incorporated more limited state cooperation than the dissenters claimed; the federally prescribed rights also required state officials' good-faith enforcement.

Conclusion

After the Civil War the precedential influence of Passenger Cases declined but then partially revived. The Court's 1875 *Henderson*, *Ger-*

man Lloyd, and *Chy Lung* decisions affirmed an expansive commerce power that undercut shippers' funding of state social welfare policies, while it circumscribed the Passenger Cases. Miller's opinions also facilitated Congress's enacting a federal tax that underwrote Chinese exclusion. After *Henderson*, the Passenger Cases maintained limited precedential influence. The triumph of preferential racial quotas in the 1924 Immigration Act rested on federal supremacy, naturalization, and treaty powers, as well as the general subordination of state police powers. From World War II on, federal supremacy did not preclude the Court incorporating inconsistent rights protections from the dormant commerce power in *Edwards*, or the Fourteenth Amendment in *Graham* that aliens and U.S. citizens shared. Both cases cited the Passenger Cases as partial authority. In *De Canas*, state illegal-immigrant regulations supported federal policies citing the Passenger Cases; by *Arizona I* and *II*, federal preemption permitted state regulation of illegal immigrants primarily within federal-state cooperation. Aliens thus shared some rights with citizens, including the right of travel, which implied without citing the Passenger Cases, notwithstanding Justice Scalia's dissent, using the commerce power to prioritize state exclusion of illegal immigrants.

Conclusions

In *Arizona v. U.S.* (2012), Justice Scalia's dissent urged that the history of police powers and the commerce power enabled greater immigrant exclusion based on state sovereignty. This study refocuses the early history, indicating that the Supreme Court construed federal and state laws generally to admit rather than exclude immigrants and free blacks, though of course certain exclusion programs were effective. Some Northern states also conferred limited citizenship upon both groups. Lawyers' legal arguments and the opinions of federal and state judges turned politics into legal issues that the Supreme Court decided. The Marshall Court first prescribed where the commerce power ended and police powers began; but it avoided addressing the status of immigrants and free blacks as legal "persons." The contested "commerce-person" distinction established in *Miln* divided the Taney Court's opinion making. In the Passenger Cases, a 5–4 majority reshaped the balance between police powers affecting immigrants and blacks and an exclusive commerce power that regulated the transport of aliens aboard ship. The new federal-state boundary influenced the coming of the Civil War and Reconstruction, including the limited rights aliens and U.S. citizens as legal "persons" acquired under the Fourteenth Amendment. Despite the precedential decline of the Passenger Cases from Reconstruction, through the rise and repudiation of immigration quotas, to contemporary struggles over "illegal" immigrants, the old case suggested the value of reconsidering commerce power history.

The Marshall Court established the first leading commerce power precedents that affected immigrants and blacks. In the 1824 *Gibbons* decision, the Marshall Court upheld the U.S. Coastal Licensing Act over New York's steamboat monopoly. Marshall avoided Justice William Johnson's concurring opinion suggesting that a dormant

Commerce Clause or a treaty resting on a commerce power might be used to overturn South Carolina's Negro Seamen Act. Marshall also rejected a concurrent commerce power Justice Smith Thompson had affirmed as a state judge. Marshall's original-package doctrine in *Brown v. Maryland* (1827) upheld a commerce power supporting a foreign trade agreement over Justice Thompson's dissent affirming Maryland's license tax on imports. In *Willson v. Black Bird Creek Marsh Co.* (1829) Marshall upheld state police powers used to improve a Delaware swamp that also interfered with navigable waterways; he dismissed a dormant commerce power and the U.S. Coasting Act. Following the end of the Napoleonic Wars European agricultural dislocation and shippers' competition prompted growing emigration to America. Congress enacted a significant regulation of the immigrant trade in the 1819 Passenger Act, relying on the commerce power and a treaty. New York passed its own passenger law in 1824 based on police powers, requiring shippers to report information about foreign immigrants.

During the 1830s the transatlantic immigrant trade further increased, resulting in the *Miln* case challenging New York's reporting regulations. After Marshall's death Story was the lone dissenter in *Miln*, who believed the reports interfered with an exclusive commerce power, foreign trade agreements, and the 1819 U.S. passenger law. New York's Justice Thompson affirmed the result, upholding the reports under police powers and a concurrent commerce power. Taney Court Democrats privately disputed the "commerce-person" distinction construing the commerce power. Jackson appointees John McLean, Henry Baldwin, James Wayne, Philip Barbour, and Roger Taney endorsed the result that New York's immigrant-reporting requirement was a legitimate exercise of police powers. But only Taney accepted Barbour's separation between "commerce," which Congress regulated, and "persons," who generally were not subject to federal regulation. Although Wayne, Baldwin, and McLean did not support Barbour's reasoning, it influenced legal arguments and state as well as U.S. Supreme Court opinions from 1837 to the Passenger Cases and beyond. Taney embraced the doctrine because it encouraged states to enforce police powers excluding free blacks and undesirable white immigrants sharing the status of legal "persons." The doctrine also undercut congressional reliance on the exclusive Commerce Clause as a possible basis for abolishing the interstate slave trade or the Negro Seamen Acts.

The Taney Court majority's private rejection of the "commerce-person" distinction had enduring impact. Baldwin separately published his concurring opinion in *Miln* primarily because he believed that the "commerce-person" doctrine threatened Marshall's commerce power compromises. In *Groves v. Slaughter* (1841) Baldwin reiterated his respect for Marshall's compromise approach; he preserved it by holding that the Fifth Amendment protected property rights in the interstate slave trade from federal commerce power regulations. Other members of the Court also applied separate reasoning to oppose the "commerce-person" distinction. McLean argued that state sovereignty enabled Northern states like Ohio to abolish slavery and to curb black laws that discriminated against free blacks. Still, in the South slavery was sacrosanct, resting on police powers that excluded free blacks as legal "persons." The federal government exclusively regulated immigrants' *transport* to the United States. Justice John McKinley's unpublished dissent in *Groves*, with which Story agreed, held that the Mississippi constitution's prohibition of the slave trade not did clash with an exclusive commerce power. But *state* slave-trade abolition made the slave traders' debt unenforceable, which perhaps violated a dormant commerce power. Wayne silently concurred with McLean, McKinley, Story, and Thompson. Taney, however, implied that the Union depended on preserving the "commerce-person" distinction.

State court litigation reflected political contestation in the Alien Tax Cases. Amid the 1837 economic panic the British consul in Boston, Robert C. Manners, initiated a protest strategy challenging the Massachusetts alien tax, which supplemented the state's poor law. The social welfare issues fragmented state-party politics facilitating conferral of citizenship upon immigrants and free blacks. Shippers paying the tax simultaneously filed a state protest seeking recovery of costs and damages (plus interest) should appeals decide that the tax was unconstitutional. Manners supported the *Norris* case challenging the tax. Losing in the Boston court, Manners funded an appeal resulting in Chief Justice Lemuel Shaw's opinion for the unanimous Supreme Judicial Court of Massachusetts. Shaw held that the tax supporting the state poor law was an exercise of police powers that did not clash with Marshall's *Gibbons* precedent; it also was consistent with the police powers upheld in *Miln*. Shaw implied, too, that the state's tax rested on police powers partly concurrent with the commerce power. The New York alien tax case arose some years later as a major increase in transatlantic immigration coincided with economic depression and the destructive potato blight traveling from the United States to Europe, Britain, and Ireland. In *Smith v. Turner* New York courts upheld the tax supporting the Maritime Hospital under police powers that also enabled conferral of citizenship upon immigrants and blacks as legal "persons."

In the Taney Court, four years of appellate arguments consolidated into the Passenger Cases channeled the legal issues and politics embracing the alien tax. Three new appointees joined the Court, confronting the transatlantic famine migration and sectional struggles arising from the Mexican territorial cession, Northern states' defiance of the fugitive slave law, and abolitionists' insistence that the commerce power enabled abolition of the interstate slave trade. These conflicts agitated anti-immigrant and racial politics within New York and Massachusetts. Daniel Webster's and John Van Buren's Passenger Cases arguments reflected state-federal bipartisan party politics promoting U.S. famine relief and passenger laws, as well as local racial and anti-immigrant political compromises promoting personal liberty laws. Within this context Webster, Van Buren, and their colleagues marshaled federal and state precedents contesting where the federal commerce power ended and state police powers began. Precedents agreed that police powers generally supported the bond-commutation system, quarantine, local pilots, and "essential inspections" states required from shippers. The alien tax, however, was levied aboard vessels based on reports of immigrants who themselves were at the same time subject to the U.S. Passenger Acts and international treaties that the federal commerce power supported.

Press reports of the Court's 4–4 deadlock in the Passenger Cases coincided with the License Cases (1847). With McKinley absent, a unanimous Court held that three New England states' police powers sustained retail license taxes regulating imported alcoholic spirits. Ten disputed opinions, however, suggested similarities between state temperance laws and the Passenger Cases regarding admission or exclusion of immigrants, free blacks, and slaves. Attentive to Ohio politics driving revision of black laws in order to alleviate racial discrimination, McLean based police powers on the same state sovereignty that Southerners asserted to defend slavery. National sovereignty, by contrast, supported exclusive federal regulation of foreign immigrants before disembarkation from vessels. Ignoring sovereignty issues, Catron accepted McLean's basic view of police powers but argued that treaties and passenger laws based on the commerce power regulated immigrants aboard ship. He also rejected a dormant commerce power. Grier agreed with Catron and McLean on the respective purposes of police powers and the commerce power, exclaiming that the former enforced a state's right of self-preservation. Daniel and Taney applied the "commerce-person" distinction to expand police powers and to limit the commerce power. Woodbury held that police powers excluded undesirable immigrants and free blacks, but he was unclear why a concurrent commerce power sanctioned such exclusion.

Webster received private notice from Taney acknowledging that McKinley likely would be the fifth vote breaking the deadlock, and from McLean indicating that the shippers would win. Unexpected however, was the bitter public exchange between Wayne and Taney publicizing the fact that a majority of the Court had never accepted the "commerce-person" distinction in *Miln*. Even so, the five justices deciding the Passenger Cases narrowly construed *Miln*, rejecting the "commerce-person" distinction. Wayne's opinion summarized a majority consensus agreeing that the alien tax clashed with federal laws and treaties consistent with Marshall's decision in *Gibbons* upholding the federal coasting statute and federal supremacy. McLean endorsed the narrow supremacy of U.S. passenger laws and treaties within dual sovereignty that enabled Northern states to abolish slavery, repeal black laws, and enact personal liberty laws. Grier insisted that state police powers excluding undesirable white immigrants and free blacks were constitutional; he also endorsed Catron's opinion overturning the tax because it clashed with federal laws and treaties without addressing the scope of either an exclusive or dormant commerce power. The nation's "cherished policy" was, Grier insisted, that admission of immigrants was the norm and exclusion exceptional. McKinley endorsed Catron's opinion but provided a unique rationale for a dormant commerce power relying on the international slave-trade clause.

A congressional vote to disseminate 5,000 copies of the Passenger

Cases reflected political contestation. The diverse opinions provided legitimacy for sectional politics shaping the 1850 Compromise: it left to "popular sovereignty" the admission or exclusion of slavery in the Western territories, enacted a stronger Fugitive Slave Act, and excluded the slave trade from the nation's capital. The majority opinions overturning the alien tax benefited the shippers' and the states' interest in admitting immigrants employing the system of bonds, sureties, and commutation. The result reinforced bipartisan support for new U.S. passenger laws that promoted the immigrant trade; it also inspired party compromises defeating most but not all Know-Nothing demands for state and federal laws that excluded immigrants. The dissenters' assertions that police powers excluded free blacks, however, facilitated passage of the 1850 Fugitive Slave Act imposing draconian federal supremacy over Northern states' resistance using personal liberty laws. The dissents also encouraged the interstate slave trade, refuting abolitionist claims that it violated an exclusive commerce power. Woodbury's attempt to balance states' expansive exclusion of immigrants and blacks employing police powers and a partially concurrent commerce power received little support. Taney's and Daniel's advocacy of the "commerce-person" distinction conflicted free and slave state police powers governing legal "persons."

The Passenger Cases maintained precedential prominence up to the 1870s. During the 1850s the decision encouraged Southern Democrats to support open immigration because it encouraged Democratic voters in Northern cities. Southerners also helped to contain the Know-Nothings' most extreme exclusionary immigration proposals in order to avoid an implication that a federal commerce power might sanction abolition of the interstate slave trade. In Northern states the decision aided Republicans' support of personal liberty laws that established limited legal equality for immigrants, free blacks, and fugitive slaves. Southerners justified secession by claiming that Northern states' personal liberty laws enabled free blacks' citizenship and defiance of the fugitive slave law, which brought about Republican victory in the 1860 presidential election, fostering Civil War. During the war the California Supreme Court cited the Passenger Cases in overturning state laws that excluded certain Chinese aliens. In 1868, however, Justice Miller distinguished away the 1849 precedent to strike down a tax on "persons" designated as passengers leaving

Nevada on stages and railroads, although dissenters urged that the tax was contrary to a dormant commerce power. In the early 1870s Justice Field's circuit opinion cited the Passenger Cases, while he also asserted that the Fourteenth Amendment guaranteed certain rights to all "persons," including Chinese aliens suffering discrimination under California's laws.

The decline of the Passenger Cases from precedential prominence suggested a reconsideration of the historical origins of states' exclusionary policies. In 1849, the Court's majority and dissenting opinions assumed that the states' police powers supported the bond-commutation system—distinct from the alien taxes—lawfully financing poor laws and health laws aiding immigrants. The majority opinions also accepted that free-state personal liberty laws could confer limited legal equality and even citizenship on free blacks, fugitive slaves, and white immigrants. Southerners, however, justified secession because they denied that state citizenship could embrace blacks. The Taney Court, as well as free- and slave-state politicians, accepted, by contrast, that the commerce power underlying treaties and the U.S. passenger laws empowered exclusive federal regulation of immigrants aboard ship. Miller's three 1875 opinions grouped under the *Henderson* case eventually ended the bond-commutation system financing state social welfare policies. His opinions also promoted a new commerce power doctrine embracing federal taxation of the immigrants that was displaced by federal regulatory supremacy based on treaty and naturalization powers enforcing federal exclusionary policies. Justice Field's opinions during the 1880s nonetheless also conferred upon aliens limited rights shared with U.S. citizens, which since World War II Congress and federal judges have steadily extended, including a right of travel affirmed in *Edwards* and *Graham v. Richardson*.

The fate of the Alabama anti-immigrant law after the Supreme Court's decisions eviscerating the Arizona law suggested the challenges federal supremacy presented. Alabama's law included the provision of the Arizona law the Supreme Court upheld in *Whiting*, enabling state employers access to the federal E-Verify database in order to avoid hiring illegal immigrants. In 2013 the state's statistics reportedly confirmed that "thousands of employers in Alabama have been ignoring [the] provision in the state's immigration law that requires them to register with the E-Verify system." In addition, each of the provisions the Supreme Court enjoined in the Arizona law exceeding federal enforcement that also appeared in the Alabama law was likewise blocked by the federal district court in Alabama or the U.S. 11th Circuit Court of Appeals, as a result of litigation won by civil liberties lawyers. Moreover, immigrants again prevailed when the federal courts stuck down Alabama's efforts to exclude immigrant children from the public schools and in the state's failed attempt to prevent churches from ministering to immigrants by targeting the right of movement. Concerning the latter right of travel, the 11th U.S. Circuit Court of Appeals overturned the Alabama law's provision that proscribed "harboring" or "transporting unlawfully present aliens." Church leaders who won the case explained, "Our concern was primarily the infringement on the obligation of the church to take care of people regardless of their status."

The Supreme Court's historical shift to federal supremacy helps to explain the shrinking success of immigration restriction since the 1940s. In the Passenger Cases, the Taney Court's disputed distinction between "commerce" and "persons" channeled the influence of free-state personal liberty laws in the immigrant and slavery crises, encouraging Southern secession. During Reconstruction the *Henderson* and *Chy Lung* decisions limited the influence of the Passenger Cases, enabling the long-term evolution of federal supremacy that empowered contradictory policies of exclusion, eventually followed decades later by open immigration. Amid this long-contested policy shift, the Court inconsistently sanctioned property and civil rights that aliens and U.S. citizens shared. Since World War II in states with significant immigrant populations, these shared rights have encouraged immigrant-group solidarity, litigation, and party politics. Thus, the Passenger Cases represented stages in a historical convergence of interests not unlike that which characterized antebellum immigrant and racial politics shaping the personal liberty laws and that which the civil rights movement established within Cold War liberalism. Even so, by the millennium, immigration-restriction proponents confronted not only foreign "others" exploiting entitlements and distributional politics. They also grappled with federal supremacy sustaining immigration regulations that linked the constitutional rights of legal and illegal aliens to the opposing side in the nation's polarized party politics and the Court's immigration decisions.

CHRONOLOGY

1787 Constitutional Convention enumerates separate naturalization and commerce powers and 1808 international slave-trade ban; reflects North-South division over import-export trade, interstate commerce, and slavery.

1788 State Constitutional Ratification Conventions, debates reflect same North-South divisions while affirming same enumerated powers.

1789 Congress affirms state regulation of pilots; Judiciary Act, sec. 25, affirms Supreme Court review of state law.

1791 Bill of Rights: nos. 1–8 apply to federal government, nos. 9 and 10 affirm state police powers.

1794 Shippers' bond system provides credit contracts aiding Massachusetts and New York poor laws; state police powers "saving clause" incorporated into commercial Jay Treaty with Britain.

1798 Federalists' restrictive Alien Act fosters weakly enforced federal naturalization process after 1801.

1817 Marshall Court's *Chirac v. Chirac* upholds federal naturalization while allowing diverse state immigration regulations; decision reflects growing postwar transatlantic immigration.

1819 With Northern and Southern congressional support, federal Passenger Act passes prescribing minimal spatial regulations of steerage immigrants aboard vessels; reflects growing postwar transatlantic immigration and compliance with treaty provisions.

1823 Justice Johnson's attempt in *Elkison v. Deliesseline* to strike down South Carolina's Negro Seamen Act fails amid local defiance; John Taylor repeats extreme states' rights constitutionalism.

1824 New York Passenger Act establishes reporting system that describes immigrants' condition, required from shipmasters upon arrival in port; reflects declining indenture-labor contract immigration amid agricultural dislocation in Britain and Europe. Marshall Court decides *Gibbons v. Ogden* based on compromise commerce power, avoiding issues of slavery and free blacks; Justice Johnson's concurring opinion suggests that South Carolina's Negro Seamen Act was unconstitutional, despite protestations of slavery defenders that such laws were supported by state police powers.

1827 Marshall Court original-package doctrine continues compromise commerce power in *Brown v. Maryland*, despite dissent; reflects growing transatlantic free trade.

1828 South Carolina and John C. Calhoun begin state-sovereignty attack on the U.S. tariff, including collection of customs duties, which help to pay off U.S. foreign debt.

1829 New York enacts alien tax funding new Maritime Hospital on Staten Island adjacent to Quarantine; tax funds separate health administration within New York City's poor-law system. Marshall Court continues compromise approach upholding state-police rather than commerce power in *Willson v. The Black-Bird Creek Marsh Co.*

1830 Shippers develop vessels for immigrant trade alone; reflects increasing ticket-based competition and freer trade with little regulation, resulting in deplorable condition aboard vessels. David Walker publishes widely circulated second edition of *Appeal to the Coloured Citizens of the World.* Britain begins partial abolition of slavery in the West Indies. American abolitionist movement begins.

1832–1833 President Andrew Jackson prevails in Nullification Controversy, ensuring federal enforcement of tariff duties; he also makes opposition to South Carolina a criterion for Supreme Court appointments.

1834 Britain abolishes slavery in West Indies; Georgia and other Southern states enact laws excluding free blacks. Marshall Court postpones decision of *New York City v. Miln*, the case challenging the immigrant-reporting system established in New York's 1824 Passenger Act.

1837 British consul in Boston, Robert Manners, begins protest challenge to Massachusetts alien tax enacted the same year in order to support the state's poor law. The newly constituted Taney Court decides the *Miln* case, affirming the New York reporting system based on state police powers; the Court's Jackson appointees privately split, with a majority opposing the person-commerce distinction employed to construe police and commerce powers.

1839 Despite the economic depression the immigrant trade grows, pushed by agricultural dislocation in Britain and Europe.

Chief Justice Lemuel Shaw and the Supreme Judicial Court of Massachusetts uphold police powers supporting the alien tax in the British-colonial *Norris* case. Massachusetts antislavery Democrats and Whigs divided by immigrant, anti-immigrant, and black voters. Similar divided racial and immigrant politics occur in New York surrounding Democrat Martin van Buren and son John in 1840 presidential election.

1841 A British captain protests paying the New York alien tax. Whig vice president Tyler begins weak presidency without political party support, including Supreme Court nominations. U.S. Supreme Court splits in deciding *Groves v. Slaughter*, revealing pronounced divisions regarding not only the "person-commerce" distinction in *Miln* concerning the interstate slave trade, but also its bearing on state exclusion or admission of destitute white immigrants and free blacks.

1842–1843 At trial and on appeal the British captain loses the New York alien tax case, *Smith v. Turner*. Immigrant politics expose corruption in the administration of New York City poor law and Maritime Hospital; result in closely divided compromise statewide politics that will enact a new Emigrant Commission. By 1843 appeals of Massachusetts and New York Alien Tax Cases to the Supreme Court delayed by Tyler's inability to overcome congressional opposition to appointments. Potato blight moves from United States to Canada and Europe.

1845–1848 Potato blight causes historic transatlantic famine migration, embracing especially Irish and Germans. Justices Nelson, Woodbury, and Grier join divided Taney Court; New York immigrant and racial compromise politics strengthen Emigrant Commission regulation of famine immigrants, and support for both personal liberty law (PLL) and stronger federal Passenger Acts; similar compromise politics in Massachusetts result in weaker PLL law. Over four terms Supreme Court hears appellate arguments of Alien Tax Cases consolidated into Passenger Cases; Webster's and John Van Buren's arguments reflect the commerce and police power theories within each state's immigrant and racial politics; Know-Nothings' proposals defeated in both states and in most respects regarding Congress's Passenger Act. Supreme Court unanimous vote for result, but ten opinions in three License Cases (1847) reveal range of police and commerce powers theories; Taney Court split 4–4 in Passenger Cases, leaving outcome to Justice McKinley's participation. Sectional politics in War with Mexico, slavery in territories, Northern states' use of PLL to defy federal Fugitive Slave Act (FSA) enforcement, abolitionists agitate interstate slave trade, all divide United States.

1849 Transatlantic famine migrations reach new level, agitating state racial and immigration politics, especially in Northern cities; Ohio repeals most black laws and enacts PLL. Webster privately learns from McLean that narrow majority overturns aliens taxes, confirming notice from Taney indicating McKinley as the fifth vote; the Court's eight opinions confirm the police and commerce power theories, while majority result, Webster says, is most important since *Gibbons*; Wayne and Taney bitter public exchange exposes the minority holding of person-commerce distinction in *Miln*. Southern congressional "Address to Constituents" employs white supremacy to rally opposition to attempted sectional compromise of slavery in territories, North PLL defiance of federal FSA, and abolition of interstate slave trade. Congressional bipartisan vote to publish 5,000 copies of Passenger Cases; bipartisan politics enacts another federal Passenger Act and defeats most extreme federal anti-immigrant proposals.

1850–1856 Compromise of 1850 diffuses issues of slavery in the territories, enacts draconian federal FSA. Taney Court attempts compromise state police and federal commerce powers in Justice Curtis's *Cooley* (1852) decision. Anti-immigrant federal and state political parties at height of influence, temporarily displacing antislavery politics and blocking 1849 federal Passenger Act; New York and Massachusetts enact deportation policies. By 1855 New York enacts immigrant receiving station at Castle Garden, signaling ebbing anti-immigrant politics, end of deportations in New York and Massachusetts, and peace in Crimean War returns transatlantic immigration to early famine levels. From the bloody Christiana, Pennsylvania, riot (1851) to the 1856 *Dred Scott* litigation antislavery politics and Northern states' use of PLL to defy 1850 FSA, polarize national politics. In New York, Massachusetts, Ohio, and other Northern states antislavery and anti-immigrant politics converge to shape PLL that confirm limited legal equality for free blacks, immigrants, fugitive slaves as legal "persons." Republican Party uses PLL to rally diverse support from Whigs, Free-

Soil proponents, antislavery and pro-immigrant Democrats. Congress passes stronger 1855 Passenger Act.

1857–1870 Taney Court's *Dred Scott* (1857) decision fosters increased Southern promotion of secession and anger at Northern states' use of PLL to defy 1850 FSA, culminating in New York high court's 1860 *Lemmon* decision, which cites Passenger Cases and other precedents to legitimate free-state sovereignty as the basis for power to confer citizenship on any chosen "persons" within its jurisdiction. South Carolina justifies secession in part by refuting the free-state sovereignty empowering conferral of citizenship upon blacks announced in *Lemmon*, as well as defiance of FSA, echoing the white-supremacy rationales in the 1849 "Address to southern constituents." Anti-immigrant groups win some curbs on certain Chinese aliens despite U.S.-China treaty allowing free labor; in 1862 California Supreme Court cites Passenger Cases as authority for supremacy of federal treaty to strike down the state's anti-Chinese police tax. As Civil War ends Nevada enacts a passenger tax on persons leaving the state, which the state supreme court affirms. The U.S. Supreme Court, with Wayne, Grier, and Nelson remaining, reviews the Nevada law; avoiding the Passenger Cases, it relies on the Supremacy Clause, striking the law down in the *Crandall* Case (1868). During Reconstruction the Fourteenth Amendment employs the "person" terminology to confer ambiguous federal citizenship, which Justice Field contends includes aliens, as well as blacks. In 1870 transatlantic immigration again increases into New York as the Western states argue for a federal tax on passengers; Emigrant Commissioner Kapp publishes a defense of state regulation that rests in part on the limited holding in the Passenger Cases.

1873–1891 Industrial depressions aggravate employment competition between American native and immigrant workers, as a momentous immigration from southern and eastern Europe and Asia transforms U.S. naturalization and immigration policies, at the point Jim Crow segregation prevails in the American South and in certain areas in the North and West. On his California circuit, Justice Field reaffirms that aliens share some rights with U.S. citizens under the Fourteenth Amendment; but in three cases from New York, New Orleans, and San Francisco in 1875 Justice Miller, noting a new majority, overturns state commutation taxes, undercutting the connection between state social welfare policies and shippers' passenger trade. The same year Congress enacts a federal passenger tax funding both exclusion of certain Chinese women and other undesirables, and the creation of a federal bureaucracy regulating immigration. In the 1882 Chinese Exclusion Act the exclusionary system is expanded; in the Chinese Exclusion Cases (1889) the Supreme Court upholds the federal tax and regulatory bureaucracy on the basis of national sovereignty and federal supremacy without reference to the commerce power, while Justice Field repeats that aliens share some rights with U.S. citizens. By 1891 New York closes Castle Garden and the federal government opens Ellis Island; it symbolizes the federal bureaucratic regulation based on national sovereignty and federal supremacy in ports and across northern and southern borders, though exclusion polices do not yet include Mexicans or others in the Americas and Caribbean. The Supreme Court affirms national sovereignty and federal supremacy as the basis for immigration, naturalization, and designated "illegal" immigrant regulations in the *Ekiu* case (1891).

1897–1924 In 1897 and 1913, Presidents Cleveland and Taft veto a literacy test devised as a basis for further exclusion of undesirable immigrants. In 1907 the Gentlemen's Agreement excludes Japanese and Koreans; in 1917, Congress overrides Wilson veto to enact the Immigration Act that imposes the literacy test and a near bar to immigration from an Asian Zone. In 1921 Congress enacts the first preferential quotas, which effectively designate members of the "Caucasian race" as those most qualified for admission to U.S. citizenship, though, because of the Civil War and Reconstruction heritage, blacks could also qualify. The Supreme Court affirms the preference for the "Caucasian race" in the *Ozawa* case (1922). The 1924 Immigration Act establishes the quotas for immigration from Eastern Hemisphere countries, instituting an annual maximum of 154,227; using the 1920 U.S. census proportions, the most preferred groups are from northern Europe and the British Isles, and restrictions apply to southern and eastern Europeans. In 1910 Congress establishes Angel Island in San Francisco Bay as the receiving station for the declining numbers of select immigrants from the Pacific Rim. Mexicans and other immigrants from the Western Hemisphere are not yet included in the quota preferences.

1924–1952 In 1943 the exclusion policy ends for China, one of the WWII Allied nations; in 1946 the exclusions end for Asian Indians and Filipinos and each group is authorized a quota of 100 visas. The 1952 Immigration and Nationality Act, which becomes law over President Truman's veto, maintains the Eastern Hemisphere preferences and annual maximum of 154,277. The law abolishes the "Asian Exclusion Zone" allotting 100 visas to each Asian nation, including Japan; it also enlarges the "national quota" system to include preferences for reason of family reunification, education, and technical skills. Numerical limitations still do not include immigrants from Latin America and the Caribbean. The Supreme Court decides *Edwards v. California* (1941) establishing right of travel, and concurring opinions suggest inclusion of alien immigrants; in an example of gradual convergence of interests, civil rights lawyer advocate to include alien immigrant groups in rights revolution during Cold War liberalism.

1965 Immigration Act: at the time President Johnson and Cold War liberals see the law as extension of the civil rights movement, including Warren Court rights revolution. The law abolishes national origins quota system, with family unification primary and education-technical skills secondary criteria for maximum 290,000 annual immigrant visas, with 170,000 and 120,000, respectively, from Eastern and Western Hemispheres.

1975 Supreme Court *De Canas v. Bicas* (1975) holds that federal supremacy sustaining federal regulation of illegal immigrants does not preclude state regulations implementing same policy. The case signals "illegal" undocumented farm workers are a policy issue in California and recognized as such by Congress.

1976 Amendments to 1965 Immigration Act establish same seven-category preferences system ranging from family unification to education and technical skills, to refugees, to ideological (anticommunist) reasons for both Western and Eastern Hemispheres. No more than 20,000 visas allotted to any one country in the Western Hemisphere.

1978 Amendments to 1965 Immigration Act: while the 290,000 maximum number of visas remains unchanged, the number applies to the entire globe, ending the unequal hemispheric division.

1980 Immigration Act establishes separate admissions policy for refugees defined by United Nations terms, rather than previous geographical or ideological categories. The maximum annual number of refugees from entire world set at 50,000, with global total reduced from 290,000 to 270,000.

1981 Congressional Report of the Select Commission on Immigration and Refugee Policy: The report signals that "illegal" or undocumented aliens have become a political issue in certain states and a transnational labor issue. Chairperson Rev. Theodore Hesburgh sums up the recommendations: "We recommend closing the back door to undocumented, illegal migration, opening the front door a little more to accommodate legal migration in the interests of this country, defining our immigration goals clearly and providing a structure to implement them effectively, and setting forth procedures which lead to fair and efficient adjudication and administration of U.S. immigration laws."

1986 Immigration Reform and Control Act (IRCA) addresses "illegal immigration" by offering amnesty and "temporary status" to "all illegal aliens" who can prove continuous residence in the United States since 1982. The act also grants farm workers a "separate, more lenient amnesty," enforces legal sanctions against "employers who knowingly hired illegal aliens," and strengthens "inspection and enforcement at U.S. borders."

1990 Immigration Act expands the 1965 act, increasing the annual global maximum immigration to 700,000, which raises the number of available visas 40 percent. Family reunification remains the main admission route, while the numbers of "employment-related" immigration double. Immigration from "underrepresented" countries is also permitted so as to increase further the diversity of immigrant groups admitted to the United States.

1996 As a global "war on terror" begins, Congress passes the Illegal Immigration Reform and Immigrant Responsibility Act (IIRIRA), providing federal funding for state officials' voluntary use of federal databases, including especially E-Verify, in order to enable state-federal cooperation in verification of the legal status (whether documented or undocumented) of immigrants seeking social welfare services and employment. Congress *rejects*, however, a provision that would have allowed states to exclude from public schools the children of illegal aliens. The state-federal cooperation in using federal databases is also adapted to national security purposes.

2010–2013 States such as Arizona enact laws that extend IRCA and IIRIRA state-federal cooperation beyond *De Canas*, *Edwards*, and other Supreme Court precedents, engendering challenges from civil liberties, religious, and business groups, as well as the federal government, arguing that the state laws are contrary to federal supremacy and preemption. In the *Whiting* (2011) case, the Supreme Court decides by a 5–3 vote that where a federal statute effectively allows, through a "saving clause," states to mandate use of E-Verify in order to enforce federal law, the Arizona law does not challenge federal supremacy or preemption. In *Arizona v. U.S.* (2012), by contrast, a different 5–3 majority strikes down all state provisions that exceed federal enforcement standards, except one that in good faith awaits state court review in order to determine whether state officials have complied with federal practices and constitutional standards. Meanwhile, the 11th U.S. Court of Appeals enjoins nearly every provision of Alabama's anti-immigrant law that exceeds the provisions of the Arizona law, including efforts to exclude immigrant children from public schools and to criminalize religious groups' missionary or ecumenical work employing right of travel. Although one provision of the Alabama law is upheld as consistent with *Whiting* precedent, the state reports that "thousands" of licensed state businesses do not use the federal E-Verify system in order to determine the status of hired workers. Over the same years, a "reform" of national immigration policy that adapts the federal policies dating from 1965 to a perceived crisis in illegal immigration and border security moves slowly through Congress toward an uncertain fate.

BIBLIOGRAPHICAL ESSAY

Note from the Series Editors: The following bibliographic essay contains the major primary and secondary sources the author consulted for this volume. We have asked all authors in the series to omit formal citations in order to make our volumes more readable, inexpensive, and appealing for students and general readers. In adopting this format, Landmark Law Cases and American Society follows the precedent of a number of highly regarded and widely consulted series.

I began thinking about the Passenger Cases as a book topic as a result of my chapter entitled "Constituting the Free-State Borderlands: New York, Pennsylvania, and Ohio," in *Freedom's Conditions in the U.S.-Canadian Borderlands in the Age of Emancipation*, ed. Tony Freyer and Lyndsay Campbell (Durham, N.C.: Carolina Academic Press, 2011), 35–83; and Tony A. Freyer and Daniel Thomas, "The *Passenger Cases* Reconsidered in Transatlantic Commerce Clause History," *Journal of Supreme Court History* 36, no. 3 (2011): 216–235. The two works that influenced my interest in the relation of these cases to immigration in the states before and during the Civil War and Reconstruction are Mary Sarah Bilder, "The Struggle over Immigration, Indentured Servants, Slaves, and Articles of Commerce, 61 *Missouri L. Rev.* 73 (1996); and Gerald L. Neuman, *Strangers to the Constitution Immigrants, Borders, and Fundamental Law* (Princeton, N.J.: Princeton University Press, 1996). The traditional constitutional history approach to the cases emphasizing slavery and the coming of the Civil War are Charles Warren, *The Supreme Court in United States History, 1821– 1855* (Boston: Little Brown, 1922); Carl Brent Swisher, *Roger B. Taney* (Hamden, Conn.: Archon Books, 1961). My incorporation of financial and institutional state-building into these approaches uses Gautham Rao, "Visible Hands: Customhouses, Law, Capitalism and Mercantile State of the Early Republic" (PhD diss., University of Chicago, 2008). For judges' multiple-motivational instrumentalism in transformative periods see Morton J. Horwitz, *The Transformation of American Law, 1780–1860* (Cambridge, Mass.: Harvard University Press, 1977); and *The Transformation of American Law: The Crisis of Legal Orthodoxy, 1870–1960* (New York: Oxford University Press, 1992). For the quote from Justice William O. Douglas see *The Court Years, 1939–1975: The Autobiography of William O. Douglas* (New York: Vintage Books, 1981), 8. I note too that in my work on civil rights I use Derrick Bell Jr., "*Brown* and the Interest-Convergence Dilemma," 93 *Harvard L. Rev.* (1980), 518–533; its application to the personal liberty laws in historical parallel with the civil rights movement and Cold War liberalism appears in chapter 6 and the conclusion of this book for the first time.

All official published case citations in this book may be located by standard title search on Westlaw, LexisNexis, or other U.S. Supreme Court databases.

Charles Warren's volume of history of the Supreme Court 1821–1855, cited above, provides many of the newspapers quoted throughout my book. The main sources for the U.S. Supreme Court precedents, opinions, and decision and impact of the Passenger Cases with biographical background of justices and lawyers are the volumes in *The Oliver Wendell Holmes Devise History of the Supreme Court of the United States*: vol. 5, Carl B. Swisher, *The Taney Court 1836–64* (New York: Macmillan Publishing, 1974); vol. 7, Charles Fairman, *Reconstruction and Reunion 1864–88, Part 2* (New York: Macmillan Publishing, 1987); vol. 8, Owen M. Fiss, *Troubled Beginnings of the Modern State, 1888–1910* (Macmillan Publishing, 1993). See also Austen Allen, *Origins of the Dred Scott Case: Jacksonian Jurisprudence and the Supreme Court, 1837–1857* (Athens: University of Georgia Press, 2006); and especially for the relationship to American slavery see Earl M. Maltz, *Slavery and the Supreme Court, 1825–1861* (Lawrence: University Press of Kansas, 2009). For the basic history of the Warren Court's due-process, voting, and apportionment revolutions see Lucas A. Powe Jr., *The Warren Court and American Politics* (Cambridge, Mass.: Harvard University Press, 2000); Morton J. Horwitz, *The Warren Court and the Pursuit of Justice* (New York: Hill and Wang, 1998); see also Tony A. Freyer, *Hugo L. Black and the Dilemma of American Liberalism* (New York: Pearson Longman, 2008). For the California Supreme Court during the postwar era see Ben Field, *Activism in Pursuit of the Public Interest: The Jurisprudence of Chief Justice Roger J. Traynor* (Berkeley: Institute of Governmental Studies, University of California, 2003).

In addition to the Supreme Court histories noted above, for several works about particular cases: for *Gibbons v. Ogden* (1824) see Maurice G. Baxter, *The Steamboat Monopoly Gibbons v. Ogden, 1824* (New York: Alfred A. Knopf, 1972); Herbert A. Johnson, *Gibbons v. Ogden, John Marshall, Steamboats, and the Commerce Clause* (Lawrence: University Press of Kansas, 2010); Thomas H. Cox, *Gibbons v. Ogden, Law and Society in the Early Republic* (Athens: Ohio University Press, 2009). Also, Justice Henry Baldwin published his concurring opinion in the *Miln Case* in *A General View of the Origin and Nature of the Constitution and Government of the United States* (Philadelphia, 1837); see also the chapter on *Cooley v. Bd. of Wardens* (1852) in Stuart Streichler, *Justice Curtis in the Civil War Era: At the Crossroads of American Constitutionalism* (Charlottesville: University of Virginia Press, 2005); and for *Groves v. Slaughter* (1841) see Maurice G. Baxter, *Henry Clay The Lawyer* (Lexington: University Press of Kentucky, 2000); for *Swift v. Tyson* (1842) see Tony Allan Freyer, *Forums of Order: The Federal Courts and Business in American History* (Greenwich, Conn.: Johnson Publishing, 1979; and his *Harmony and Dissonance: The* Swift *and* Erie *Cases in American Federalism* (New York: New York University Press, 1981).

For the origins and meaning of legal "persons," the term that appears in the Constitution and runs through all the cases discussed in the text of this book, within the legal context of the antebellum period see Joseph Story, "Manuscript Digest Reported Cases and Treatises [1808–1812?]," 3 vols., Special Collections Harvard Law School. From this source too I began to understand the Massachusetts poor law's inclusion of poor whites (including foreign immigrants), free blacks, and slaves, which are developed in my book. The term and doctrinal idea reappears, often with the many of the same sources discussed in the "Digest," in Story's *Commentaries on the Conflict of Laws* (Boston: Hilliard, Gray, 1834). Story's doctrinal use of "persons" echoes Attorney General Taney's responses regarding black seamen quoted in the text from two *Opinions Attorney General* (1831); and R. B. Taney to Edward Livingston, "With communication relative to the law of South Carolina," June 9, 1832 (National Archives, College Park, RG 59 microfilm publication, *#m1794*: Miscellaneous Letters of the Department of State, 1789–1906, Roll 73, file: Taney to Livingston dated June 9, 1832 (frames 301–309) [I thank John Taylor, NA senior archivist, for this cite]. Reinforcing the citations and commentary in Story's "Digest" and *Conflict of Laws*, and Taney Attorney General opinions, is the most illuminating George H. Moore, *Notes on the History of Slavery in Massachusetts* (New York: D. Appleton, 1866) [thanks to Professor Bernard Bailyn for this source].

For the period prior to *Gibbons*, when commerce power issues indirectly arose concerning foreign affairs, see Kevin Arlyck, "Plaintiffs v. Privateers: Litigation and Foreign Affairs in the Federal Courts, 1816–1822," *Law and History Review* 30, no. 1 (Feb. 2012): 245–278. For how the Negro Seamen Acts conflicted the commerce power see Michael Schoeppner, "Navigating the Dangerous Atlantic: Racial Quarantines, Black Sailors and United States Constitutionalism" (PhD diss., University of Florida, 2010); Philip M. Hamer, "Great Britain, and Negro Seamen Acts, 1822–1848," *Journal of Southern History* 1, no. 1 (Feb. 1935): 26; Philip M. Hamer, "British Consuls, and the Negro Seamen Acts, 1850–1860," *Journal of Southern History* 1, no. 2 (May 1935): 144; Edlie L. Wong, *Neither Fugitive nor Free: Atlantic Slavery, Freedom Suits, and the Legal Culture of Travel* (New York: New York University Press, 2009), 183–239. For police powers, generally, see Tony Freyer, *Producers versus Capitalists: Constitutional Conflict in Antebellum America* (Charlottesville: University Press of Virginia, 1994); and on the distinctiveness of American state police powers contrasted with British North American colonies, see Lyndsay Campbell, "Governance in the Borderlands: Upper Canadian Legal Institutions," Bradley Miller, "British Rights and Liberal Law in Canada's Fugitive Slave Debate, 1833–1843," and Lyndsay Campbell, "The Northern Borderlands: Canada West," in Freyer and Campbell, *Freedom's Conditions*, 109–140, 141–172, 195–227.

The biographies of the members of the Supreme Courts that discuss the precedents for and opinions of the Passenger Cases are C.B. Swisher's biography of Chief Justice Taney, noted above; R. Kent Newmyer, *John Marshall and the Heroic Age of the Supreme Court* (Baton Rouge: Louisiana State University Press, 2001); and his *Supreme Court Justice Joseph Story: Statesman of the Old Republic* (Chapel Hill: University of North Carolina Press, 1985); Alexander A. Lawrence, *James Moore Wayne: Southern Unionist* (Chapel Hill: University of North Carolina Press, 1943); Francis P. Weisenburger, *The Life of John McLean: A Politician on the United States Supreme Court* (Columbus: Ohio State University Press, 1937; reprint, New York: Da Capo Press, 1971); John P. Frank, *Justice Daniel Dissenting: A Biography of Peter V. Daniel, 1784–1860* (Cambridge, Mass.: Harvard University Press, 1964); Donald Malcolm Roper, *Mr. Justice Thompson and the Constitution* (New York: Garland Publishing, 1987); Donald G. Morgan, *Justice William Johnson, the First Dissenter: The Career and Constitutional Philosophy of a Jeffersonian Judge* (Columbus: University of South Carolina Press, 1954); Steven P. Brown, *John McKinley and the Antebellum Supreme Court: Circuit Riding in the Old Southwest* (Tuscaloosa: University of Alabama Press, 2012); Richard H. Leach, "Benjamin R. Curtis: Case Study of a Supreme Court Justice" (PhD diss., Princeton University, 1951). Also useful for certain details are the entries to the members of the Supreme Court in Clare Cushman, ed., *The Supreme Court Justices: Illustrated Biographies 1789–1993* (Washington, D.C.: Supreme Court Historical Society, Congressional Quarterly, 1993). See also the leading biography of Lemuel Shaw, Leonard W. Levy, *The Law of the Commonwealth and Chief Justice Shaw* (Cambridge, Mass.: Harvard University Press, 1957). For Samuel Miller, Charles Fairman, *Mr. Justice Miller and the Supreme Court, 1862–1890* (Cambridge, Mass.: Harvard University Press, 1939); useful for commerce power development to 1890 is Samuel F. Miller, *Lectures on the Constitution of the United States* (New York: Banks and Brothers, 1891).

For Daniel Webster's role in the commerce power litigation though the aftermath of the Passenger Cases see Maurice G. Baxter, *Daniel Webster and the Supreme Court* (Amherst: University of Massachusetts Press, 1966); and his *One and Inseparable Daniel Webster and the Union* (Cambridge, Mass.: Harvard University Press, 1984). The Webster correspondence quoted from in chapter 4 of this book is in Andrew J. King, ed., *The Papers of Daniel Webster: Legal Papers*, vol. 3, *The Federal Practice, Part 2* (Hanover, N.H.: University Press of New England, 1989), 707–732; the same source provides some references to Webster's support for the 1847 and 1849 Passenger Acts. For other references to Webster's support for those laws and Irish famine relief see the notes to the *Congressional Globe* cited in Freyer and Thomas, "The *Passenger Cases* Reconsidered," full cite above.

The Freyer and Thomas article also includes the citations to John C. Calhoun and Illinois Democratic congressman T. J. Turner, as well as other commentary appearing in the *Congressional Globe* concerning the 1847 passenger bill. For Calhoun's support for Irish immigration through New York Port, famine relief, and the dissemination of the 5,000 copies of the Passenger Cases opinions in 1849, see *The Papers of John C. Calhoun, 1848–1849*, vol. 24, ed. Clyde N. Wilson and Shirley Bright Cook (Columbia: University of South Carolina Press, 2001); in this same volume the editors reprint the text, from which the quotes in chapter 5 of this book are cited: "The Address of Southern Delegates in Congress, To Their Constituents [1849]." Sources for Calhoun, Jackson, and nullification are William W. Freehling, *Prelude to Civil War: The Nullification Controversy in South Carolina, 1816–1836* (Harper & Row, 1966); Richard E. Ellis, *The Union at Risk: Jacksonian Democracy, States' Rights, and the Nullification Crisis* (New York: Oxford University Press, 1987); John C. Calhoun, "Exposition Reported to the Committee," in *The Papers of John C. Calhoun*, vol. 10, ed. Clyde N. Wilson and W. Edwin Hemphill (Columbia: University of South Carolina Press, 1977), 444–535. Compare Calhoun's theories to John Taylor, *New Views of the Constitution of the United States* (Washington, D.C., 1823; reprint, New York: Da Capo Press, 1971). For Congressman Turner, the Freyer and Thomas article provides the citations to his comments also appearing in *Congressional Globe*; our article also includes the passages quoted from supporters of the 1847 passenger bill, and the Know-Nothing (Native American Party) critics.

The influences of free trade and slavery, including the interstate slave trade, in the Constitution's framing and early national development are drawn from the following sources. The enumeration of powers generally, and the commerce powers embraced in the Commerce Clause more particularly, are examined in Forrest McDonald, *Novus Ordo Seclorum: The Intellectual Origins of the Constitution* (Lawrence: University Press of Kansas, 1985); Gordon Wood, *The Creation of the American Republic, 1776–1787* (New York: W. W. Norton, 1972); Albert S. Abel, "The Commerce Clause in the Constitutional Convention and in Contemporary Comment," *Minnesota L. Rev.* 25, no. 4 (March 1941): 432–494. In ch. 1 the Framers' quotations from the 1787 Constitutional Convention are from Max Farrand, ed., *The Records of the Federal Convention of 1787*, 4 vols. (New Haven, Conn.: Yale University Press, 1911); Jonathan Elliot, *The Debates in the Several State Conventions on the Adoption of the Federal Constitution, as Recommended by the General Convention at Philadelphia in 1787. Together with the Journal of the Convention, Luther Martin's Letter, Yates's Minutes, Congressional Opinions, Virginia and Kentucky Resolutions of 1798–99, and Other Illustrations of the Constitution in Four Volumes* (1836); Herbert Storing and Murray Dry, eds., *The Complete Anti-Federalist*, 2 vols. (Chicago: University of Chicago Press, 1981); Alexander Hamilton, James Madison, and John Jay, *The Federalist*, ed. J. R. Pole (Indianapolis, Ind.: Hackett Publishing, 2005). Also in ch. 1, the sources for quoted passages of Charles Pinckney, Annals 16th Congress, 1st sess., II, 1318; and James Madison to J. C. Cabell, Feb. 13, 1829 (3 *Farrand* 478). For slavery and the interstate slave trade see George William Van Cleve, *A Slaveholders' Union: Slavery, Politics, and the Constitution in the Early American Republic* (Chicago: University of Chicago Press, 2010); David L. Lightner, *Slavery and the Commerce Power: How the Struggle against the Interstate Slave Trade Led to the Civil War* (New Haven, Conn.: Yale University Press, 2006). Two treatises advocating abolition of slavery, including use of the Commerce Clause, are William Goodell, *American Constitutional Law in Its Bearing upon American Slavery*, 2nd ed. (Utica, N.Y.: Lawson & Chaplin, 1845); Joel Tiffaney, *A Treatise on the Unconstitutionality of American Slavery: Together with the Powers and Duties of the Federal Government in Relation to That Subject* (Cleveland, Oh.: J. Clayer, 1849). The related issues of sojourner slaves and enforcing the fugitive slave clause, and racial identification are discussed in Gautham Rao, "The State the Slaveholders Made: Regulating Fugitive Slaves in the Early Republic," Stephen Middleton, "The Judicial Construction of Whiteness in the Borderlands of the Northwest Territory, 1803–1860," Aviam Soifer, "Constrained Choices: New England Slavery Decisions in the Antebellum Era," John Werthheimer, Daphne Fructman, et al., "*Willis v. Jolliffe*: Love and Slavery on the South Carolina-Ohio Borderlands," in Freyer and Campbell, *Freedom's Conditions*, full cite above, 85–108, 173–194, 227–256, 257–285.

Discussion of immigration and its relation to shipping regulations is drawn from the following: Aristide R. Zolberg, *A Nation by Design: Immigration Policy in the Fashioning of America* (Cambridge, Mass.: Harvard University Press, 2008); Walter T. K. Nugent, *Crossings: The Great Transatlantic Migrations, 1870–1914* (Bloomington: Indiana University Press, 1995); Oliver MacDonagh, *A Pattern of Government Growth 1800–60: The Passenger Acts and Their Enforcement* (London: MacGibbon & Kee, 1961); Robert Greenhalgh Albion and Jennie Barnes Pope, *The Rise of New York Port 1815–1860* (New York: Charles Scribner's Sons, 1939; reprint, 1970). On nativist groups opposing immigration see John Higham, *Strangers in the Land: Patterns of American Nativism* (New York: Atheneum, 1975). The best work on Western immigration policies is Elliott Robert Barkan, *From All Points: America's Immigrant West, 1870s–1952* (Bloomington: Indiana University Press, 2007). An illuminating account of how the reception process operated as a regulatory system at Ellis Island is "Conceivable Aliens," in Alan Trachtenberg, *Shades of Hiawatha: Staging Indians, Making Americans, 1880–1930* (New York: Hill and Wang, 2004). For the Chinese exclusion struggle see Charles J. McClain, *In Search of Equality: The Chinese Struggle against Discrimination in Nineteenth-Century America* (Berkeley: University of California Press, 1994); Erika Lee, "Enforcing the Borders: Chinese Exclusion along the U.S. Borders with

Canada and Mexico, 1882–1924," *Journal of American History* 89, no. 1 (June 2002): 54–86; Erika Lee and Judy Lung, *Angel Island: Immigrant Gateway to America* (New York: Oxford University Press, 2010); Erika Lee, *At America's Gates: Chinese Immigration during the Exclusion Era, 1882–1943* (Chapel Hill: University of North Carolina Press, 2003). The reference to German immigrants in Louisiana is Ellen C. Merrill, *Germans of Louisiana* (Gretna, La.: Pelican Publishing, 2005); in addition to Zolberg, noted above, the references to the German migration driven by the famine, 1845–1855, are in William L. Langer, *Political and Social Upheaval, 1832–1852* (New York: Harper, 1969). The primary source about New York City immigrant regulations and the bond-commutation system quoted in the text is Friedrich Kapp, *Immigration and the Commissioners of Emigration of the State of New York* (New York: Nation Press, 1870). For the pilot law petition quoted in the text see *Speech of Hon. John A. Dix of New York on the Pilot Laws in the Senate of the United States, June 30, 1848* (Washington, D.C.: Congressional Globe Office, 1848).

From a quite large literature on the Irish famine migration I begin with Kerby A. Miller, *Emigrants and Exiles: Ireland and the Irish Exodus* (New York: Oxford University Press, 1988); for the 60 percent of the Irish who upon arrival in British North America went to the United States see Elizabeth Jane Errington, "British Migration and British America," in *Canada and the British Empire*, ed. Phillip Buckner (Oxford: Oxford University Press, 2008), 140–159. In addition to O. MacDonagh, *Pattern of Government*, cited above, a work describing the tragic weakness of regulation under the Passenger Acts is Edward Laxton, *The Famine Ships: The Irish Exodus to America* (New York: Henry Holt, 1997); see also Herman Melville, *Redburn: His First Voyage* (1849; republished, New York: Library of America, 1983). Other references to the famine migration are taken from John Feehan, "The Potato: Root of the Famine," David Nally, "The Colonial Dimensions of the Great Irish Famine," Peter Gray, "British Relief Measures," Helen Hatton, "The Largest Amount of Good: Quaker Relief Efforts," Kerby A. Miller, "Emigration to North America in the Era of the Great Famine, 1845–55," in *Atlas of the Great Irish Famine*, ed. John Crowley, William J. Smyth, and Mike Murphy (New York: New York University Press, 2012), 28–37, 64–74, 75–84, 100–106, 214–227.

My essay "Constituting the Free-State Borderlands," cited above, sets out the arguments for the state politics and law involving the personal liberty laws, free blacks, fugitive slaves, and immigrants. The argument assumes the chronologies of laws enacted in New York, Massachusetts, and Ohio set out in Thomas D. Morris, *Free Men All: The Personal Liberty Laws of the North, 1780–1861* (Baltimore: Johns Hopkins University Press, 1974), and Paul Finkelman, *An Imperfect Union: Slavery, Federalism, and Comity* (Chapel Hill: University of North Carolina Press, 1981). The three state politics involving free blacks and immigrants are from Jonathon H. Earle, *Jacksonian Antislav-*

ery and the Politics of Free Soil, 1824–1854 (Chapel Hill: University of North Carolina Press); William E. Gienapp, *The Origins of the Republican Party, 1852–1856* (New York: Oxford University Press, 1987); Michael F. Holt, *The Rise and Fall of the American Whig Party: Jacksonian Politics and the Onset of the Civil War* (New York: Oxford University Press, 1999); Ronald P. Formisano, *The Transformation of Political Culture Massachusetts Parties, 1790s–1840s* (New York: Oxford University Press, 1983); Daniel J. Hulsebosch, *Constituting Empire: New York and the Transformation of Constitutionalism in the Atlantic World, 1664–1830* (Chapel Hill: University of North Carolina Press, 2005). The free-black and immigrant politics discussed in the preceding political histories are augmented by racial tensions between Irish immigrants and free blacks in Noel Ignatiev, *How the Irish Became White* (New York: Routledge, 1995); Kerby A. Miller, "Green over Black: The Origins of Irish-American Racism, 1800–1863," (unpublished paper, permission granted); Stephen Middleton, *The Black Laws: Race and the Legal Process in Early Ohio* (Athens: Ohio University Press, 2005); Nikki M. Taylor, *Frontiers of Freedom: Cincinnati's Black Community, 1802–1868* (Athens: Ohio University Press, 2005); Leslie M. Harris, *In the Shadow of Slavery: African Americans in New York City, 1626–1863* (Chicago: University of Chicago Press, 2003); James A. Colaiaco, *Frederick Douglass and the Fourth of July* (New York: Palgrave Macmillan, 2006). For the comparison between free blacks and Irish immigrants concerning educational curriculum, racial segregation, and minimal desegregation, see Philip Hamburger, *Separation of Church and State* (Cambridge, Mass.: Harvard University Press, 2004); Davison M. Douglas, *Jim Crow Moves North: The Battle over Northern School Segregation, 1865–1954* (New York: Cambridge University Press, 2005); James Oliver Horton and Lois E. Horton, *In Hope of Liberty: Culture, Community, and Protest among Northern Free Blacks* (New York: Oxford University Press, 1997).

For the significance of mainstream and radical Christians see: David Walker, *Walker's Appeal in Four Articles*, ed. William Loren Katz, 3rd ed. (1830; reprinted, 1848; reprinted, 1969, Arno Press); *David Walker's Appeal to the Coloured Citizens of the World*, ed. Peter P. Hicks (University Park: Pennsylvania State University Press, 2000); Richard J. Carwardine, *Evangelicals and Politics in Antebellum America* (New Haven: Yale University Press, 1993); and Martha S. Jones, *All Bound Up Together: The Women Question in African American Public Culture 1830–1900* (Chapel Hill: University of North Carolina Press, 2007). An example of politics, racial and immigrant conflict, and religion dividing a community in a major fugitive slave crisis: Thomas P. Slaughter, *Bloody Dawn: The Christiana Riot and Racial Violence in the Antebellum North* (New York: Oxford University Press, 1991). Compare the above to Leon Litwack, *North of Slavery: The Negro in the Free States, 1790–1860* (Chicago: University of Chicago Press, 1961).

For the economic and legal history of immigration see Michael R. Haines, "The Population of the United States, 1790–1920," in *The Cambridge Economic History of the United States*, vol. 2, *The Long Nineteenth Century*, ed. Stanley L. Engerman and Robert E. Gallman (Cambridge: Cambridge University Press, 2000), 143–206; Carol E. Heim, "Structural Changes: Regional and Urban," Richard A. Easterlin, "Twentieth Century American Population Growth," Claudia Goldin, "Labor Markets in the Twentieth Century," in *The Cambridge Economic History of the United States*, vol. 3, *The Twentieth Century*, ed. Stanley L. Engerman and Robert E. Gallman (Cambridge: Cambridge University Press, 2000), 93–190, 505–548, 549–624; Christopher Tomlins, "Law, Population, Labor," in *The Cambridge History of Law in America*, vol. 1, *Early America (1580–1815)*, ed. Michael Grossberg and Christopher Tomlins (Cambridge: Cambridge University Press, 2008), 211–252; Kunal M. Parker, "Citizenship and Immigration Law, 1800–1924: Resolutions of Membership and Territory," in *The Cambridge History of Law in America*, vol. 2, *The Long Nineteenth Century (1789–1920)*, ed. Michael Grossberg and Christopher Tomlins (Cambridge: Cambridge University Press, 2008), 168–203.

My attempt to summarize the evolution of federal policy toward immigrants in relation to Supreme Court opinions and federal-state relations since World War II follows, for general themes, Zolberg, cited above. Emanuel Celler, *You Never Leave Brooklyn: Autobiography of Emanuel Celler* (New York: J. Day, 1953), is a leading participant's view of the gradual repeal of preferential quotas between 1943 and 1952. The legislative history of the more open immigration policies from 1965 to 1995 can be found in "Three Decades of Mass Immigration: The Legacy of the 1965 Immigration Act," *Center for Immigration Studies*, September 1995, 1–8, http://www.cis.org/1965 ImmigrationAct-MassImmigration. An overview of the Warren Court, in addition to major works cited above, is Tony A. Freyer, "The Warren Court as History," in *Transformations in American Legal History Law, Ideology, and Methods: Essays in Honor of Morton J. Horwitz*, vol. 2, ed. Daniel W. Hamilton and Alfred L. Brophy (Cambridge, Mass.: Harvard Law School, 2010), 375–399; and for the changes in federalism since then wrought by the Rehnquist and Roberts Courts, see Mark Tushnet, *A Court Divided: The Rehnquist Court and the Future of Constitutional Law with a New Epilogue* (New York: W. W. Norton, 2006).The legislative intent and judicial travails of Alabama's anti-immigrant law enacted in 2011 are incisively examined in Scott A. Gray, "Federalism's Tug of War: Alabama's Immigration Law and the Scope of State Power in Immigration," *Alabama L. Rev.* 64, no. 1 (2012): 155–186. The connections among citizenship, naturalization, sovereignty, and national border are developed in the essays in Mary L. Dudziak and Leti Volpp, eds., *Legal Borderlands: Law and the Construction of American Borders* (Baltimore: Johns Hopkins University Press, 2006).

The differing legal and economic statuses of African Americans under Southern Jim Crow versus the Northern and Western states, 1930s to 1950s, is suggested in Risa L. Goluboff, *The Lost Promise of Civil Rights* (Cambridge, Mass.: Harvard University Press, 2007). See the contrast between civil rights lawyers in the South and the chapter on California African American lawyer and judge Loren Miller in Kenneth W. Mack, *Representing the Race: The Creation of the Civil Rights Lawyer* (Cambridge, Mass.: Harvard University Press, 2012); and the race cases in Field, *Chief Justice Traynor*, cited above. Compare the broader political and social history of racial pluralism in California by Mark Brillant, *The Color of America Has Changed: How Racial Diversity Shaped Civil Rights Reform in California, 1941–1978* (New York: Oxford University Press, 2010). Professor Brillant's book provides a social-policy focus compared to Elliott Robert Barkan's *From All Points*, cited above, emphasizing California's heritage of racial pluralism, encompassing all the diversity of the Pacific Rim, Mexico, the Caribbean, Central and South America, and Europe. A fascinating case study of the influence on the early origins of this California pluralism is a Reconstruction figure in Charles McClain, "California Carpetbagger: The Career of Henry Dibble," 28 *Quinnipiac Review* 4 (2010), 885–968; see also the end of Chinese exclusions in McClain's *In Search of Equality*, and Erika Lee's *At America's Gates*, cited above.

The comparative inequities, inequalities, and selectively fulfilled hopes of citizenship for legal and illegal aliens during and after the Cold War are suggested by Mae M. Ngai, *Impossible Subjects: Illegal Aliens and the Making of Modern America* (Princeton, N.J.: Princeton University Press, 2004); Cindy I-Fen Cheng, *Citizens of Asian America Democracy and Race during the Cold War* (New York: New York University Press, 2013); John S. W. Park, *Elusive Citizenship Immigration, Asian Americans, and the Paradox of Civil Rights* (New York: New York University Press, 2004); Ronald T. Takaki, *From Different Shores: Perspectives on Race and Ethnicity in America* (New York: Oxford University Press, 1987); Ronald T. Takaki, *Double Victory: A Multicultural History of America in World War II* (Boston: Little, Brown, 2000); Nayan Shah, *Stranger Intimacy: Contesting Race, Sexuality, and Law in the North American West* (Berkeley: University of California Press, 2011); Karen Leonard, *Making Ethnic Choices: California's Punjabi Mexican Americans* (Philadelphia: Temple University Press, 1992); Bill Ong Hing, *Deporting Our Souls: Values, Morality, and Immigration Policy* (Cambridge: Cambridge University Press, 2006); Kelly M. Greenhill, *Weapons of Mass Migration: Forced Displacement, Coercion, and Foreign Policy* (Ithaca, N.Y.: Cornell University, 2010).

INDEX

www.ingramcontent.com/pod-product-compliance
Lightning Source LLC
LaVergne TN
LVHW050629100826
845148LV00011B/1799